MEN, MYTHS, AND MOVEMENTS
IN GERMAN LITERATURE

MEN, MYTHS, AND MOVEMENTS IN GERMAN LITERATURE

A VOLUME OF HISTORICAL AND CRITICAL PAPERS

by

WILLIAM ROSE

KENNIKAT PRESS, INC./PORT WASHINGTON, N. Y.

116506

MEN, MYTHS, AND MOVEMENTS IN GERMAN LITERATURE

Originally Published in 1931
This edition published in 1964 by KENNIKAT PRESS

Library of Congress Catalog Card No: 64- 24466

PREFACE

THE present volume offers the fruits of research extending over a period of eight years. Four of the papers were delivered in the form of lectures to the English Goethe Society, two were originally prepared as public lectures in the University of London, King's College, and all except *Goethe and the Jews* and *The Spirit of Revolt in German Literature* have appeared elsewhere, though not necessarily in quite the same form.

In the last three papers will be found some slight overlapping of material, which was inevitable in the attempt to treat a short period of literary history from three different angles.

To Professor H. G. Atkins of this College my thanks are due for his invaluable help in reading the proofs.

WILLIAM ROSE

THE UNIVERSITY OF LONDON,
KING'S COLLEGE, *July,* 1931

CONTENTS

MEN, MYTHS, AND MOVEMENTS
IN GERMAN LITERATURE

THE MEDIEVAL BEAST EPIC

THERE are two fundamental problems in connection with the medieval Beast Epic which have not yet been satisfactorily elucidated, for, though the literature on the subject is voluminous and comprehensive, the views of scholars are very much at variance and in some cases even diametrically opposed to each other. One school of thought claims that the Beast Epic developed out of popular tradition, and another regards it as being originally the work of monastic poets. The second point at issue is whether France or Germany has the better claim to be regarded as the country from which it sprang. With regard to the former question, there are not only ardent supporters of the two extreme views, but many scholars advocate theories which pursue the golden mean; and, in order to ascertain the present state of our knowledge as to the origin of the Beast Epic, it will be necessary to go back ninety years or so to the beginnings of research in the subject. It will only be possible to trace in outline the development of the widely divergent conceptions put forward, since the investigations of numerous scholars in Germany, France, Holland, Scandinavia, and Russia, while clearing up many obscure points, have rendered the main question all the more involved and puzzling.

The starting-point of all the theories is the view expressed by Jacob Grimm, in the Introduction to his edition of *Reinhart Fuchs*, published in Berlin in the year 1834, that there has existed since prehistoric times a Beast Saga, which was common to all the Indo-Germanic races, but only reached full epic development among the Germans. In prehistoric times men lived in intimate connection with the animal-world, observed its peculiarities, and found in animals beings of a similar nature to themselves. They imagined them as actors in a world of their own, and thus erected a bridge by means of which they could be allowed into the realm of human actions and events; and in this way there arose legends and mythologies giving expression to the belief in the transformation of men into animals and of animals into men. The legend of the Werwolf is, of course, well known. All popular poetry accords a large space to animals, and Grimm quotes the ancient formula with which stories of some obscure and long-distant age are wont to begin—"When animals could still speak." He recognised the striking affinity between Hindu, Greek, and German legends, but this was due to the nature of the fable, as an allegory, and to the prehistoric relationship of the nations. The German Beast Saga was not borrowed from abroad, and it was absurd to attribute its origin to Greek, Latin, or Oriental fables, since Æsop, the *Hitopadesa*, and the German fable have all three an innate dissimilarity. The Beast Saga sprang from oral tradition and was specifically German. Even the lion did not belong to it originally, but had gradually usurped the place of another native animal. The royal beast was in the first place most probably the *bear*, the real king of the German forests.

Grimm at first found many supporters for his theory, but it was not long before a reaction set in. Had there really existed a universal Saga deeply implanted in the minds of the Indo-Germanic races, then not only would there be earlier traces in epic literature, but, when the legend was eventually cast into epic form, we should expect to find something much more grandiose than the poems which have come down to us. It was proved that much of what Grimm had taken for primitive Germanic legendary material had, as a matter of fact, been borrowed by monastic poets from collections of the fables of antiquity and thence introduced into the Beast Epics. There is no definite trace either in Germany or in Northern Europe of a coherent epic Beast

Saga such as Grimm had attributed to the Indo-Germanic races, and, as far as we know, the earliest epic treatment of the subject took place in the monasteries of the Middle Ages. There were numerous collections of fables in existence at that time, and the Latin version of Æsop formed one of the most important primers in the monastic schools. The Greek verse translation by Babrios, in the second or third century A.D., of the original Greek prose Æsop, was in turn rendered into Latin distiches by Avianus in the fourth or fifth century. In addition, there was the Latin verse adaptation of Æsop by Phædrus in the reign of Tiberius, which was known to the Middle Ages in the prose version of *Romulus*. Both Avianus and *Romulus* in turn underwent various adaptations.

The fables of Æsop probably came originally from India, which has given us the Sanskrit collection of stories and fables known as the *Panchatantra* and the summary of the latter, the *Hitopadesa*. In the European fable and epic there appears the relationship between the lion and the fox, which does not occur in reality, but in the Indian fable we have the jackal in the place of the fox, and the connection between fox and wolf is common both to the Indian and European stories. In the *Physiologus*, where the nature of the animals is interpreted symbolically, it is religious conceptions, in the fables it is social conditions that are reflected.

Thus the theory of Grimm was thrown overboard, and the Beast Epic was considered to have a definitely monastic origin. This was the prevailing view until a French savant, Léopold Sudre, published in the year 1893 the results of his researches in his book entitled *Les Sources du Roman de Renart*. Sudre sets out to prove that the Hindu and Greco-Latin compilations reflect the animal folklore of antiquity, and the medieval epics that of the Middle Ages. The *Panchatantra*, the Æsopic apologues, and the French epic are fragments of an immense edifice of popular oral tradition. Sudre makes use of the investigations of the Finnish scholar Kaarle

Krohn, who came to the conclusion that there had been a cycle of beast-legends in Northern Europe which was, from the point of view of its subject-matter, independent of the Southern cycle of legends as well as of the Southern fable and epic literature. In these Northern stories the chief protagonist was the bear, whose opponent was always the fox. It was the bear who was continually being duped by the fox, but in the stories of Central and Southern Europe the bear was replaced by the wolf or some other animal. In the Oriental tales we find the lion and his two satellites, the jackal and the hyena; these two servants of the lion are in a state of constant rivalry, and the former is characterised by an extreme cunning, the latter by insatiable gluttony and brutal ferocity. These Oriental stories (the hostility of the jackal and the hyena developing into that of the fox and the wolf) were more numerous than the Northern tales of the fox and the bear, and were doubtless established in the Franco-German borderlands before the importation of the latter, and so they naturally imposed their form upon them. The two cycles became assimilated, since in each of them the fox played the same rôle, and the wolf remained his chief antagonist. Thus two story-cycles, based on different conceptions, and originating the one in the North and the other in the East, became fused into one harmonious unity. That is to say, the animal folklore of Central Europe, such as we have it, is for the most part a composite production, though that does not eliminate the probability of there having been beast-stories in those regions before this double importation.

By reducing to a minimum the probability of the Beast Epic having a monastic origin, based on foreign and especially classical sources, and tracing it preponderantly to popular, oral tradition, Sudre returned to a great extent to the theory of Grimm, though he denied the existence of an Indo-Germanic Beast Saga. His conclusions were almost universally accepted and controversial ardour became somewhat cooled.

The next considerable piece of independent research was undertaken by another French scholar, Lucien Foulet, who, in his book *Le Roman de Renard*, published in 1914, proceeded to demolish the arguments of Sudre and to demonstrate that in the first half of the twelfth century there is no trace either of a Beast Epic in the French language or of popular tales having as heroes Reynard the fox and Ysengrim the wolf. All he could find was a fugitive echo of the jests and pastimes of a small circle of clerics who were amateurs of Latin literature. The argument in favour of a folklore origin was based on the fact that beast-stories are found in such large numbers and in very different and widely distant countries, but, as Foulet truly points out, such a deduction is lacking in scientific accuracy. The stories which are now collected in obscure villages may quite plausibly have been handed down for centuries, but, since it is possible that the oral tradition sprang in the first place from the *Roman de Renard* itself or from one of the other Beast Epics, it is only arguing in a circle to suggest that because there is an oral tradition nowadays there was also an oral tradition in the Middle Ages. For the argument to have any validity, it would be necessary to prove that the present-day legends descend from legends which were extant before the time of the written epics. The twelfth century must be explained by the twelfth century, and not by the nineteenth.

The origin of the names of the two protagonists has not been satisfactorily explained. The German word *Reinhart* means "very hard" (and not "strong in counsel," as it is usually explained). *Ysengrim* means "the one with the iron helmet or mask." The German word for the fox replaced in France the French word *goupil*. The principal names are German, some being the actual names of persons and others denoting some characteristic of the animal.

It is not only in literature that are to be found proofs of the popularity of the beast-stories during the Middle Ages. In the Cathedral of Strassburg there were formerly to be seen opposite the pulpit two reliefs illustrating the funeral of the fox, who was pretending to be dead, but they have since been carved away; and a relief in the Cathedral of Basel represents a fox playing a fiddle to another animal. Guibert de Nogent, referring to disturbances at Laon in A.D. 1112, says that a man was called Ysengrim by an opponent, so that the term appears to have been quite intelligible to everybody, and there are other historical references which point to a widespread knowledge of the tales.

Whereas the Beast Fable is international in character, the Beast Epics in many respects bear the marks of the country in which they were written. There is one anecdote which forms the nucleus of all the Beast Epics, and that is the Æsopic fable of the healing of the sick lion by the fox, who recommends him to wrap himself in the wolf's skin. The oldest medieval version of this story is found in the Latin poem written by Paulus Diaconus at the Court of Charlemagne about 782-6. The lion falls sick and summons all the animals to bring him remedies. They all obey the call, with the exception of the fox, who is calumniated in his absence by his enemy, the bear, and condemned to death by the lion. He at last turns up, however, and informs the lion that he has been on a long journey in search of a remedy, which he has succeeded in discovering. The only cure for the lion is that he should be wrapped in the skin of the bear. The latter is thereupon flayed, and the fox not only justified in the eyes of the lion but also revenged on his old enemy. The substitution of the bear for the wolf is peculiar to this version, and does not occur elsewhere.

The same story constitutes the greater part of the oldest Beast Epic of which we have any trace, the *Ecbasis cuiusdam captivi per tropologiam* (The Escape of a Captive, in an allegory). This Latin poem in hexameters with internal rhyme, containing about 1,200 lines, consists of an outer and an inner story:—

In the month of April at the time of the full moon, a

young calf escapes from his stall in the Vosges into the forest, where he is captured by the wolf and carried off to the den of the latter, who is living there as a monk. The wolf informs him that, as he has refrained from meat for a long time and is tired of fasting, he will devour his captive on the morrow. The calf succeeds in persuading him to postpone the execution until early mass. After the wolf has had his supper, his two servants, the otter and the hedge-hog, arrive, and the former is ordered to guard the prisoner, while the latter lulls his master to sleep with a song accompanied on the zither. The wolf has a bad dream and wakes up, and though the otter interprets the dream to mean that the wolf will come to the gallows, the calf be freed, and the fox rejoice at his enemy's downfall, the villain only hardens his heart and gives the hedge-hog further orders concerning the preparation of his Easter meal. The next morning the shepherd discovers the absence of his calf, and the bull and the cow lament the loss of their child. The dog, however, who knows his way about the mountains and had heard the bleating of the calf the previous evening, now leads the whole herd, chief among them the powerful bull, to the wolf's den. The wolf springs up in alarm, but then calls to his two vassals to prepare for the battle, of which he is not afraid: the only animals he fears at close quarters are the boar and the stag, but his castle is unscalable. The fox might be able to undermine the fortress, but he does not appear to be among the hostile force. The two servants ask their master why he regards the fox as his worst enemy, and the wolf thereupon relates to them at great length the inner fable, the story of the sick lion and the wolf's skin, the victim having been an ancestor of the present wolf. Since that time there had existed a state of mortal enmity between the wolf and the fox, especially as the latter had been rewarded with the wolf's castle.

When the wolf has finished his story, the otter climbs the hill, and whom should she see but the fox, who bears in his hand a document from the king granting him in fief the castle of the wolf. The otter and the hedge-hog desert, and the castle is stormed. The fox, to avoid bloodshed, requests the wolf to come out, in order that all may see the handsome, noble, learned, generous and brave prince. The wolf is enticed by these flatteries to come out into the open, and the bull fixes him to a tree with his horns. The calf has meanwhile escaped. The fox sets an epitaph over the executed wolf and takes possession of the castle. On the way home the calf relates his experiences, and thanks God for his rescue.

Though the inner fable is of classical origin, the outer story is an adaptation of the parable of the lamb that was caught by the wolf and taken back by the shepherd. The lamb has given place to a calf, just as in the fairy-tale of *Red Riding Hood* it is a child who nearly becomes the victim of the wolf. The allegorical intention of the author is obvious from the title of the poem, and the moral is that of renunciation of the world. The idea of the wolf as a monk may have been suggested by the Gospel of St. Matthew, vii. 15, which is a warning against false prophets who come in sheep's clothing but inwardly are ravening wolves. To understand the circumstances in which the *Ecbasis* was written, it will be necessary to examine the historical background.[1]

The second half of the ninth century and the beginning of the tenth were not favourable to the monasteries of the West Franconian countries. The reforms introduced by Louis the Pious through the agency of Benedict of Aniane in 817 had been gradually destroyed by internal and external strife, and the monasteries were lacking in strong personalities who might have checked decay. They fell into the hands of lay abbots, and with the secularization of their possessions there went hand in hand a slackening of discipline. The diminished revenues were no longer sufficient to keep the monks in food, and many of them left their cells and wan-

---

[1] The following historical sketch is based upon the Introduction to Ernst Voigt's edition of the *Ecbasis captivi* (*Quellen und Forschungen*, vol. viii. Strassburg, 1875).

dered about the country, where they soon began to show signs of the corrupting influences of the outer world.

It was not only the monasteries in the neighbourhood of large towns that were exposed to these temptations; the most extravagant signs of degeneracy were sometimes exhibited by those established in the solitude of the mountains. Lorraine in particular, which had lost its national independence after the death of Lothar II in 869, was one of the worst victims of the internal wars of the time. It was taken possession of by the West Franks, then in 870 divided between the West and the East Franks; in 880 the whole country was won by the latter, in 911 by the former and in 925 again by the latter, until during the years 939–42 Otto I confirmed his possession of the state after severe fighting. Thus Lorraine fluctuated between the two nations, and suffered in addition from the encroachments of the dukes and betrayal by its bishops.

In the South of France, however, there arose a powerful impulse for reform. The Benedictine monastery of Cluny was founded in 910 by William the Pious, Count of Auvergne and Duke of Aquitaine, who appointed Berno as its first abbot. The latter carried out the earlier reforms of 817 with the utmost strictness, but it was his successor, St. Odo (927–942), who spread the fame of the Cluniac discipline throughout France and even beyond its borders. He directed all his energies towards making Cluny the centre of a reform, and among other monasteries which came under his influence was that of St. Evre in the neighbourhood of Toul. This monastery was reformed by Gauzlin, Bishop of Toul, on the basis of the discipline of Cluny, and one of the members of this monastery was the author of the *Ecbasis*. The poem was inspired by this reform, and its theme is the return from careless vagrancy to the strict discipline of monastic life.

All our knowledge of the author has to be deduced from the poem itself. He was probably born in the year 912, and the preponderance of Germanisms in the language, together with other hints, makes it probable that he lived on that side of the border where the Germanic language was spoken. He was of noble birth, and born presumably in the neighbourhood of Luxemburg, but there is no clue to his name. He appears to have led a pleasant, lazy existence at St. Evre, until the reform of the monastery in 936 brought about a tightening of discipline. The introduction and the outer fable inform us of his subsequent experiences. He could not bring his mind to concentrate on regular work, warnings and punishments were of no avail, so he was imprisoned in the monastic dungeons. He escaped to the Vosges, but was recaptured and thrown into prison once more. He not only had to submit to corporal punishment but his imprisonment was to be for life, unless he could give proof of his moral and spiritual conversion. In order to regain his freedom, he began to write, most probably between 936 and 940, shortly after the reform of the monastery had been accomplished, his poem, the *Ecbasis captivi*, in which he decided to portray his own experiences and his return to the fold. Like the erring calf, he had been tempted by the world and fallen into the hands of the devil, but with the help of the brethren had been rescued and brought back into the true path.

The author demonstrates his classical education by numerous quotations. About 250 lines are borrowed wholly or partly from Horace, especially from the *Satires* and the second book of *Epistles*; and among other Latin authors whom he utilised were Prudentius, Virgil, and Ovid. Though there is little trace of creative imagination, the author cannot be denied a certain amount of poetic talent, more particularly in the working out of some of the scenes. There are numerous references to ecclesiastic and political affairs, but it is doubtful whether the satirical tendency, so marked in the later Beast Epic, is yet intentional.

Although the *Ecbasis* testifies to the epic treatment of the theme in ecclesiastical circles, it has no direct connection with the subsequent Beast Literature. It is not until two hundred years later that we meet with the second Latin

Beast Epic, *Ysengrimus*, which was written about 1152.[1] In this poem the animals are for the first time individualised by means of proper names, and it is no longer a question of a fox and a wolf, but of *Reinardus* and *Ysengrimus*; the lion is *Rufanus*, the bear *Bruno*, the ass *Balduinus*, and so forth. Although there are borrowings from classical writers, particularly from Ovid, on whom in some respects he modelled his style, the poet gives the impression of original talent and considerable plastic power. The intention is quite definitely satirical, and, unlike the *Ecbasis*, the picture is in the main objective. Brute strength is shown to be inferior to wisdom, and the educated layman superior to a sensual and ignorant clergy. The vices of the latter which the poet especially attacks are greed, laziness, and simony; the bishops appear to be rapacious, the abbots gluttonous, the whole of the clergy shows a frivolous sophistry in the evasion of Biblical and disciplinary regulations, and the author even attacks the right of the papal hierarchy. The accusations against the Court and Society are more moderate, but the power of wealth is deplored which puts in the shade the hereditary nobility. This expression of dislike for the *nouveau riche* sounds strangely modern.

Ysengrimus contains about 6,600 lines and the following are the twelve adventures it relates:—

Reinardus, who has insulted the wife and children of Ysengrimus, meets the latter in the forest, and the wolf announces his intention of devouring him, or, as he puts it, of giving him safe shelter in his belly. Reynard, however, offers to procure for Ysengrim a slaughtered pig which a peasant is just carrying by. This he succeeds in doing, and Ysengrim devours the pig, leaving only a gnawed fragment of intestine for the fox. Reynard plans revenge. The next time he meets Ysengrim, who is represented as a monk, he

---

[1] *Ysengrimus* was formerly known as *Reinardus Vulpes*. There is a shorter version, known as *Ysengrimus abbreviatus*, which was formerly thought to be older than the so-called *Reinardus Vulpes*, but has now been proved to be merely a later abridgement.

advises him to avoid the sin of eating meat and to keep to a fish diet. They go at night to a frozen pond and, on the advice of the fox, Ysengrim dips his tail in the water. Reynard slips into the village, steals a fowl from the priest, and so induces the villagers to pursue him to the pond, where the wolf's tail has become frozen in. A peasant-woman aims a clumsy blow at Ysengrim with the axe, but only succeeds in amputating his tail, and he escapes. Reynard, who has crept away to devour his fowl, hears the wolf uttering lurid threats, but with tears in his eyes he comes forward and consoles him with the assurance that the mutilated tail will contribute to his greater holiness, and offers him the opportunity of obtaining compensation for his injury. There are four rams contending about the partition of a field, and Ysengrim can settle the dispute. They go to meet the rams, and Ysengrim stands in the middle of the field, so that the rams can run towards him, one from each boundary, and so decide the partition—the first to arrive receiving the largest share. They do so, and the wolf is nearly butted to death. The next incident is the tale of the sick lion, Rufanus. When Reynard eventually arrives at Court, he exhibits a number of pairs of worn-out shoes, and informs the lion that he has undertaken the arduous journey to Salerno (where the great medical school of the Middle Ages was situated), and has brought back medicinal herbs. It is, however, also necessary for the lion to sweat beneath the skin of a $3\frac{1}{2}$-year-old wolf. Ysengrim can lend his, and have it back when the lion has finished with it. When the king is convalescent, Bruno the bear is ordered to relate further adventures for the entertainment of the Court. Bruno thereupon gives a poem, which he has himself composed, to Grimmo the boar, who reads the following three adventures:

Bertiliana the doe and seven other animals go on a pilgrimage. An old wolf tries to approach the company, and Reynard thinks out a scheme. He cuts the head from another wolf, which he finds hanging on a tree, and tells Joseph the

ram what to do if the old wolf should appear as a guest. At
nightfall the travellers sit down to supper, and the wolf
enters their hut with peaceful greetings. They bid him sit
down, and Bertiliana asks: "What shall we give our guest to
eat?" Joseph answers: "We have nothing but old wolves'
heads." "Bring one of them along," says the fox. Joseph
fetches the head, and the wolf begins to wish he were somewhere else. Reynard cries: "This one is no good, fetch a
bigger one." Joseph goes, and brings back the same head.
So the game continues, until the wolf suddenly remembers
that his wife and children are waiting for him at home,
begs to be excused, and takes his leave. He collects all the
wolves of his tribe, and the pack falls on the pilgrims, but
is eventually routed. The next morning Sprotinus the cock
and Gerardus the gander decide to desert the company.
Reynard follows Sprotinus and requests him to continue the
pilgrimage, but the cock refuses. Reynard captures Sprotinus
by cunning, but the latter is equally clever and escapes.
The third adventure describes how the wolf becomes a
monk. Reynard meets a cook, whose lambs he had once
protected from the wolf, and who now gives him a dish of
fritters. The fox schemes to get the better of the wolf and
has himself tonsured. When he meets Ysengrim, he tells him
how he has joined a monastery and is now able to eat his
fill. He allows the wolf to share his fritters, and to be persuaded to become a monk. After being tonsured, Ysengrim
follows Reynard to the monastery of Blandinium, where he
is to look after the flocks. Meanwhile Reynard slips off to
Ysengrim's house, fouls his children, and violates his wife.
The wolf behaves with his usual uncouthness in the monastery, and is ordained by the monks with blows and mockery,
so that he is glad to escape. On discovering Reynard's
treachery he swears eternal revenge. It is this anecdote
which explains the grudge borne by Ysengrim against
Reynard at the beginning of the poem.

The boar ceases his recital, and the story continues with
the further adventures of the excoriated wolf. Ysengrim

meets Corvigarus the horse, and demands his skin in replacement of that which he has lost. Corvigarus replies: "You have lost your hood, but your tonsure has grown; I will shave it for you with my knife." Corvigarus carries his knife on his hoof, which is shod with iron rings. Ysengrim refuses to be tonsured again, and reproaches the horse with having stolen the rings from the monastery doors. Corvigarus pretends to be repentant and asks for indulgence: he holds his foot out to the wolf, and, when the latter is about to take it, drives it into his face. Later on, Ysengrim again meets Reynard, who tells him that Joseph the ram is responsible for the loss of his skin, and bids him come to Joseph's stable to take his revenge. Ysengrim demands payment for the land he has measured, twelve-fold interest, and the ram himself. Joseph is agreeable and offers to jump into the wolf's maw. Ysengrim plants his feet firmly on the ground, opens his vast jaws, and Joseph butts him again, covering him with wounds. Subsequently Reynard takes the lion on a visit to Ysengrim's house, but, as the latter has no entertainment to offer, they all go out and hunt a calf, which the wolf is to divide. He makes three equal shares, and receives from the king a blow which tears a strip of skin from shoulder to tail. Reynard is then ordered to do the sharing out, and allots the chief portion to the lion, the second to the lioness, and the third to the lion cub. He reserves for himself only a foot, which, however, the lion may have for himself if he so wishes. Rufanus is content, and allows Reynard to keep the foot, but asks who has taught him to divide the booty so skilfully. Reynard replies: "My uncle, the wolf." Ysengrim's next misfortune is to lose a foot in a trap, again through the cunning of Reynard, and his last adventure is a meeting with Salaura the sow, who possesses more cunning than nine abbots. He calls her aunt, and asks for a kiss of peace. She makes fun of his amputated foot and tells him to pinch her ear as soon as she begins to sing. Her piercing shrieks summon a whole herd of pigs, who fall upon the wolf and tear him to pieces.

The poem concludes with speeches by Salaura and Reynard about the way of the world; the former makes bitter accusations against the Pope, and Reynard says that, if Ysengrim were still alive, he would not tolerate Salaura's audacious language, but would revenge the innocent Pope.

The story of the loss of the wolf's tail, while fishing, is similar to a widespread legend which is told in Northern Europe about the bear, to explain the shortness of his tail.

One of the most striking features of *Ysengrimus* is that the more cultivated animals are supposed to come from France. Both their manners and their language are those of the romance countries, whereas the wolf and the donkey, the types of laziness, stupidity, and coarseness, live in Germany Voigt[1] considers that the author was a German, praising French culture at the expense of his native land; that he was born in the Rhineland, but lived and wrote his poem in Flanders, where he was a monk in the monastery of Blandigny in Ghent and was intimately connected with the local church of St. Pharahilda. Willems,[2] on the other hand, thinks that such an antipathy to things German could not have been expressed by a writer of German origin. He declares that the author was not resident in the Flemish part of Flanders but in the French part, and that he had never been to Germany at all: his home was probably in Lille, and his mother-tongue French. The latter theory has, however, received but little support.

One of the manuscripts which have handed down to us the story of *Ysengrimus* states that the author was called *Nivardus* and that he was a *magister*. He was most probably of noble birth, but though the name itself is common, it has not been possible to trace in other documents a magister Nivardus, who might have been the author of *Ysengrimus*. The poem contains numerous references to contemporary events and personalities, and the catastrophe of the Second

[1] E. Voigt, *Ysengrimus* [Halle a. S., 1884].
[2] L. Willems, *Etude sur l' Ysengrinus* [Ghent, 1895].

Crusade appears in particular to have made a deep impression upon the poet's mind.

For the next development in the history of the Beast Epic, we have to look to France. Between 1170 and 1250 the "branches" of the *Roman de Renard*,[1] twenty-seven in all, came into existence. In both the *Ecbasis captivi* and *Ysengrimus* the wolf was the chief character, but from now on the fox takes the foremost place. The *Roman de Renard* is not a coherent unity, but a collection of stories, or "branches," whose number and sequence is different in the various manuscripts and some "branches" contain more than one adventure. The sequence is often arbitrary, and the "branches" were composed at different periods and by different authors. The title "roman" is somewhat misleading, and there are even some stories where the fox does not appear at all.

The first "branche" commences with an announcement of the author's intention to supplement the story of Perrot, who is no doubt Pierre de St. Cloud, the author of the sixteenth "branche." He therefore relates the story of the summoning of the animals to the Court of Noble the lion, the accusation of Renard the fox by Ysengrin the wolf and Chantecler the cock, and the arrival of Renard at the Court. Noble has a gallows erected to hang Renard, but finally grants the latter's wish that he be permitted to proceed "beyond the sea" to implore God's pardon. Renard becomes a pilgrim, but after leaving the Court, he captures Couart the hare, and, from the top of a hill overlooking a valley where the lion and his barons are assembled, he throws down his cross, his pilgrim's wallet and staff, and hurls insults at the royal retinue. He is pursued, but escapes wounded to his castle of Maupertuis, which is forthwith besieged. The king proclaims that whoever captures Renard should put him to death without more ado. After various

---

[1] The edition to which reference is made in this article is the standard text of E. Martin, published at Strassburg, 1882–7.

adventures, Renard jumps through a window, falls into a dyer's vat, and is dyed yellow. Meeting Ysengrin, he disguises his voice, and, being already unrecognizable owing to his change of colour, he succeeds in passing for an English *jongleur*. He plays a trick on Ysengrin, who arrives home badly wounded only to be expelled from home by Hersent the she-wolf. Renard arrives home in time to find his wife Hermeline marrying again, as she believed him dead. He lures the new bridegroom into a trap, where he is torn to pieces by dogs, and puts Hermeline out of doors, as well as Hersent, who had come to prepare the nuptial bed. The two ladies quarrel, a fight ensues, and Hermeline's life is only saved by a pilgrim, who succeeds in reconciling them to their husbands.

This "branche" is important as being the main source of the Flemish poem *Van den vos Reinaerde*, and it is interesting to note that there is in the *Panchatantra* a story of a jackal who plunges into a vat of indigo, comes out blue, and is not recognised by the dogs who are pursuing him.

Only three of the "branches" mention the names of their authors; the ninth is by a "prêtre de la Croix en Brie," the twelfth by Richard de Lison, a Norman, who tells us that he has pursued ecclesiastical studies, and the sixteenth, already mentioned above, by Pierre de St. Cloud. The twenty-seventh "branche" is distinguished from the others by being written in a dialect which is half French, half Italian. The majority of the other "branches" are by poets from Picardy or the Ile de France, and the extent of the work may be judged by the fact that it contains over 30,000 lines.

As we have seen, the Latin Beast Epics were the work of monks or priests, but the "branches" of the *Roman de Renard* were composed by the *trouvères*, the medieval Court-poets of Northern and Central France. When we come to the question of the origin of the various "branches," we find it necessary to deal again with the theories of Sudre and Foulet, whose general views on the Beast Epic have already been noticed.

Sudre endeavours to prove that the *Roman de Renard* is

entirely a work of tradition, that the *trouvères* only rewove material which had already been elaborated by numerous predecessors whose work has not come down to us. He does not deny all connection between the "branches" and the antique apologues, or the Latin poems which are derived from the latter, but he finds it impossible to establish between these two types of literary production anything but an indirect link and a distant relationship. The *trouvères* were not translators, except in the case of the eighteenth "branche," which is a faithful copy of a Latin poem called *Sacerdos et Lupus*. The *trouvères*, in composing their poems, drew for the most part upon their memories, in which was stored up a vast treasure of ancient folklore, though they did not wholly ignore the minor literary sources of classical fable and clerical epic.

Foulet's theory is that the *Roman de Renard* comes from books, but that it was written for the people, and it is the people who have been responsible for its success. All the echoes of contemporary folklore which investigators have pretended to recognise in writings of the thirteenth century are really echoes of the *Roman de Renard*, which had become the property of the people. Foulet thinks that the immense popularity of this work during the Middle Ages has not been sufficiently emphasised, and that attempts have been made to explain the "branches" by modern legends which are derived from those very "branches." The *Roman de Renard* was in fact the work of a score or so of clerics of the twelfth and thirteenth centuries; the *trouvères* were people who had studied at the schools, and either taken orders or had at one period the intention of doing so. They did not draw directly from the sources of antiquity, but found their models in the prose *Romulus*, possibly in the *Ecbasis captivi* and above all in *Ysengrimus*.

When views are so conflicting as these, the truth is most probably to be found in the middle way. Foulet goes too far in his underestimation of folklore, and Sudre does not lay sufficient weight on the influence of the monasteries.

There can be little doubt that a popular tradition existed before the composition of the various "branches," but it is even more certain that the main inspiration for the *Roman de Renard* came from *Ysengrimus*, which was the source of some of the best-known stories. All the stories in *Ysengrimus* are to be found in the French epic, with the exception of the final one, which relates the death of the wolf. The issue is even more confused by the fact that the *trouvères* imitated and copied each other. They wrote their poems, however, in the first place, to amuse their hearers. The French Beast Epic parodies the Heroic Epic and the Romance of Chivalry, but the inconspicuous satirical and didactic tendencies are later developments and not intrinsic elements, as they are in *Ysengrimus*.

The next two Beast Epics were both derived from the "branches" of the *Roman de Renard*: one was written in a High-German dialect, the other in Flemish.

About 1180, a travelling minstrel named Heinrich der Glîchezâre, who came from Alsace, wrote his poem of *Reinhart Fuchs*, based upon the oldest "branches" of the French epic.[1] Whereas in Bavaria and Austria the epic poetry both of the knights and wandering minstrels (*Spielleute*) was based on the national tradition, that of Western Germany was deeply indebted to French sources. Heinrich's poem, which was written about 1180,[2] has come down to us complete, with the exception of a small hiatus, in a manuscript of the thirteenth century, but we also have a badly

[1] It has been submitted by various investigators that *Reinhart Fuchs* is a translation, not of "branches" which have come down to us in manuscripts, but of older "branches" of which these are but later versions. Others think that both *Reinhart Fuchs* and the *Roman de Renard* sprang, independently of one another and at different periods, from a cycle of Beast Poems. Finally, as though to leave no possible theory unuttered, it has been suggested that it is the "branches" of the French poem which are adaptations of *Reinhart Fuchs*! This latter theory is hardly tenable, since it was the fashion in the twelfth and thirteenth centuries for German poets to take their material from the French and not vice versa.

[2] Cf. *Reinhart Fuchs*, hrsg. von Karl Reissenberger. 2nd ed. [Halle a. S., 1908].

mutilated fragment of an earlier manuscript, which used to be known by the title of *Îsengrînes nôt*.

Reinhart Fuchs, which runs to 2,266 lines, contains a large number of adventures :—

Reinhart is first of all outwitted by the smaller creatures, the cock, the titmouse, the raven, and the cat. Then he seeks the comradeship of Isengrin, and the latter continually gets the worst of it. Among other tricks Reinhart tempts him into the wine-cellar of a monastery, where he becomes intoxicated, begins to sing, and escapes only with great difficulty when the monks come upon the scene. The two beasts separate : Reinhart builds himself a house which he calls *Übelloch* (= Fr. *Maupertuis*), and one day the hungry wolf comes along and makes his peace with Reinhart, after smelling the eels which the latter is roasting. Isengrin is willing to become a monk in order to enjoy such good food, and Reinhart prepares him a tonsure by pouring boiling water on his head. The poor wolf is then led to a frozen pond to fish, and loses his tail. Reinhart's violation of Isengrin's wife is the last straw, and the wolf resolves to bring the matter before the King.

An ant had crept into the ear of King Vrevel the lion, and was tormenting him because he had destroyed the castle of the ants who refused to recognise his sovereignty. The lion thinks this is a divine punishment because he has neglected to hold a court of justice for some time. He therefore summons all the animals to attend, and Isengrin submits his accusation against the absent Reinhart. Krimel the badger endeavours to defend the accused by suggesting that Hersent the she-wolf was not averse to his advances, and that, as she was bigger than he, the crime of which Reinhart was accused could not have been committed by him. Nevertheless the fox is condemned to be hanged, but a camel suggests he should be summoned three times to appear before the Court. Bruno the bear is sent to fetch him, but is persuaded by the fox to put his head in a split tree, where there is supposed to be a store of honey. Reinhart withdraws the wedge, and Bruno is caught. He escapes with the loss of his ears and the skin of his head, and returns to the Court. This time Dieprecht the cat is sent to Reinhart's castle, but he also is lured into a trap. When the third summons is brought by Krimel the badger, Reinhart goes back, equipped as a doctor, with the messenger. He walks calmly up to the King, greets him on behalf of Master Bendin, a physician of Salerno, and gives a medicine for his illness. Vrevel must in addition be wrapped in the skins of a wolf and a bear, and the hood of a cat, with a strip of stag's skin from the nose to the tail. In order that the King may have a dish of bacon and boiled fowl, the hen Pinte is killed and a joint cut from the haunch of the boar. Thus Reinhart revenges himself on all his enemies. He gives the King a hot bath and wraps him in the animals' skins, until this Turkish bath makes things too warm for the ant, who creeps out from the King's ear—and Vrevel is cured.

In the Latin and French epics, this adventure concludes with the showering of honours upon Reinhart. In this poem, however, the fox plays tricks even upon his friends: he persuades the King to invest the elephant with the kingdom of Bohemia, and to appoint the camel abbess of the Alsatian convent of Erstein. The consequence is that the elephant is driven out of Bohemia with blows, and the camel thrown in the Rhine by the nuns. Finally, Reinhart poisons the King and leaves the Court with Krimel the badger, his only friend. The poem ends with the moral that many an impostor is more esteemed at Court than an honest man.

It will be seen from the above summary that after the appearance of the fox at Court, the versions of the first "branche" of the *Roman de Renard* and *Reinhart Fuchs* diverge completely. The latter combines the story of the trial of the fox with that of the sickness of the lion, as in the Latin Epics, but when once Reinhart has appeared at Court, the trial is forgotten. The order of the adventures is peculiar, the fox being first of all the victim of his weaker enemies, and the climax is formed by the story from which all the Epics

31

appear to have sprung, so that Reinhart's revenge is complete. The references to Bohemia and the convent of Erstein are obscure, but there is an interesting reference to the Nibelungen Hoard. If Heinrich der Glîchezâre based his poem on half a dozen of the French "branches," he was by no means merely a literal translator. His work was more or less contemporary with that of the earlier *trouvères* from whom he took his subject-matter, and he must be granted credit for a certain share in the arrangement of his material, and for occasional satirical touches, though there is little sign that he wrote his Epic with consistent, satirical intention.

Heinrich's name is mentioned, both by himself and by the man who revised the poem in the thirteenth century; and, from the fact that he is alluded to as "her," he must have been of noble birth, though poor, since he was a wandering minstrel singing for money. On one occasion he says "swer des niht geloubet, der sol mir drumbe niht geben" ("whoever does not believe me, need not give me anything"), and again, "swer wil, daz ez gelogen sî, den læt er sîner gâbe vrî" ("whoever thinks this is a lie, is exempted from giving a present"). Glîchezâre means "simulator" or "dissembler," New-High-German "Gleissner," and was probably an inherited cognomen.

The literary influence of the High-German epic was insignificant, and it is to a poem written in the Netherlands in the Flemish tongue that the subsequent popularity of the Beast Stories, which has endured down to the present day, is ultimately due. *Van den vos Reinaerde* is the basis of all the versions which have helped to keep the fame of Reynard alive since the Middle Ages.

The Flemish epic, containing 3,476 lines, is the work of two men, Arnout and Willem, of whom the former was the older poet, while the latter continued the work and added a new introduction.[1] It must have been written in East

[1] It was only in 1908, when a new manuscript was discovered in the Castle of Dyck, near Neuss, by Düsseldorf, that it was proved beyond doubt that Willem was not the sole author.

Flanders, since most of the places mentioned in the course of the poem lie between Ghent and Antwerp. The date of composition was about 1250, and the source of the poem was the first of the French "branches," though the authors have also made use of other "branches" and added original touches. They relate how Reinaert, summoned to appear at Court, plays tricks on the first two messengers, the bear and the cat, but follows the badger, when he is summoned for the third time. He is condemned to death, but now the story diverges from that of the *Roman de Renard*. He deceives the King with a story of a secret conspiracy between the bear and the wolf, and at the same time informs him of a hidden treasure of which he knows the whereabouts. The King pardons him and allows him to go on a pilgrimage to Rome, after the bear and the wolf have been imprisoned and compelled to supply him with pieces of skin for shoes and a wallet. Soon after leaving the Court, the fox kills and eats Cuwaert the hare, and sends Belijn the ram back to the King with his wallet. The stupid ram thinks this contains letters for the King, but Reinaert had put in it the head of Cuwaert. The bear and the wolf are set free, and the ram and his tribe delivered up to them for all time as their lawful prey, while Reinaert and his family are outlawed. From now on, it is the trial of the fox, and no longer the sickness of the lion, that forms the central point of the adventures. The authors take both laity and clergy as butts for their satire, and the form of their poem is a parody of the serious epic.

About 1375, an unknown West Flemish poet revised the epic of Arnout and Willem and added a continuation of over 4,000 lines. This version, which is known as *Reinaerts Historie*, is inferior to the earlier work and written with a distinct didactic tendency. The continuation not only employs motives from the original poem, but the author has consulted other French "branches" and a Flemish version of *Romulus*, in addition to inserting matter of his own. The unity of the tale is disturbed, and in his anxiety to point a moral, the author often falls out of the rôle of the story-teller into that of the preacher.[1]

Even before the composition of *Reinaerts Historie*, about 1267–1274, there had been a translation into Latin verse of *Van den vos Reinaerde* by a monk, probably of Bruges, named Balduinus.

Reinaerts Historie was resolved into prose, supplied with an introduction and headings for the various anecdotes, and printed by Gheraert Leeu at Gouda 1479, under the title *Die historie van reynaert de vos*. It was this book, the first on the subject to be printed in any language, that William Caxton translated, and published as the *Historye of reynart the foxe* in 1481. A reprint of the Flemish book appeared at Delft in 1485.

In 1487, there was issued from the printing-works of Gheraert Leeu at Antwerp, a version, divided into chapters and provided with a gloss, by Hinrek van Alckmer. Of this version there is only extant a fragment of 223 lines, belonging to the first part of *Reinaerts Historie*; this fragment is now in the University Library at Cambridge and contains, in addition to the text, two fragments of glosses, four chapter-headings, and three woodcuts.

The gloss, containing political, social, and religious moralisations, was an innovation, and this fragment is important, since the version of Hinrek van Alckmer was the direct source of the Low-German epic *Reynke de vos*.

In the preface to *Reynke*, doubtless translated from the Flemish original, Hinrek van Alckmer describes himself as "scholemester unde tuchtlerer des eddelen, dogentliken vorsten unde heren hertogen van Lotryngen" ("school-master and tutor of the noble, virtuous prince and lord duke of Lorraine"). The book was printed anonymously at Lübeck in 1498, and for centuries, owing to this preface, it was thought that Hinrek was the author. The suggested authorship of Nicolaus Baumann has also been refuted, and the problem remains unsolved. The fact remains, however,

[1] Introduction to E. Martin's edition of *Reinaert* [Paderborn, 1874].

that so far as comparison is possible with the fragments of Hinrek's work, the Low-German translation can contain very little that is original.

In 1539 there appeared an edition of *Reynke* at Rostock, with considerable alterations. In particular, the gloss which in the *editio princeps* of 1498 was Catholic, was adapted to Protestant needs with polemics against the Catholic Church. The poem was praised by Martin Luther as a "living counterfeit of court life." The Flemish original was put on the *Index librorum prohibitorum* at Antwerp in 1570.

In 1544 there was printed anonymously at Frankfort-on-the-Main a translation of *Reynke* into High-German, with many mistakes and omissions, and from this High-German version Hartmann Schopper composed his Latin translation in four-foot iambics, which was published at Frankfort in 1567 under the title *Opus Poeticum de admirabili fallacia et astutia Vulpeculae Reinikes.* Schopper says that the author of the High-German version was Michael Beuther.

The Flemish folk-book, based on the prose edition of 1479, divided into chapters and combined with moralisations, was published at Antwerp in 1564.

There have since been innumerable editions, based either upon the Flemish or the Low-German version, and the best known of all the later adaptations is Goethe's *Reineke Fuchs*, based on the Low-German, which is written in hexameters, and was first published at Berlin in 1794.

The Beast Epic thus appears to have been limited to Flanders, the North of France and the West of Germany, though Beast Stories are found in all parts of the world. Before the publication of Caxton's translation in 1481, there is hardly any trace of the Beast Story in English literature. Chaucer took the story of his *Nonne Preestes Tale* from a fable which is related in the poems of Marie de France. It is the story of the capture of Chauntecleer by Russel the fox and the cock's clever escape, the same adventure which is met with in the Beast Epic.

Owing to Caxton's translation, it is the Flemish version which has formed the basis of nearly all the English reprints. There are, however, three editions, which have as their source the Low-German *Reynke*, and one which comes from the work of Schopper.

An anonymous English version in five-foot rhymed iambics, after Hartmann Schopper's Latin translation, was published in London by John Nutt in 1706, as *The Crafty Courtier: or the Fable of Reinard the Fox: Newly done into English Verse, from the Antient Latin Iambics of Hartm. Schopperus*. The "Argument" to the first chapter runs as follows:—

> "The Lion thro' his Realms decrees
> A Festival, and solemn Peace:
> His Subjects far and near resort,
> And croud their Passage to his Court.
> The wily Fox some danger ghess'd,
> Suspects it, and avoids the Feast."

Then come the first four lines:—

> "Nor Arms I sing, nor of Adventurous Deeds,
> Nor Shepherds playing on their Oaten Reeds,
> But civil Fury, and invidious Strife,
> With the false Pleasures of a Courtiers Life."

The moral "Conclusion" provides a pompous finale:—

> "Cease, cease thy Allegories, peevish Muse,
> Beware, lest Satyr sinks into Abuse;
> To Better Judgements leave the Publick Cares,
> And turn thy Splenetick Complaints, to Pray'rs
> For *England*, and for all in Place and Pow'r,
> Whose hearts are *English*, and whose Hands are Pure;
> Present the Reader with a Nobler Scene,
> A Court refin'd, a Senate; and a Queen
> A Fair Defender of our Faith, and Law;
> And only Worthy to succeed NASSAU."

The first translation from the Low-German, by D. W. Soltau, was published at Hamburg in 1826 as *Reynard the Fox: A burlesque Poem of the 15th Century*. Soltau says in his preface that he has endeavoured to mitigate as much as possible some passages in the poem, "which savour a little of the indelicate taste of the middle age," and has thought it expedient to transplant the scene of action from Germany to England.[1]

A version by Samuel Naylor in four-foot rhymed iambics, the metre of *Hudibras*, was published in London by Longmans in 1844 (dated 1845). Naylor says he worked from the Low-German edition, "hovering between translation and paraphrase." He has also taken care "that no immodest word offend the ear." The title is *Reynard the Fox; a renowned Apologue of the Middle Age, reproduced in Rhyme.*

In 1852 E. W. Holloway translated *Reynke* into English verse, following to a great extent the metre of the original, but altering or qualifying in several instances the sense of passages which "if literally translated, would have been offensive to the taste of his readers, and must necessarily have had the effect of excluding the work from the family circle." The translation was published as *Reynard the Fox, a Poem in twelve Cantos*, by A. H. Payne in Dresden and Leipzig and W. French in London, and was embellished with thirty-seven engravings in steel, after designs by H. Leutemann.

It was not only in England that the Flemish version established its predominance, but also, of course, in the Netherlands, and, strange to say, in France. In the latter country, the *Roman de Renard* was forgotten until the end of the eighteenth century, and the French renewed acquaintance with Reynard through the medium of translations from the Flemish. The Low-German version has prevailed, not only in Germany (chiefly through the popularity of Goethe's poem), but also in Denmark and Sweden, and it even appears to have been translated into Icelandic. The latest, and not the least striking, example of the eternally human appeal of the Beast Tale, is to be found in the American stories of Uncle Remus.

[1] The original MS. of this translation, with thirteen fine sepia drawings, was apparently sent by the author to the Duke of Cambridge, to whom he dedicated his poem, and is now in the possession of Professor R. Priebsch, of University College, London.

BIBLIOGRAPHY

E. Voigt: *Ecbasis Captivi* (*Quellen und Forschungen*, No. viii. Strassburg, 1875).

E. Voigt: *Ysengrimus* (Halle, 1884).

E. Martin: *Le Roman de Renart*, 3 volumes and Supplement, containing *Observations sur le Roman de Renart* (Strassburg, 1882–7).

K. Reissenberger: *Reinhart Fuchs* (2nd edn., Halle, 1908).

E. Martin: *Reinaert* (containing *Van den vos Reinaerde* and *Reinaerts historie*. Paderborn, 1874).

F. Prien: *Reinke de Vos* (*Altdeutsche Textbibliothek*, No. 8. Halle, 1887).

J. W. Muller and H. Logeman: *Die Hystorie van Reynaert die Vos* (critical edn. of the 1479 prose text. Zwolle, 1892).

L. Sudre: *Les Sources du Roman de Renart* (Paris, 1893).

L. Foulet: *Le Roman de Renard* (Paris, 1914).

L. Willems: *Etude sur l' Ysengrinus* (Ghent, 1895).

L. Willems: *Bulletin de la Société d'Histoire et d'Archéologie de Gand* (*Re* the newly discovered MS. of *Reinaert*. Pp. 125–141. Ghent, 1908).

H. Degering: *Van den Vos Reynaerde* (the text of the newly discovered MS. Münster, 1910).

Kaarle Krohn: *Bär* (*Wolf*) *und Fuchs* (translated from the Finnish. Helsingfors, 1889).

Karl Breul: *The Cambridge Reinaert Fragments* [*Culemann Fragments*] (Cambridge, 1927).

THE HISTORICAL DOCTOR FAUST AND THE FOLK-BOOK

THE story of the man who sells his soul to the powers of evil in return for material gain, is one of the most ancient in the history of humanity. It is perhaps as old as humanity, for when the light of self-consciousness first began to dawn on man, he no doubt desired to know more than his limited intellect could tell him, or to possess something that the world could not or would not give him. When he looked around, and was frightened at his own littleness, he created gods for his protection, and these gods he endeavoured to propitiate, until they became his tyrants. They were the symbols of his hopes and fears, so that when he was propitiating his gods he was stereotyping the limitations of his own mind. And the most important of those limitations was that he must not look beyond his manufactured gods for the hidden causes of things. A profound instinct nevertheless urged him to probe beyond, and the resulting spiritual unrest, which has always manifested itself spasmodically in the human race, underwent various personifications at different times. The elements of the Faust story were already present in the Garden of Eden—the Tree of Knowledge, the personification of Evil in the Serpent, and the Woman who was tempted to overstep the bounds of what was permitted by the orthodox authority, in order to grasp the Forbidden Fruit. It is significant for the peculiar construction of the human mind that it was always the Spirit of Evil which led the way to spiritual emancipation. In order to give concrete expression to his almost unconscious thirst for greater knowledge, man had to pretend to himself that this craving was pernicious. His very attempts to free himself from superstition provide the strongest evidence of the tortuous way in which his mind had to work, for it could only rise to a higher conception of its own worth by playing a game of self-deception.

The Faust problem was not peculiar to the Christian era. The Jews had their Solomon and the Greeks their Prometheus, but it was only at the end of the Middle Ages, when the old world was in the melting-pot, that there arose the most famous of all these legends, the most curious element in which is perhaps the fact that there was at the source of it an actual person.

I

The Historical Personage

The first record of an actual magician or adventurer of the
name of Faust occurs in a letter written in Latin by the
Abbot Trithemius of Würzburg, formerly of the Benedictine
monastery of Sponheim, near Kreuznach in the Palatinate,
to the mathematician and Court astrologer, Johann Virdung, on the 20th of August, 1507. The learned abbot, whose
name is the Latinized form of Johannes Tritheim, writes
to his friend in Heidelberg to warn him against a certain
Faust from whom the astrologer is expecting a visit:—

"That man, about whom you have written to me, Georgius
Sabellicus, who has ventured to call himself the prince of
necromancers is a vagabond, an empty babbler and a
knave: worthy to be whipped, that he might no longer
profess publicly abominable matters which are opposed
to the holy Church. For what are the titles which he assumes,
other than the signs of a most stupid and senseless mind,
which proves that he is a fool and no philosopher? Thus he
has adopted the following title: *Magister Georgius Sabellicus,
Faustus junior*, fountain of necromancers, astrologer, *magus
secundus*, chiromancer, aëromancer, pyromancer, second in
hydromancy. Behold the foolish temerity of the man; what
madness is necessary to call oneself the fountain of necromancy. A man who is, in truth, entirely devoid of education, should rather call himself a fool than a *magister*. But
his wickedness is not unknown to me. When some years ago
I was returning from the March of Brandenburg, I met this
man in the town of Gelnhausen, where I was told in the inn
of many frivolous things promised by him with great
audacity. When he heard of my presence, he fled forthwith
from the inn and could not be persuaded by anyone to
present himself to me.

He sent to me also by a citizen the advertisement of his foolishness, which I remember he sent to you. In that town I was told by priests, that he had said in the presence of many people that he had attained such great knowledge and memory of all wisdom, that if all the works of Plato and Aristotle, together with all their philosophy, had been absolutely wiped out of human memory, he would restore them, like a second Hebrew Ezra, by his genius, totally and more excellently than before.

When I was later on in Speyer, he came to Würzburg, and is said to have boasted with similar conceit in the presence of many people, that the miracles of our Redeemer Christ are no cause for astonishment; he himself could do everything that Christ had done, as often as and whenever he wished. This year, during the last days of Lent, he came to Kreuznach, where he made vast promises in a similar swaggering manner, and said that in alchemy he was the most perfect of any that had ever lived, and knew and could perform whatever the people wished. During this time the office of schoolmaster in this town was vacant, and it was conferred upon him through the intercession of Franz von Sickingen, the steward of your prince, a man who is exceedingly ardent with regard to mystical matters. But soon afterwards he began to practise a most infamous kind of fornication, forsooth, with the boys, and he fled, when the matter came to light, from his imminent punishment.

This is what is evident to me, according to the most certain testimony, concerning that man whose visit you are awaiting with such eagerness."

The accusations of the abbot are to be taken with a pinch of salt, for he was himself suspected of dabbling in magic, and his indignation may have been coloured by more than a tinge of jealousy. He is known to have declaimed before the Emperor Maximilian against the followers of the black art, and there is a letter, written by him only four days before the above epistle to Virdung, in which he protests against the imputing to him of magic practices. He was even rumoured to have conjured up the spirits of the dead in the presence of the Emperor. At any rate, he does not seem to have been anxious for popular inclusion among the necromancers. Neither is it at all certain that there is any truth in the scandal about the school at Kreuznach, for that was the sort of vice which it was usual to attribute to dissolute magicians.

It cannot be explained why Faust should have called himself *junior*, for there is no trace of any earlier magician of the same name. Whether *Sabellicus* was his real name, and *Faustus junior* a kind of professional title, or whether George Faust attached the title *Sabellicus* to his name as an allusion to the magic art of the Sabines, is likewise a mystery. It will be noticed that he is called *George*, and the same Christian name occurs again, six years later, in the second existing reference to Faust.

Conrad Mutianus Rufus (Conrad Mut, Canon at Gotha, called Rufus on account of his red hair), a friend of Reuchlin and Melanchthon, and one of the most cultured of the Humanists, makes the following statement in a letter written from Erfurt to his friend Heinrich Urbanus on the 7th of October, 1513:—

"There came a week ago to Erfurt a certain chiromancer named Georgius Faustus, *Helmitheus Hedebergensis*, a mere braggart and fool. The professions of this man and of all the fortune-tellers are vain. The rude people marvel at him, the priests should denounce him. I heard him swaggering at the inn. I did not reprove his boastfulness, for why should I bother about the foolishness of others?"

These two George Fausts are obviously the same person. The term *Helmitheus Hedebergensis* may be meant for *Hemitheus Hedelbergensis*, half-god of Heidelberg, where the charlatan perhaps pretended to have studied.[1] There was a Bachelor named Johann Faust, of Simmern, at Heidelberg

[1] H. Düntzer: *Die Sage von Dr. Joh. Faust* [Scheible's Kloster, 1847].

in the year 1509, but it is unlikely that he has any connection with our Faust.

There is a legend that Faust was given asylum at the monastery of Maulbronn by the Abbot Entenfuss in the year 1516, and that he there pursued his alchemistic activities. The well-known "Faust tower" which is still shown there was, however, not built until nearly a hundred years later.

The next reference we find is an entry in the account book of the Bishop of Bamberg by the latter's chamberlain, under the date 12th of February, 1520:—

"Item 10 gulden given and presented to Doctor Faustus *philosophus* in honour of his having cast for my gracious master a nativity or *indicium*, paid on Sunday after Scholastica by the order of Reverendissimus."

A less flattering entry is that in the minutes of the resolutions of the Town Council of Ingolstadt in 1528:—

"To-day, Wednesday after St. Vitus, 1528. The fortune-teller shall be ordered to leave the town and spend his penny elsewhere." This is supplemented by another entry in the record of expulsions: "To-day, Wednesday after St. Vitus, 1528, one who calls himself Dr. Jörg Faustus of Heidelberg has been told to spend his penny elsewhere, and has promised not to resent or mock such summons of the authorities."

It will be noticed that the same Christian name again occurs, in conjunction with the reference to Heidelberg.

There is then a gap of some eleven years before we meet the name again in the *Index Sanitatis* of the physician Philipp Begardi of Worms, published in 1539:—

"There is also to be found a renowned and bold man; I did not wish to have mentioned his name, but it will not be hidden or unknown. For some years ago he wandered through almost every province, principality and kingdom, made his name known to everybody, and boasted loudly of his great art, not only in medicine, but also in chiromancy, necromancy, physiognomy, crystal-gazing and more of such arts. And not only boasted, but also gave himself out to be and wrote himself as a famous and experienced master. He also himself acknowledged and did not deny, that he was, and was called Faust, and signed himself *Philosophus Philosophorum*, etc. There has, however, been a great number of people who have complained to me that they have been swindled by him. His promises were as great as those of Thessalus. Similarly his fame, like that of Theophrastus also; but the fulfilment, as I learn, was found to be very small and fraudulent; yet he was not slow in taking money, and at his departure many people were cheated. But what can one do about it, gone is gone."

When Philipp von Hutten, the cousin of the more famous Ulrich von Hutten, was about to start on his first expedition to Venezuela in 1534, Faust prophesied that the voyage would be unfortunate, and he was right, for von Hutten, in a description of the voyage written in 1540, writes: "I must acknowledge that the philosopher Faustus divined it correctly, for we have had a very bad year." A rival fortune-teller, Joachim Camerarius, who had declared that the voyage would be lucky, asks in a letter to a friend, written in 1536, what Faust can prophesy about the German Emperor's next battle with the King of France.

Johann Gast, a Protestant clergyman at Basel, relates two anecdotes of Faust in the edition of his *Sermones Convivales* which appeared in 1548:—

"Concerning the Necromancer Faust

He once turned into a very wealthy monastery, in order to spend the night there. A brother sets before him ordinary, weak, not very tasty wine. Faust asks him for better wine from another barrel, which is usually given to distinguished guests. The brother says: 'I haven't the keys. The prior is asleep, and I may not rouse him.' Faust replies: 'The keys

45

lie in that corner; take them and open that barrel on the left and bring me a drink!' The brother refuses and declares that he has no permission from the prior to give the guests other wine. When Faust hears this, he says: 'In a short time thou wilt experience strange things, inhospitable brother!' Early next morning he went away full of bitterness, without taking leave, and sent a raging devil into the monastery, who made an uproar day and night, and set everything in motion in the church and in the rooms of the monks, so that they had no peace, whatever they did. At last they consulted as to whether they should abandon the monastery or totally destroy it. They therefore announced their misfortune to the Count Palatine, who took the monastery under his protection and sent away the monks, to whom he allows every year what they need, keeping the rest for himself. Some assert that even now, when monks enter the monastery, there arises such a tumult, that the inhabitants have no peace. The devil knows how to manage that.

Another Instance of Faust

When I was dining with him in the great College at Basel, he gave the cook birds of various kinds, concerning which I did not know where he had bought them or who had given them to him, since at that time none was being sold in Basel, and they were birds such as I have never seen in our neighbourhood. He had with him a dog and a horse, which, as I believe, were devils, since they could do everything. Some people told me that the dog had sometimes assumed the form of a servant and brought him food. The wretched man came to a terrible end; for the devil strangled him; his corpse lay on the bier on its face all the time, although it was turned round five times."

The chronicler appears to have been a superstitious person, and he is the first to refer to Faust as being in league with the Devil, for Trithemius had looked upon him as a dissolute, wandering scholar, and Begardi thought him little more than a common charlatan. None of the last three authorities quoted above has mention of Faust's Christian name, but he appears as *Johannes* in a book compiled by Johannes Manlius (Johann Mennel) in 1563, *Locorum Communium Collectanea*, which consists mainly of reports of conversations with Melanchthon, to whom the following reminiscence is also to be attributed:—

"I knew a man named Faustus of Kundling, a little town near my home. When he studied at Cracow, he had learned Magic, which was formerly keenly studied there and where public lectures were delivered about this art. Later he wandered about in many places and spoke about secret things. When he wanted to create a sensation at Venice, he announced that he was going to fly into the heavens. The devil then lifted him up in the air, but let him fall to earth again, so that he nearly gave up the ghost. A few years ago, this Johannes Faustus sat very downcast on his last day in a village in the duchy of Württemberg. Mine host asked him why he was so downcast, this not being his custom or habit; for he was usually a graceless rogue, who led a dissolute life, so that at one time and another his love affairs had nearly brought him to his death. He thereupon replied to the host in that village: 'Do not be frightened to-night!' At midnight the house was shaken. Since on the next morning Faustus had not risen and it was already noon, the host went into his room and found him lying beside the bed with his face twisted round, as the devil had killed him. During his life, he kept a dog, which was the devil. . . . This Faustus escaped from our town of Wittenberg, when the excellent prince, duke Johann, had given the order that he was to be arrested. In a similar way, he is said to have escaped likewise in Nuremberg. At the beginning of the meal, he felt warm; he immediately rose from the table and paid his scot to the host. He was hardly outside the door when the minions came and asked for him. This magician Faustus, an infamous beast, a cesspool (*cloaca*) of many devils, boasted that all the victories which had been won by the imperial armies in Italy, had been obtained for them by him through his magic, which was a most shameless lie."

This story is repeated by Andreas Hondorff in his *Promptuarium Exemplorum*, which appeared five years later, in 1568:—

"Such a necromancer was Johann Faustus, who practised many tricks through his black art. He had with him always a black dog, which was a devil. When he came to Wittenberg he would have been arrested by order of the Prince Elector, if he had not escaped. The same would have happened to him in Nuremberg also, where he likewise escaped. But this was his reward. When his time was up, he was in a tavern in a village of Württemberg. Upon the host asking him why he was so downcast, he replied, 'Do not be afraid to-night, if you hear a great banging and shaking of the house.' In the morning he was found lying dead in his room, with his neck twisted round."

There is a casual reference to Faust in the *Table-talk of Martin Luther*, edited by Johannes Aurifaber (Johann Goldschmidt) in 1566:—

"But when in the evening, at table, mention was made of a necromancer named Faustus, Doctor Martin says earnestly, 'the devil does not employ the services of magicians against me; had he been able to do me hurt, he would have done it long ago. He has no doubt had me often by the head, but he nevertheless had to let me go again.' "

In a chronicle concluded in the same year by the Count Froben Christoph von Zimmern, the scene of Faust's death is given as Staufen in Breisgau:—

"But that the practice of such art (of soothsaying) is not only godless, but extremely perilous, that is undeniable, as is proved by experience, and we know how it went with the famous necromancer Faustus. He, after many wonderful things which he did during his life, about which one could write a special treatise, was at last, at an advanced age, slain by the evil spirit in the province of Staufen in Breisgau."

And there is further a reference to his revenge on the inhospitable monks:—

"About that time (i.e. after 1539), Faustus died at, or at least not far from Staufen, the little town in Breisgau. During his life, he was a strange necromancer, who in our times could be found in German provinces and had so many strange dealings, that he will not easily be forgotten for many years. He lived to be an old man, and, as is said, died wretchedly. Many people have thought that he was killed by the evil spirit, whom in his lifetime he only called his brother-in-law (*Schwager*). The books which he left behind have come into the possession of the lord of Staufen, in whose province he died, and many people have afterwards tried to obtain them, and in my opinion desired in them a perilous and unlucky treasure. He charmed a spirit into the monastery of the monks of Lüxheim in the Vosges, which they could not get rid of for many years, and which troubled them strangely; for the sole reason that they had once been unwilling to give him shelter for the night, that was why he had procured for them this turbulent visitor; at the same time, it is said, that a similar spirit was attached to the former abbot of St. Diesenberg by an envious wandering scholar."

The last considerable reference, before the publication of the folk-book, is in the edition of *De Praestigiis Daemonum* by Johannes Wierus (Johann Weyer, or Wier), which appeared in 1568. A German edition of this book was published eighteen years later. Wierus was one of the most distinguished and enlightened physicians of his time, and he fought for years, at first with some success, against the fanatical persecution of witches which was providing human torches in every village in Germany. In this book on the illusions of the devils, he protests against the witch-burnings, and it is noticeable that he does not definitely refer to Faust's alleged compact with the Devil:—

"When formerly at Cracow in Poland necromancy was taught publicly, there came one of the name of Johannes Faustus, of Kundling, who in a short time understood this art so well, that a short time ago, before the year 1540, he practised it to the amazement of many and with many lies and frauds in Germany, publicly and without fear. What a strange hoaxer and adventurer he was, and what strange tricks he was able to perform, I will here only demonstrate to the reader by one instance, but with the instruction that he promise me beforehand that he will not imitate him. When on one occasion this necromancer Faustus on account of his wicked tricks was imprisoned at Battenburg, which lies on the River Maas and borders on the Duchy of Geldern, in the absence of the Count Hermann, the chaplain of that place, Dr. Johann Dorsten, a pious, simple man, showed him much kindness, because he had promised to teach him many good arts and make him a profoundly experienced man. Therefore, when he saw that Faust was very fond of drink, he sent him wine so long till the barrel was empty. But when the magician Faustus noticed that, and the chaplain also prepared to go to Graven to get a shave, he told him that if he would procure for him more wine, he would teach him an art, how to remove his beard without a razor or anything. When the chaplain forthwith agreed, he bade him take some arsenic and rub well his beard and chin with it, not telling him to prepare it beforehand and mix it with other things. When he did this, his chin began to burn, so that not only the hair fell out, but the skin and flesh came off as well.

"I knew another man who had a black beard, and was yellowish of face on account of his melancholy complexion. When he visited the magician Faust, the latter said to him: 'Really, I thought you were my brother-in-law, my sister's husband; and so I looked immediately at your feet, to see whether you had long, crooked claws!' Thus he compared the good man, because he was swarthy, to the devil, and called him also, as was always his custom, his brother-in-law. But he received his reward at last. For, as is said, he was found dead one morning beside his bed in a village in Württemberg, his face turned towards his back, and the previous night there was such a turmoil in the house, that the whole house shook."

And lastly, there is a reference to Faust's conjuring up the dead in Wolffgang Bütner's *Epitome Historiarum*, in 1576 :—

"I have heard that Faustus, at Wittenberg, showed to the students and to an exalted man N——, Hector, Ulysses, Hercules, Æneas, Samson, David and others, who came forth with fierce bearing and earnest countenance and disappeared again, and princely personages are also said to have been present at the time and to have looked on."

At this point it will be well to summarise what we have learnt about Faust from contemporary references. The difficulty with regard to his Christian name has already been mentioned. If his real name was *Georg*, it may have been forgotten and replaced by the more common one of *Johann*, or there may have been two magicians of the name of Faust, the older one named Georg and the later one Johann, who may have taken the name of Faust because it had already been rendered famous by his predecessor. The latter hypothesis is, however, extremely unlikely, and there seems very little reason to doubt that all the references are to the same individual. It has been suggested that the name Johann may have originated through confusion with Johann Fust, the printer, but the latter died in the year 1466, and it was only during the seventeenth century that the Faust legend was attributed to him. The earliest investigators thought that the whole story was a mere legend, and possibly invented by the monks as an expression of their hatred of the inventor of printing, though, as a matter of fact, it was only through financial sharp practice that Fust obtained possession of the printing outfit of the real inventor, Gutenberg.

As early as 1683, however, a professor of theology at Wittenberg brought forward evidence of the actual existence of an individual of the name of Faust.[1]

According to Manlius-Melanchthon, Faust was born in Knittlingen and studied at the University of Cracow, though he appears later to have said he came from Heidelberg. About the year 1505, the Abbot Trithemius came in contact with him at Gelnhausen, though he did not speak to him, and does not even say that he actually saw him. He was later in Würzburg and in 1507 he came to Kreuznach where he obtained a post as schoolmaster, though he was soon compelled to flee on account of alleged immorality. In the year 1513, he was in Erfurt, where he called himself the half-god of Heidelberg. He may have stayed at Maulbronn during the year 1516, but we hear nothing definite until he casts the horoscope of the Bishop of Bamberg in 1520. Eight years later, he was expelled from Ingolstadt, and six years after we find Philipp von Hutten seeking his advice about a forthcoming expedition. Another five years elapse, and a physician of Worms refers to the complaints of people who had been swindled by him; the remark "gone is gone" may allude to the disappearance or death of Faust, though it is more likely that it refers to the money of the victims. The Zimmern Chronicle mentions the village of Staufen, near Freiburg in Breisgau, as the scene of his death, and gives the date as some time after 1539. Wierus places the period of his activity before 1540, and when Gast writes in 1548, he refers to Faust as being already dead. He appears to have travelled extensively, for there are additional allusions to his presence in Wittenberg, Nuremberg, Battenburg on the Maas, and Basel, where Gast met him.

There seems no doubt that Doctor Faust surpassed all the

[1] J. G. Neumann: *Disquisitio historica de Fausto Praestigiatore.*

wandering scholars of his time both in pretensions and notoriety. His attempts to fly and to conjure up spirits, to say nothing of the boast that he could restore lost manuscripts of classical authors, are all intelligent anticipations of what has been done or pretended in the present century. He was rather indiscreet in declaring that he had helped the Imperial army to victory in Italy, but he may have been emboldened by patronage such as that of Philipp von Hutten and the Bishop of Bamberg, though the distinguished humanists and reformers would have nothing to do with the braggart. The students appear to have been greatly impressed by him and he certainly imposed on the uneducated people.

Soon after his death the historical facts became blurred, and the mysterious circumstances surrounding his disappearance may have given an additional impulse to the subsequent legend, which appears, indeed, to have started even during his lifetime. The later contemporary references are already coloured with imaginative detail, and anecdotes relating to his various pranks, real or alleged, were circulating among all classes of the people. These soon became the nucleus of a large collection of stories, some of which had formerly been related of other magicians and were now fathered on Faust, until in the year 1587, scarcely fifty years after his death, the first printed account of the life of "Dr. Johann Faust, the notorious Magician and Necromancer" was published, as a warning to all readers, at Frankfort-on-the-Main. It is astonishing that he should so soon have become a myth, but an explanation may perhaps be sought in the ferment and unrest of an age which stands between the medieval and the modern, when old conceptions were tumbling and new worlds, both material and intellectual, were being discovered. Literature was no longer a diversion for the upper classes, and the dreams and traditions of the people were finding their way into print. Till Owlglass, the Wandering Jew, Doctor Faust are all types in which have been concentrated the lore and myths of centuries. In these representative figures, the people have focussed their longings and their aversions, their hopes and fears, and none of the wizards of popular superstition was more familiar to them than the man who had put forth his pretensions in all the market-places of Germany.

The Zimmern Chronicle declares that when Faust died, he left behind him various books which came into the possession of the lord of Staufen, and that many people had endeavoured to obtain these works. Whether there is any truth in this statement is a matter for considerable doubt, but the booksellers were not long in turning the belief to their own advantage and supplying the demand for books of an occult nature. There were at first manuscripts in circulation, which gave instructions how to practise the various magic arts attributed to Faust, the most famous of them being the *Höllenzwang*, or *Conquest of Hell*. They were usually disposed of secretly by disreputable people at exorbitant prices,[1] but later the publishers brought out volumes which they ascribed to the authorship of Faust, and some of these were even supplied with false dates, to give them an appearance of antiquity.

One such manuscript bears the following title :—

"Secret and hidden, highly authenticated Magic Writings, for the advantage of all, which have been truly tested by me, Doctor Johann Faust, and found trustworthy in each and every case, to the purpose that I have set down herein honestly and without falseness or deceit the principles of all the arts of the world, how I have practised them all myself and come thereby to great fortune; likewise I have presented openly everything which I have herein recounted to my successors, necromantic as well as cabalistic, that I may be well remembered; all Spirits have been subject to me through these my Writings, they have been compelled to fetch for

[1] One enthusiast in Holland is said to have paid eight thousand gilders for four magic seals contained in a book of this kind.

me and do all my bidding. Nothing further have I written but these twelve parts. Let him who finds and obtains them use them with caution and take strict heed of all therein, that you may not endanger body and life, against which I warn you in all sincerity."

A *Höllenzwang* printed in the year 1607 explains in greater detail the benefits to be attained by its aid:—

"Dr. Johann Faust's Juggler's Bag, concerning all kinds of unheard-of, secret, merry feats, mysteries and inventions whereby a man may interpret dreams, tell fortunes, open locked doors, cure the gout, recognise adulterers and fornicators, inspire strange men, women and maids with love, increase his height by some ells, make himself invisible or invulnerable, change his shape, rouse the thunder and lightning, collect and disperse snakes, catch pigeons, fish or birds in his hands, overcome his enemies, and perform other innumerable, incredible and extravagant feats, both merry and advantageous, together with five other extravagant, excellent and authentic devices. Now for the first time from the Original written with his own hand by Dr. Faust, published for the particular pleasure of all artists by Johann de Luna, Christoph Wagner's former disciple and well-experienced in the Magic Arts."[1]

[1] K. Engel: *Zusammenstellung der Faust-Schriften vom 16. Jh. bis Mitte 1884* [Oldenburg, 1885], pp. 150 and 158.

II

The German Faust Book

It was not long before a publisher saw the business possibilities of the legend, for in the autumn of the year 1587 there appeared at Frankfort-on-the-Main the first printed account of the life and death of Faust:—

Historia Von D. Johann Fausten, dem weitbeschreyten Zauberer unnd Schwartzkünstler, Wie er sich gegen dem Teuffel auff eine benandte zeit verschrieben, Was er hierzwischen für seltzame Abentheuwer gesehen, selbs angerichtet und getrieben, bisz er endtlich seinen wol verdienten Lohn empfangen. Mehrertheils ausz seinen eygenen hinderlassenen Schrifften, allen hochtragenden, fürwitzigen und Gottlosen Menschen zum schrecklichen Beyspiel, abscheuwlichen Exempel, und treuwhertziger Warnung zusammen gezogen, und in den Druck verfertiget. Iacobi IIII. Seyt Gott underthänig, widerstehet dem Teuffel, so fleuhet er von euch. Cum Gratia et Privilegio. Gedruckt zu Franckfurt am Mayn, durch Johann Spies. M.D.LXXXVII. [History of D. Johann Faust, the notorious Magician and Necromancer, How he sold himself for a stipulated Time to the Devil, What strange Things he saw, performed and practised during this Time, until at last he received his well-merited Reward. For the most Part extracted and herewith printed from his own posthumous Writings as an awful and abominable Example and sincere Warning to all presumptuous, inquisitive and godless Persons: "Submit yourselves to God. Resist the Devil, and he will flee from you" (James iv). Cum Gratia et Privilegio. Printed at Frankfort-on-the-Main by Johann Spies. M.D.LXXXVII.]

The story is preceded by a dedication to two friends of the publisher, and a *Preface to the Christian Reader*, in the former of which there is reference to the widespread popularity of the legend: "Since many years ago there was great and universal talk in Germany about the various adventures of Doct. Johannes Faustus, the notorious magician and necromancer, and everywhere there is a great demand for the history of the said Faustus at entertainments and gatherings, and since likewise there is now and then mention in the works of some modern historians of this magician, his devilish arts and fearful end, it has often been a matter of astonishment to me that nobody has composed a regular account of this fearful story, and published it as a warning to the whole of Christendom. I have also not hesitated to enquire from scholars and wise people whether this history has perhaps already been written down by anyone, but I have never been able to discover anything certain, until recently it was communicated and sent to me by a good friend in Speyer, with the request that I should publish and present it as a fearful example of devilish deceit, murder of body and soul, as a warning to all Christians." This dedication is dated Monday, the 4th of September, 1587, and signed by Johann Spies himself. The *Preface to the Christian Reader*, amid much quoting of the Bible, declares that, "The exorcisers of the devil seldom come to a good end, as is to be seen in the case of Dr. Johann Faustus, who was alive within the memory of man, signed a compact and league with the devil, experienced many strange adventures and practised abominable infamy and vice, with guzzling, swilling, fornication and all kinds of sensual pleasure, until at last the devil gave him his deserved reward and wrung his neck in a dreadful manner."

This little volume must have been enormously popular, for although it appeared so late in the season, there were before the end of the year at least four reprints, a new original edition, and a further edition containing eight new chapters. The *editio princeps* (of which there is a copy in the British Museum) contains 69 chapters.

It is not long since an older version of the *Historia* in manuscript, dating from the 'seventies or early 'eighties of the sixteenth century, was discovered.[1] It contains a different preface and two more chapters, one of which describes how Faust releases a nobleman and old schoolfellow named von Reuttpüffel from captivity in Turkey, and brings him home just after his wife has married again. The story is told with all the hearty bawdiness of the time, and the wife is made to feel thankful that her vigorous first husband has returned to her, after her single, disappointing experience with the second one. There are in addition a few prophecies made by Faust in his last year concerning the Papacy, including one concerning the Massacre of St. Bartholomew in 1572. It was written, of course, after the event. The preface states that the manuscript was translated from the Latin, but whether the first version of the Faust book was really written in any other language than German it is impossible to say.

It is already obvious from the preface to the Faust book that the publication of the wicked life and dreadful doom of Faust was intended as a warning to all who could not find peace and content in the bosom of the Church, but would seek to explore beyond, with the treacherous aid of science, which at that time, of course, included magic. Curiosity in theological matters was regarded as an unhealthy symptom, and was only playing into the hands of the Devil, who, in the words of the Epistle of Peter, quoted in the preface, as a roaring lion, walketh about, seeking whom he may devour. Faust represents the spirit of enquiry, which was regarded as fatal to the soul, but nobody seems to have wondered whether a soul that had to be so jealously guarded and could be so easily lost was worth having at all. The strong Lutheran tendency which was a characteristic of the activi-

[1] By Gustav Milchsack in the library at Wolfenbüttel, and edited by him in *Historia D. Johannis Fausti des Zauberers* [Wolfenbüttel, 1892-7]. Milchsack promised at the time to follow up this publication with a second volume containing the results of his researches, but he has not yet done so, and according to German custom, other scholars have hitherto refrained from trespassing on his preserves, so the problems raised by the discovery of this manuscript have not yet been fully investigated.

ties of Spies as a publisher is also a marked feature of the Faust book. Martin Luther himself shared the prevailing view of the time, that the world is divided into two camps, that of God and that of the Devil, and the latter is mentioned frequently in his writings. Faust can, with some reservation, be looked upon as the great counterpart of Luther; they are the two poles of the sixteenth century. In the book, the contrast is all the more striking since it does not appear as an intentional element in the work. The views of Luther are not definitely defended, but are taken as a matter of course, and the contrast between the theologian and the sceptic develops naturally from the theme, though the Lutheran doctrine occasionally comes prominently to the fore. Both the Faust of the legend and Luther were Doctors of Theology and closely connected with Wittenberg, the cradle of the Reformation. Starting from the same point, they reached goals which were diametrically opposed. They both lectured on the culture of antiquity, and they had both been in Rome, but whereas Luther had set out with feelings of reverence, only to return in disappointment and indignation, Faust was merely amused and contemplated with cynical complacency the licence of the Vatican, where the priests were no better than himself. Luther married in accordance with the tenets of the Church, but Faust rejected the sacrament of marriage for the pagan Helena. Luther based his faith on the Bible, Faust was not content to accept the Holy Writ, but sought to penetrate the forbidden mysteries beyond it. Faust entered into league with the Devil, while Luther hurled his inkstand at him.[1]

It is true that it was not in the spirit of Luther to conceive of the defection from orthodox theology as defection from God, and the ridicule to which the Church of Rome and its priests are exposed in the Faust book, even the Devil himself appearing in the guise of a monk, would quite possibly even have appealed to his robust sense of humour. Nevertheless, there seems little reason to doubt

[1] W. Scherer: *Das älteste Faustbuch* [Berlin, 1884].

that the book was written from the Lutheran standpoint. Since, however, in the field of German literary research it seems impossible for any definite point of view, with whatever weight of proof it may be supported, to be maintained for very long, before a scholar brings forward its exact opposite, which he defends with equally weighty evidence, there has recently been an attempt to prove that the tendency of the Faust book was not Lutheran but Catholic.[1] The author of this theory does not deny that the intention of some passages is obviously hostile to Catholicism, but he declares that they are later interpolations, and endeavours to prove that the book is a parody on Luther, who is represented as a modern Bacchus and companion of the Devil. The first direct anti-clerical reference is the taunt at the celibacy of the clergy in Faust's conversation with Mephostophiles concerning the former's desire to take a wife. The Devil endeavours to dissuade him by declaring that marriage is a divine institution, but Faust retorts that the monks and nuns do not marry. This passage is lacking in the Wolfenbüttel MS. In the chapter which deals with the journey through Europe, Faust remarks at Cologne that the Devil is in the Church of St. Ursula with the 11,000 virgins. The MS. has *Tempel* instead of *Teufel*. When Faust arrives in Rome, he spends three days and nights invisible in the Pope's palace, finding that "these pigs at Rome are fattened and all ready to roast and cook," and after his experience in the harem at Constantinople, he mounts up in the air in the vestments of a pope. These last two adventures are also to be found in the MS., but Dr. Wolff declares them to be interpolations. His evidence, however, is not convincing, and there is little reason to assume that the spirit of any literary version of the Faust book which may have been extant before 1587 was different from the tendency of the edition published by Spies.

The development from historical fact to legend was influenced considerably by contact with other myths of the same

[1] Eugen Wolff: *Faust und Luther* [Halle, 1912].

type. There were numerous alleged covenanters with the Devil in the Middle Ages, of whom the most akin to Faust was Theophilus of Adana. But Theophilus was saved eventually from eternal damnation by the intervention of the Virgin Mary, and if the Faust book had really been of Catholic origin, there is little doubt that the Madonna and the Saints would have saved him. The fires of Hell are essential to the spirit of the Faust book; the pact is irrevocable. Many features formerly attributed to other wizards were transferred to Faust, including the Devil in the form of a black dog which always accompanied Cornelius Agrippa of Nettesheim, the enchanted garden conjured up by Albertus Magnus for the Emperor in the midst of winter, and the exorcising of the spirit of Alexander the Great and other Greek heroes by the Abbot Trithemius. The incident of Helena may be due to the connection with Simon Magus, who was accompanied on his journeys by a courtesan named Helen. The fame of all these magicians sank into obscurity, and the one figure that carried on into future centuries the memory of their deeds was Faust.

When the oral legend was cast into literary form, the anonymous author appears to have consulted many works of reference. The long chapter which describes the journey of Faust and Mephostophiles, as well as the description of Paradise, is based on the *Book of Chronicles* of Hartmann Schedel, which appeared in 1493. The peculiar zigzag nature of the journey is due to the fact that Schedel gives the towns in chronological order, according to the supposed year in which they were founded, and the author of the Faust book has copied them mechanically. Similarly, he has taken from the German-Latin dictionary of the Swiss humanist Dasypodius, in alphabetical order, the list of fish, game and wine with which Faust entertains his guests at the court of the Count (really Prince) of Anhalt. For example, the fish are mentioned in the following order: *Aal, Barben, Bersing, Bickling, Bolchen, Aschen, Forell, Hecht, Karpffen, Krebs, Moschel, Neunaugen, Platteissen, Salmen* and *Schleyen,* and the wines are *Burgunder, Brabänder, Coblentzer, Crabatischer, Elsässer, Engelländer, Frantzösische, Rheinische, Spanische,* etc. The conversations concerning the physical sciences and celestial phenomena can be traced to *Elucidarius,* a collection of scientific dialogues.

Augustin Lercheimer's (pseudonym for Professor Hermann Witekind of Heidelberg) *Christliche Bedenken und Erinnerung von Zauberei,* which first appeared in 1585, was formerly thought to have been a direct source of the Faust book, but it is possible that Lercheimer himself borrowed from an earlier manuscript of the Faust book. He anticipates modern science when he protests against the witch-burnings, and declares that witches should be sent to the physician rather than to the judge. In the third edition of his book, which was published in 1597, Lercheimer denounces the Faust book as a libel on the University and Church of Wittenberg :—

"It is all malicious lies. . . . He had neither house nor yard at Wittenberg, or elsewhere, was never at home, lived like a vagabond, was a parasite, guzzled, swilled and lived by his conjuring. How could he have a house and yard by the outer gate of the town in the Scheergasse, since there never was a suburb and therefore no outer gate? Neither was there ever a Scheergasse there. That in such a University, a man whom Melanchthon used to call a cesspool of many devils should have been made Master, to say nothing of Doctor of Theology, which would be an eternal disgrace to the degree and honourable title, who believes that? . . . About all the other vanity, lies and *Teufelsdreck* in the book, I will say nothing. . . . It is, to be sure, nothing new and no cause for surprise that such calumnies are issued by the enemies of our religion, but it is unwarrantable and lamentable that our printers also should publish such books without shame, whereby honest people are slandered and inquisitive youths led to attempt similar magic feats; to say nothing of the abuse of the beautiful and noble art of printing, which has been conferred on us by God." The fact that Lercheimer, who was an ardent adherent of Luther, should have condemned the book in such terms, cannot be regarded as evidence of its anti-Lutheran tendency.

Another important manuscript was discovered recently in Nuremberg.[1] A certain Christoph Rosshirt, a teacher of Nuremberg, who had studied in Wittenberg, copied into an album about the year 1575, amidst other matter, anecdotes relating to various magicians, including Doctor Faust. It will be noticed that Faust's Christian name is given here as *George*. The Faust stories are four in number :—

1. When Dr. Georgius Faustus is lecturing to the students at the University of Ingolstadt on philosophy and necromancy, he invites some friends to dinner, and tells them that the food and drink they are enjoying come from the wedding-feast of the King of England. He instructs them to hold on to the edge of the towel when water is brought for them to wash their hands, and he will take them to the dance at the King's wedding. When they are discovered in the ball-room, they are taken for spies and arrested. They are condemned to be hanged, but Faust rescues them in the same way that he had brought them there. They wash their hands in England and dry them in Germany.

2. Faust asks a Jewish merchant at the Frankfort Fair to change him some French money into good talers. The merchant promises to call on Faust at his inn and bring him the money, but when he arrives, Faust is lying on a couch, apparently asleep. The Jew puts his bag of talers on the table and shakes Faust by the arm, but cannot rouse him; he becomes annoyed and shakes him violently by the leg, which comes off in his hand. He rushes in terror from the house, leaving behind him cloak and money-bag, which are shared by Faust and his servant.

3. Faust sells a swineherd in Bamberg some fat pigs, but

[1] By Wilhelm Meyer, and edited by him in *Nürnberger Faustgeschichten* [Munich, 1895].

warns him against driving them into flowing water. On the next day the swineherd neglects the warning and the pigs are turned into bundles of straw. By this time Faust is well on the way to Nuremberg.

4. On the evening before he is due to fulfil his pact with the Devil, Faust arrives at a village inn and asks for a room for the night. In the tap-room there is a crowd of drunken, noisy peasants, who refuse to be quiet when Faust asks them. The magician bewitches them so that they remain sitting with their mouths wide open, and he is able to have his last meal in peace. He pays his bill, tips all the servants, and goes to bed, but is persuaded by the host to disenchant the drunken clowns. On the next morning, Faust is found dead in bed.

As some of these stories had already been in circulation about other magicians, it is obvious that Faust was already becoming in popular imagination the prototype, and it is possible to see the myth in progress of development. The magician who sold his soul to the Devil was not a new factor in the superstitious fantasy of the people, but it was convenient to father all the floating rumours on some outstanding personality of whom everybody had heard and who had, in the memory of many, boasted in public of his wicked art. It is of interest to note that whereas Bütner declares that it was at Wittenberg, the leading Lutheran University, that Faust conjured up the Greek heroes, this Nuremberg manuscript transfers his teaching activities in philosophy and necromancy to the centre of Catholic doctrine, Ingolstadt. Later on the scene is shifted to Erfurt, the seat of humanism.

The enlarged edition which appeared in 1587, with a different sequence of chapters and eight new ones added, has drawn for its new matter mainly on the *De Praestigiis Daemonum* of Wierus and the *Christliche Bedenken und Erinnerung von Zauberei* of Augustin Lercheimer, where the anecdotes are related for the most part about other magicians.

The title-page of this edition states that it was printed by Spies, but his printer's ornament is lacking, so the statement is most probably false.

The stories are as follows:—

1. Faust meets a peasant who has lost his horse, and tells him that he has just seen a man riding away on it. The peasant hurries after the supposed thief and there is a gory fight, until he notices that the other man's horse is a stallion, whereas his own was a gelding.

2. Faust meets a priest in Cologne hastening to church with his breviary in his hand, and turns the sacred book into a pack of cards.

3. Faust enters an inn, where he is refused entertainment, as there is no food in the house. He taps the window with his finger, and says "Bring what you have"; then putting his hand outside the window, he draws in a large dish of boiled pike and a large can of good Rhine wine.

4. A castle in which Faust is living is besieged by the Spanish troops of the Emperor Charles. He shoots fragments from a tree under which a Spanish colonel is sitting, although the latter is not visible from the castle, and catches the Spanish cannon-balls in his hands.

5. Faust swallows a servant in an inn, because he fills the glasses too full, and washes the morsel down with a bucket of water. The servant is afterwards discovered in the yard all wet and dripping.

6. Faust cuts off a man's head in an inn, but is prevented from setting it on again by the mysterious influence of one of the spectators; so he causes a lily to grow on the table, from which he slices off the head, and immediately one of the spectators falls decapitated from his seat. Faust then sets the first man's head on his shoulders again.

7. Faust invites some gentlemen to dinner, but when they arrive they find the table empty. Their host bids his spirit fetch food from a neighbouring wedding-party, and after the feast the guests ask him to show them one of his tricks.

He causes a vine to grow on the table, with grapes for each of his guests, and tells each one to pick his own fruit with one hand and put his knife to the stalk with the other, but to be very careful not to cut. He then leaves the room, and when he returns they are all grasping their own noses with one hand and holding their knives in dangerous proximity with the other.

8. Faust teaches a chaplain how to remove his beard with arsenic.

The edition of 1589 is important, because it contains the six extra "Erfurt Chapters," which were most probably based on local tradition in that town. Faust is seen here as a lecturer at the University. The following is a summary of these extra chapters :—

1. Some students invite Faust to accompany them to the Leipzig Fair, and after they have inspected the town and the University they come to a wine-cellar, where some draymen are endeavouring without success to roll out a huge barrel. Faust mocks their efforts, and they return his jeers with interest, but the owner of the barrel offers to make a present of the contents to whoever can lift it out. Faust goes into the cellar, sits astride the barrel as though it were a horse and rides out. The host has to keep his promise, and Faust shares the contents with his companions.

2. Faust was for some years at Erfurt and lectured at the University. On one occasion, when he is lecturing on Homer, the students request him to conjure up the ancient heroes of Greece. He promises to do so at his next lecture, which is consequently very fully attended. The heroes duly appear in their armour—Menelaus, Achilles, Hector, Priam, Alexander, Ulysses, Ajax, Agamemnon and others, followed by the one-eyed giant Polyphemus, with the extremities of a man he is eating still projecting from between his teeth. The spectators are terrified, but Faust laughs and orders the spirits to go away again, which they all do with the exception of Polyphemus, who looks as though he would like

to devour one or two of the students. However, he also is
persuaded to retire, but the students do not ask Faust to
repeat the experiment.

3. Faust offers to bring to light the lost comedies of
Terence and Plautus, though only for a sufficient length of
time to enable them to be copied. The theologians and
members of the University council, however, think that
there are enough books in existence from which the students
can learn Latin, and in any case there is the possibility of
the Devil inserting in the newly discovered works all kinds
of poison and bad examples, and the disadvantage might
outbalance the gain. So Faust is not given the opportunity
this time of proving his skill.

4. While Faust is in Prague, a friend of his, who is giving
a party in Erfurt, desires his presence, and presently there
is a knock at the door and Faust is seen to have just alighted
from his horse. He says he cannot stay long as he must be
back in Prague on the morrow. He gets intoxicated, and
asks the guests whether they would not like to try some
foreign wines. He thereupon bores four holes in the table
and puts plugs into them. Glasses are fetched, Faust draws
the plugs and serves each man with the wine he desires. It
appears that his horse, who is devouring all the oats in the
stable and looking for more, is really Mephostophiles.
Early in the morning Faust rides away, and the guests who
accompany him to the door see his horse rise with him into
the air.

5. Faust invites some friends to his lodging, and when
they arrive there is neither food nor drink, fire nor smoke.
Their host raps on the table with his knife, and a servant
comes in. Faust asks, "How swift are you?" and the reply is,
"Like an arrow." "No," says Faust, "you cannot serve me,
go back whence you came." He raps again, and another
servant enters, who tells Faust that he is as swift as the wind.
He also is sent away. A third servant is as swift as thought
and is accepted by Faust, who orders him to bring food and
drink for the feast. The goblets are put on the table empty,

but Faust asks each of his guests what kind of wine or beer he would like, holds the goblet out of the window and draws it in again full of the desired liquor.

6. A famous Franciscan monk, named Dr. Kling, who was well acquainted with Dr. Martin Luther, endeavours to convert Faustus. But Faust declares it would be dishonourable to go back on his pact with the Devil, which he has signed with his own blood. "The Devil has honourably kept his part of the bargain, therefore I will keep mine." The monk reports this conversation to the Rector and Council of the University, and Faust is compelled to quit Erfurt.

These stories are also to be found in a seventeenth-century manuscript chronicle of Thuringia and the town of Erfurt, based on an Erfurt chronicle of the previous century which is now lost. The author of this earlier chronicle appears to have heard the anecdotes, in the year 1556, from a neighbour of the Franciscan monk who tried to convert Faust. The story of how Faust rode the barrel of wine out of the cellar is recorded in two paintings on the wall of Auerbach's wine-cellar in Leipzig, which bear the date 1525, but are in reality no earlier than the seventeenth century. The wine-cellar itself was not built till 1530.

There were further editions of the Faust book in 1590 and 1592, as well as a rhymed version, which appeared at Tübingen in the winter of 1587–8. It is probably the authors of this book who are referred to in the complaint of the ducal commissioners to the senate of the University of Tübingen, which is recorded in the minutes of the senate on the 15th of April, 1588. The publisher and authors are ordered to be incarcerated for a couple of days, and sternly reprimanded.

In the year 1599 there was published at Hamburg a considerably enlarged edition, of which the end of each chapter was adorned with an edifying commentary, called an *Erinnerung*, or Remonstrance, and it is this version which became the basis of the subsequent editions. The story becomes more anti-Catholic than in the earlier editions, and the anti-papal moral is driven home in each *Erinnerung*. The editor, Georg Rudolf Widman, has successfully eliminated any element of titanism or poetry which may have been present in the original book, and Faust becomes merely a young man led astray by the Church of Rome. Widman has even been delicate enough to condense the Helena episode to a mere reference in a footnote.

Widman's version was again subjected to rearrangement in the year 1674, by the Nuremberg physician Johann Nicolaus Pfitzer, who modified the former polemic against the Catholic Church, and in 1725 Pfitzer's version was published in abbreviated form by an anonymous editor who called himself a *Christlich-Meynender*, or Man of Christian Sentiments. This volume is exceedingly slim, but it was sold everywhere and became the popular chap-book. It is important in that it contains the germ of the Gretchen episode in Goethe's drama. Faust tries to seduce a servant-girl, but she is proof against temptation and he offers to marry her; Lucifer, however, dissuades him and gives him Helena instead.

III

Faust in England

The earliest mention of Faust in England is in a translation by R. H. of a book by the Swiss Ludwig Lavater, *Of Ghostes and Spirites*, published in 1572 :—

"There are also conjurers founde even at this day, who bragge of themselves that they can so by inchauntments saddle an horse, that in a fewe houres they will dispatch a very long journey. God at the last will chasten these men with deserved punishment. What straunge things are reported of one Faustus a German, which he did in these our dayes by inchauntments?"

The History of the Damnable Life and Deserved Death of Doctor John Faustus, which was published in London in 1592, was, as the title-page announces, newly printed and in places amended, so there must have been an earlier edition of which all trace is lost. This was in all likelihood translated from the *editio princeps* of 1587, but as we are uncertain of its date, it is not impossible that one of the slightly later German editions was used. There occurs in the Stationers' Registers under the date 28th of February, 1589, the entry of "A ballad of the life and deathe of Doctor FFAUSTUS the great Cunngerer. Allowed under the hand of the Bishop of London."

This ballad has been preserved only in later versions of the seventeenth century, and it is not possible to say definitely whether or no it was founded on the English translation of the German Faust book, though that is the most likely theory. There is little doubt that the latter appeared before the ballad. In any case, *The Tragical History of Doctor Faustus*, by Christopher Marlowe, which was in all probability on the stage as early as 1589, was based directly, as is shown by internal evidence, on the English Faust book, and it is unlikely that Marlowe was acquainted with the German version.[1] So even if the ballad was founded on Marlowe's tragedy, which is very improbable, and not on the English Faust book, the latter must have been published an astonishingly short time after the appearance of the original German *Historia*. The translator is called P. F. *Gent*. (i.e. Gentleman, and not, as some editors have thought, his surname), but in later editions these initials appear as P. R. or P. K. His identity cannot be established, and it is not even possible to estimate definitely his knowledge of German. To quote Logeman: "That P. F. . . . must have known some German is of course evident from the whole of the translation and more especially from some passages where a smaller light would have blundered. But that his own cannot have shone very brightly is apparent from the number of lesser and greater blunders in which we have caught our translator, and also from the fact that some passages which present considerable difficulties will be found to have been omitted." We cannot, however, judge a sixteenth-century translator by present-day standards, for he was at liberty to adapt or modify as he listed. For example, where the German original states that Faust blew in the pope's face, the translator renders *blew* by *smote*, thus altering the whole sense, and it is doubtful whether the false translation is due to P. F.'s sense of humour or his ignorance of German. The description of Florence is even more confused than in the original, and he adds strange lore of his own, such as the mythical story of the Brazen Virgin on the bridge at Breslau, who was used for the disposal of unruly children. It is possible that P. F. had really visited eastern Germany and the Polish or Galician regions, such as Prague and Cracow, but it is just as likely that he obtained his extra knowledge from a travelled friend. He frequently tones down the German author's denunciation of Faust's wicked ways, and emphasises the fantasies and cogitations rather than the

[1] *Marlowe's Faustus, etc.*, edited by A. W. Ward [4th ed., Oxford, 1901] and *Faustus-Notes*, by H. Logeman [Gand, 1898].

presumption and arrogance of the sorcerer. The English Faust book is therefore the first step in the deepening of the Faust character, and this conception is developed by Marlowe.[1]

There is in the original legend of Faust little of that titanic discontent with the spiritual limits of humanity which is now regarded as the fundamental characteristic of the Faustian nature. It is not the desire to solve the riddle of the universe that drives him to the pact with the Devil, but the less worthy desire for power and pleasure. It is true that "he took to himself eagles' wings and wanted to fathom all the causes in heaven and earth," but the Promethean defiance which some scholars have sought to establish as his guiding motive, was a preconception implanted in their own minds by a study of the Faust of Goethe. The Faust of the *Historia* obliges the Devil to answer all his questions and shows afterwards a lively interest in the organisation of heaven and hell, but the first-fruits of the pact are food, wine and women. Even Marlowe's Faustus promises himself merely treasure, delicacies and power from intercourse with the spirits; philosophy, medicine, law and theology are all inadequate for the man who longs to "raise the wind, or rend the clouds," but when his league with hell has endowed him with supernatural powers, the only use he finds for them is to gratify his sensual desires or indulge in practical jokes. It cannot be said that Marlowe has realised in his tragedy the potentiality of the legend, though he seems to have had an inkling of it. The Helen episode gives rise to the finest poetical passage in the play:—

> "Was this the face that launch'd a thousand ships,
> And burnt the topless towers of Ilium?"—

and the final scene, with Faust's death presaged by the striking of the clock, is impressive, but the author has done little to raise the conception to a higher plane.

After the production of Marlowe's play the name of

[1] R. Rohde: *Das Englische Faustbuch und Marlowes Tragödie* [Halle, 1910].

Faustus appears to have become a household word, and there are various allusions to the character in contemporary writings, including a reference in Shakespeare's *Merry Wives*. William Prynne relates in his *Histrio-Mastix, The Players' Scourge*, 1663, a curious incident which occurred during a performance. He is quoting the tragic end of many who have been slain in playhouses in London, "Nor yet to recite the sudden fearful burning even to the ground, both of the Globe and Fortune Playhouses, no man perceiving how these fires came: together with the visible apparition of the Devil on the Stage at the Belsavage Playhouse, in Queen Elizabeth's days (to the great amazement both of the Actors and Spectators) whiles they were there profanely playing the History of Faustus, . . . there being some distracted with that fearful sight."

There was no further development of the theme in this country, for it degenerated into a subject for farce and pantomime. There were further editions of the English Faust book, and in the year 1664 there was published in London *The History of Doctor John Faustus; Compiled in Verse, very pleasant and Delightfull*, with a doggerel dedication to the reader:—

> "Reader, I would not have you think,
> That I intend to waste my ink,
> While Faustus Story I reherse,
> And here do write his life in verse.
> For seeing Fryer Bacons Story,
> (In whom Oxford still may glory)
> For want of better pen comes forth,
> Compos'd in Rymes of no great worth:
> I call'd my Muse to task, and pend
> Faustus life, and death, and end.
> And when it cometh forth in print,
> If you like it not, the Devil's in't."

A farce by the actor W. Mountford, *Life and Death of Doctor Faustus, with the Humours of Harlequin and Scaramuch*, was acted at the Queen's Theatre in Dorset Gardens between 1684 and 1688, and revived later at the theatre in Lincoln's

Inn Fields. It was borrowed for the most part, with the exception, of course, of the harlequinade, from Marlowe.

The poet Alexander Pope declares that Faust was the subject of a set of farces, which lasted in vogue two or three seasons, and in which both Drury Lane and Covent Garden strove to outdo each other for some years. John Thurmond, a dancing master, composed a *Harlequin Dr. Faustus*, which was performed at Drury Lane, and published in the year 1724, and there is a record of a *Harlequin Dr. Faustus, Pantomime; altered from the Necromancer*, by a Mr. Woodward, which was acted at Covent Garden as late as 1766. These are but casual references to what must have been numerous Faust farces, and there were in addition performances of Faust puppet-plays in the Punch and Judy Theatre of Martin Powell opposite St. Paul's Church in Covent Garden. Neither the pantomimes nor the puppet-plays appear to derive from Marlowe, but since the appearance of the latter's tragedy, the Faust story appears definitely to have abandoned the epic form for the dramatic, and it is in its original home, Germany, that further development took place. Although in England the theme degenerated until it was employed for the most insipid type of theatrical entertainment, it was the English dramatist who first gave it the form in which, two centuries later, it was to inspire the greatest of all the poets who have sought to express the strivings of humanity in the figure of Faust.

IV

The Faust Drama in Germany

Throughout the stagnant literary period of the seventeenth century and the first half of the eighteenth, it was not the various editions of the Faust book that keep the legend green in Germany, but the popular drama which developed from Marlowe's *Faustus*. Towards the end of the sixteenth century, companies of English actors began to tour the Continent, and in their repertories were the plays of the Elizabethans, much mangled and adapted to the taste of their uncultivated audiences. The popularity of these *English Comedians*, as they were called, was greatest in Germany, and we find traces of them throughout the first half of the seventeenth century. Acting as a profession began in Germany with these English companies. At first they played only in English, but later they produced German translations of their repertory, even German original plays, and recruited their ranks from among German actors. Soon German troupes were formed on the same lines, who still, however, called themselves "English Comedians," since the advertisement was of value. The English actors laid great weight on visual effect, for the language difficulty had at first to be surmounted. The actors themselves were for the most part minstrels and dancers, and the most important character was the clown who appeared in every production, however tragic it might be. Even when the play was performed in English, the clown spoke German, and he was known under various names, such as *Pickelhäring*, while later on he was called *Hans Wurst*. The plays were not written down and there was plenty of scope allowed for gagging, so that eventually they were distorted out of all recognition and were practically the work of the actors themselves. Among the plays which were produced and gradually adapted in this manner was Marlowe's tragedy, and in its more spectacular form it provided the public with the two somewhat contradictory essentials, plenty of coarse humour and plenty of blood.

The earliest record of a performance of Marlowe's play by the English strolling players is one at Gräz in 1608. In 1626, a *Tragödia von Dr. Faust* was produced at Dresden on the 7th of July, and this was no doubt also Marlowe's play. We know what the main outline of the popular drama must have been from a comparison of the various puppet-plays which were performed in comparatively recent times in Germany and Austria, for when the Faust drama ceased to be performed by living actors, it was taken over by the proprietors of marionette theatres, and in this form it survived till well into the nineteenth century. The main points which the popular drama possessed in common with Marlowe's tragedy were the expository opening monologue, the appearance of the good and evil angels, and the presaging of Faust's impending end by the striking of the clock. The humorous and melodramatic scenes had no doubt been supplemented and exaggerated by other hands even on the English stage. There is no ground for assuming that there was already a Faust play of German origin on the German stage before the arrival of the English Comedians.

The following is an amusing specimen of the type of programme which was issued by the strolling players. It refers to a performance by the famous Neuber troupe in Hamburg, on the 7th of July, 1738:—[1]

"The wicked Life and fearful End of the World-famous Arch-sorcerer D. Johann Faust.

The following Scenes will be presented, among others: A great outer Court in the underworld Palace of Pluto, by the Rivers Lethe and Acheron. On the River comes Charon in a Boat, and to him Pluto on a fiery Dragon, followed by the whole of his underworld Retinue and Spirits.

[1] K. Engel: *Zusammenstellung der Faust-Schriften* [Oldenburg, 1885, pp. 188 ff.].

Dr. Faust's Study and Library. An agreeable Spirit of the upper World will sing the following touching Aria, accompanied by tender Music:

[A song of three verses.]

A Raven flies out of the Air and fetches the Manuscript of Dr. Faust. Hans Wurst breaks in accidentally on his Master, Dr. Faust's Magic. He must stand still and cannot move from the spot until he has taken off his Shoes. The Shoes then dance together in a merry Manner.

An insolent Court-menial, who mocks Dr. Faust, is endowed with a pair of Horns.

A Peasant buys a Horse from Dr. Faust, and as soon as he rides it, the Horse turns into a Bundle of Hay. The Peasant wants to call Dr. Faust to Account, Faust pretends to be asleep, the Peasant tugs him and pulls off his Leg.

Hans Wurst wants to have a lot of Money, and to please him, Mephostophiles causes him to rain Money.

The lovely Helena sings, to the Accompaniment of pleasant Music, an Aria which is unpleasant to Dr. Faust, for it presages his Doom.

Dr. Faust takes Leave from his Famulus Christoph Wagner. Hans Wurst also departs, and the Spirits fetch Dr. Faust to the Accompaniment of Fire-works, which play in an ingenious Manner.

The underworld Palace of Pluto is seen once more. The Furies have Possession of Dr. Faust and dance a Ballet round him, because they have brought him safely into their Domain.

The Rest will be more pleasant in the Seeing than here in the Reading.

Commencement at half-past four, in the so-called Opera House in the Goosemarket at Hamburg."

Another programme from Frankfort of the year 1742 announces that after the play there will be a dance, after the dance a ballet, and, if time permits, after the ballet there will be a merry comedy.

It will thus be seen to what depths the story of Faust had fallen, before the time came to raise it to the plane of the world's greatest tragedies. It was Lessing who first saw the potentialities of the theme, and he pointed them out in the famous seventeenth *Literaturbrief* of the 16th of February, 1759, which commenced a new era for German literature, henceforth to turn away from French models and seek inspiration from Shakespeare. The stilted superficiality of French literature was to yield to the more congenial vigour of the English. It is true that Lessing did not recognise the worth of Marlowe, who stood in the shadow of his greater contemporary, but he declares that the old German plays had possessed much of the English quality. "To mention only the best known of them: *Doctor Faust* has a number of scenes, which could only have been imagined by a Shakespearean genius. And how deeply was, and in part still is, Germany in love with her Doctor Faust! One of my friends possesses an old draft of this tragedy, and he has communicated a scene to me in which there is undoubtedly much that is great." He then prints a scene, which was really composed by himself, and among his papers after his death were found sketches relating to his plan for a Faust drama. It is certain that Lessing intended to reject the obsolete orthodox view that Faust must necessarily pay for his sins by an eternity of damnation. The Catholic theologians had permitted sorcerers to be saved by repentance, but the spirit of the Reformation demanded that Faust forfeit his soul, and from this inevitable doom there was no appeal. The age of Enlightenment, on the other hand, looked upon the intellect as supreme, and it was obviously absurd that Faust's attempt to solve an intellectual problem should lead to the loss of his soul. It is to Lessing that is due the fundamental change in the conception of the Faust problem, whereby Faust is not damned but saved. The longing to penetrate the mysteries of the universe is no longer regarded as an instinct implanted in humanity by the Devil.

So far as we can judge from the fragments, Lessing's

Faust was to be driven to the pact solely by his thirst for knowledge. Goethe was to create the eternal type, the man who seeks to encompass the universe, who demands complete and ultimate satisfaction for the limitless craving of the human soul. The first impulse to create a Faust drama of his own came to Goethe from a marionette version of the popular drama, a performance of which he saw in Leipzig in his student days, for he never saw it performed by living actors, and neither the Folk-book nor Marlowe's tragedy came into his hands until much later. It was a task which occupied him all his life. His original draft, the *Urfaust*, has only been discovered in manuscript in recent times, but in the year 1790 he published *Faust. A Fragment.* The first part of the completed tragedy appeared in 1808, and the second part in 1833, a year after Goethe's death.

The fundamental difference between Goethe's conception of the problem and all that had gone before is typified in the fact that it is not a *pact* into which Faust enters with Mephisto, but a *wager*. There are indeed two wagers. In the Prologue in Heaven, Mephisto discusses Faust with the Lord and says:—[1]

"What will you bet? There's still a chance to gain him,
　If unto me full leave you give,
　Gently upon *my* road to train him!"

The Lord enters into the spirit of the thing and replies:—

　　"As long as he on earth shall live,
　　So long I make no prohibition,
　　While Man's desires and aspirations stir,
　　He cannot choose but err.

　　·　　·　　·　　·　　·

　　A good man, through obscurest aspiration,
　　Has still an instinct of the one true way."

The opening monologue, which shows Faust in his study fighting with the realisation that "here, poor fool! with all my lore I stand, no wiser than before," is an echo of the initial

[1] Bayard Taylor's translation.

79

monologue of Marlowe's tragedy, which came to Goethe through the medium of the popular drama and the puppet-show. Hitherto the pact had been for a definite period of twenty-four years, during which Faust was to enjoy all that the Devil could give him and then to fulfil without hope of mercy his part of the bargain. Goethe's Faust, however, demands more than the fulfilment of transitory desires. He wants to grasp the moment of supreme satisfaction, and if Mephisto cannot give him that, Faust's soul remains his own :—

> "When on an idler's bed I stretch myself in quiet,
> There let, at once, my record end!
> Canst thou with lying flattery rule me,
> Until, self-pleased, myself I see,—
> Canst thou with rich enjoyment fool me,
> Let that day be the last for me!
> The bet I offer! . . .
>
> .   .   .   .   .
>
> When thus I hail the Moment flying:
> 'Ah, still delay—thou art so fair!'
> Then bind me in thy bonds undying,
> My final ruin then declare!"

That is the important point. Mephisto plunges Faust in the pleasures of revelry, love, power and classic beauty, but in spite of his burning craving for supreme happiness, he is incapable of enjoying the blissful moment. There never is a fleeting moment to which he can say, "Ah, still delay—thou art so fair!" There is no absolute truth or absolute beauty, and therefore no absolute happiness. The blissful moment does not exist, and the only satisfaction which man is free to enjoy is in striving after an imaginary absolute. Faust never becomes absorbed in a moment of ecstasy, and therefore the Devil loses the wager. By using his power unselfishly to further the lot of others, he is the instrument of his own salvation; he redeems himself by an ever higher and purer form of activity, as Goethe himself said, and dies with the conviction that

> "He only earns his freedom and existence,
> Who daily conquers them anew."

When Mephisto summons his devils to carry the soul to hell, a host of angels flies from heaven to repel them, and as they bear Faust's immortal soul into the upper air, they proclaim

> "Whoe'er aspires unweariedly
> Is not beyond redeeming."

The Devil had not given Faust the blissful moment, but had only enabled him to find a compromise between dream and reality by creative work. Faust's craving remained unfulfilled, and his reconcilement to the conditions of life was only temporary. But as that is the only possibility, as man's highest aspirations never can be completely satisfied, the wager was from the first destined to be unfulfilled.

In Goethe's *Faust* the theme received the highest treatment of which it was capable. At the time when he first came in contact with the story, Faust dramas were being announced by authors from all corners of Germany, and perhaps it would not be too much to say that every German poet since Goethe has cherished the hope of some day creating his own Faust. Of the tragedies, farces, operas, pantomimes, ballets, novels, short stories, poems, folk-songs and even parodies on the subject, it may be said that their name is legion, and it appears to have been cast into every possible art-form. It will, perhaps, suffice to mention here a dance-poem which was written by the poet Heinrich Heine in 1851 for performance at Drury Lane. Lumley, the director of the theatre, had already made preparations for the production, when it was laid aside as unsuitable. One of the latest treatments of the theme is *Faust and the City*, by Lunacharski, formerly Minister of Education in Soviet Russia.

BIBLIOGRAPHY

H. LOGEMAN: *The English Faust Book of* 1592 *(Recueil de Travaux de l'Université de Gand,* 24ᵉ fascicule. Ghent, 1900).

A. E. RICHARDS: *The English Wagner Book of* 1594 *(Literarhistorische Forschungen,* XXXV. Heft. Berlin, 1907).

W. J. THOMS: *Early English Prose Romances* (2nd. Ed. Vol. III. London, 1858).

R. PETSCH: *Das Volksbuch vom Doktor Faust* (Reprint of the first edition of 1587. *Neudrucke,* Nos. 7, 8, 8a, 8b. Halle, 1911).

G. MILCHSACK: *Historia D. Johannis Fausti des Zauberers* (Reprint of the Wolfenbüttel MS. Wolfenbüttel, 1892–7).

W. MEYER: *Nürnberger Faustgeschichten (Abhandlungen der philosoph.-philolog. Klasse der königl. bayrischen Akademie der Wissenschaften,* Bd. XX. Abt. 2. Munich, 1895).

S. SZAMATÓLSKI: *Das Fäustbuch des Christlich Meynenden (Deutsche Literaturdenkmale des* 18. *und* 19. *Jh.,* No. 39. Stuttgart, 1891).

J. SCHEIBLE: *Das Kloster* (Vols. 2, 3, 5 and 11. Stuttgart, 1846–9).

A. TILLE: *Die Faustsplitter in der Literatur des* 16. *bis* 18. *Jhdts.* (Berlin, 1898–1904).

K. ENGEL: *Zusammenstellung der Faust-Schriften vom* 16. *Jh. bis Mitte* 1884 (Oldenburg, 1885).

C. KIESEWETTER: *Faust in der Geschichte und Tradition* (Leipzig, 1893).

E. FALIGAN: *Histoire de la légende de Faust* (Paris, 1888).

E. SCHMIDT: *Faust und das* 16. *Jahrhundert (Charakteristiken,* 1. Reihe, 2. Aufl. Berlin, 1902).

E. SCHMIDT: *Faust und Luther (Sitzungsberichte,* 1896).

E. WOLFF: *Faust und Luther* (Halle, 1912).

W. CREIZENACH: *Versuch einer Geschichte des Volksschauspiels vom Doctor Faust* (Halle, 1878).

A. W. WARD: *Marlowe's Tragical History of Dr. Faustus* (4th Ed. Oxford, 1901).

R. ROHDE: *Das Englische Faustbuch und Marlowes Tragödie* (Halle, 1910).

H. LOGEMAN: *Faustus-Notes* (*Recueil de Travaux*, 21^e fascicule. Ghent, 1898).

J. FRITZ: *Ander theil D. Johañ Fausti Historien* (Reprint of first edition of *German Wagner Book*. Halle, 1910).

H. G. MEEK: *Johann Faust, the Man and the Myth* (Oxford, 1930).

GRIMMELSHAUSEN AND HIS
SIMPLICISSIMUS

THE course of German literature has been compared to a succession of hills and valleys, of which the most striking are the Golden Age of medieval poetry in the thirteenth century, the sterile period of the sixteenth and seventeenth centuries, and the zenith of German literature which was reached in the latter half of the eighteenth century. The thirteenth century saw the popular epic at its height with the composition of the *Nibelungenlied* and *Gudrun*, the masters of the Court Epic, Wolfram von Eschenbach and Gottfried von Strassburg, and the greatest of all the Minnesingers, Walther von der Vogelweide. During the eighteenth century rose the twin stars, Goethe and Schiller. Between these two epochs lies a period of gradual decadence, culminating in the seventeenth century, when German literature sank to its lowest ebb. It was the age which gave Shakespeare and Milton to England, and Corneille, Racine and Molière to France, but during the whole of the period, roughly from the death of Hans Sachs in 1576 to the publication of the first cantos of Klopstock's *Messias* in 1748, there is hardly anything in German literature which has any intrinsic worth, or other than historical interest, except a few hymns and those of the works of Grimmelshausen which are connected with the name of *Simplicissimus*. The *Nibelungenlied* and the Court Poetry were alike forgotten, and the essential characteristic of the writers of the seventeenth and early eighteenth centuries was their abject dependence on foreign models, at first the literature of Spain and later that of France. Even when Lessing, after a great effort, was successful in pointing out to the writers of Germany the way to better things, it was by showing them in the first place not only that the path to salvation lay through the rejection of French models, but further, that they must begin their education anew by turning to the literature of England, which would teach them more wholesome and fruitful principles than they could imbibe from France.

In England and Spain, literature had already drawn new strength from the Renaissance, without losing its own national characteristics, and was thus able to appeal not only to the educated classes, but to every rank of society. Italy and France had likewise a literature in the popular tongue which was appreciated by the ruling caste, but in Germany the state of affairs was very different. As far as literature was concerned, the national marrow appeared to have dried up. The reigning house of Austria, the traditional head of the "Holy Roman Empire of German Nationality," was completely estranged from German culture, and the Emperor Charles V declared that German was a language for horses. Even in the eighteenth century, Frederick the Great held the German language in contempt, and while he ignored Lessing, he bestowed his patronage on Voltaire. After the Renaissance, there was an unbridged gulf between the vernacular popular literature and the Latin literature of the scholars, which lasted well into the seventeenth century, for there was no mutual fusion of the popular literary elements with the new art form that had sprung from the humanistic movement. When literature took new shape, it was cultivated by scholars and intended to appeal only to the educated. For the common people there was a corrupted popular literature which did not fail to appear regularly at the spring and autumn fairs, and from which inspiration was later to be drawn by no less a person than Goethe.

The seventeenth century was a transition period, when the national consciousness was almost annihilated by the religious and political struggles which made Germany a cockpit for half the nations of Europe. The claim of Frederick the Elector Palatine to the throne of Bohemia was the initial episode of the Thirty Years War, which began in 1618 as an internal conflict, developed into a European war, and was only concluded in 1648 by the Treaty of Westphalia. The combination of religious, political and feudal quarrels brought upon German soil ill-disciplined hordes of French, Walloon, Italian, Spanish, Swedish, Danish and Croat mercenaries, to say nothing of Scotch and Irish soldiers of fortune, who fought for the most part not for any particular cause, but for the master who paid them. In consequence there was little restraint put upon looting and violence, and the soldier and citizen looked upon each other as natural enemies. The overrunning of the country with these foreign armies, the degeneration of social life to the verge of barbarity, even to cannibalism, and the decadence of literature to a mere means of frivolous amusement, present a picture of utter national degradation, which lasted far beyond the conclusion of peace. The ruin to which the country was brought may be judged by the fact that the population of the Empire sank during the period of the war from 16 million to 6 million, a diminution of about two-thirds. The startling transition to the Golden Age of German literature in the latter half of the eighteenth century, to the highest pinnacle it has ever reached before or since, is therefore perhaps the most amazing phenomenon in the whole of world literature. It is evident that some of the roots of the tree which put forth such magnificent blossoms must stretch back into the previous century, and though the trunk was dormant for so long, the roots continued to draw a nourishment, which was meagre, but sufficient to preserve the life-force in the midst of the foreign, parasitical growth by which it was threatened. Grimmelshausen, who did more than any other writer of the age to keep alive the national spirit in literature by fusing the popular and the learned elements, stands almost isolated, and his peculiar importance will best be understood by examining the state of the German novel before the publication of *Simplicissimus*.

The first novels in German literature were the long epic poems of the medieval Court poets, but the invention of printing gave an enormous impetus to the composition of stories in prose. The prose novel was at its origin dependent for its subject-matter on French sources, just as the medieval poets had borrowed their plots from the *troubadours*, and until the first half of the seventeenth century, the German novel-reading public was fed almost exclusively on translations and adaptations of foreign works. About the middle of the sixteenth century, the novelist Jörg Wickram, who was also a Meistersinger, wrote original novels, in which, to be sure, he exhibited no remarkable talent, but since he was not dependent on foreign sources for his subject-matter, he is looked upon as the father of the German novel. His attempts to found a novel of common life were unsuccessful, and were soon forgotten, for in the second half of the century there came from France the famous cycle of novels, or romances of chivalry, known as *Amadis of Gaul*.

The first *Amadis* was Spanish, and was written in the second half of the fifteenth century by Garcia Ordoñez de Montalvo, who based his story on an older version which is now lost. He added adventures of Amadis' son, other Spanish authors continued the story with the adventures of further descendants, and Nicolas Herberay des Essarts translated the first eight books freely into French in the first half of the sixteenth century. Other Frenchmen continued to add to the stories, and in the year 1569 there began to appear free translations into German, which continued until the seventeenth century. In addition, the German public was supplied with novels of equally interminable length, manufactured on the same plan, and containing the same elements of pseudo-chivalry, marvellous adventures and erotic interludes as the originals.

When the readers tired of the impossible adventures of *Amadis* and the other romances of chivalry, it was again to foreign sources that the authors turned. The desire to escape into a world of dreams, which had already been noticeable in the popularity of the idealistic romances of chivalry, was now directed into another channel, that of the idealistic pastoral romance, which was just as pseudo-pastoral as the *Amadis* romances were pseudo-chivalrous. They were both aspects of the Golden Age for which humanity is always yearning. The *Arcadia* of the Italian Jacopo Sannazaro, at the beginning of the sixteenth century, became the model both for the Spaniard Montemayor's *Diana*, which appeared in 1545, and for Sir Philip Sidney's *Arcadia*, which appeared in 1590, after the author's death. Honoré d'Urfé's *L'Astrée*, the first and most famous of the French pastoral romances, appeared during 1610–27, and Sidney's novel was translated into German by Martin Opitz in 1629.

The pastoral romance, however, in its turn had to make way for a new form of novel, to which it was closely related. Chiefly through the influence of Martin Opitz, who translated in 1626 the allegorical political novel *Argenis*, written in Latin, of the Scotsman John Barclay, the heroic-gallant novel was introduced into Germany. *Argenis* describes under a thin veil the conditions of France, torn by party quarrels, under the last of the Valois. This introduction of contemporary persons and politics, which was the outstanding feature of Barclay's *roman à clef*, was imitated in Germany by authors who wrote romances full of similar hidden allusions, but lacked the Scotsman's political judgment and sense of balance. They also filled their novels with long didactic disquisitions, without any attempt to adapt them to the story, so that the sole reason for their insertion appears to have been in order to exhibit the authors' more or less useless learning. Opitz's translation was of great importance for the development of the German novel, and from now on the divorce between the literature of the people and that of the educated classes became more acute, since the novelists were not only mostly of aristocratic birth, but they were alienating themselves intentionally from the national, popular tradition.

The heroic-gallant novel exhibits on the surface its descent from the romance of chivalry, for although the magic equipment and fairy-tale atmosphere have disappeared, the chief characters are still princes and princesses, and the adventures they undergo are vastly estranged from the realm of probability. They are also indeed the same people we meet in the pastoral romances. The only difference is in the setting.

The first original novelist after Jörg Wickram was Philipp von Zesen, who, unlike any of his contemporaries, looked upon his writing as a profession. The seventeenth century regarded literature as a hobby, as an amusement for a man's leisure hours, and Zesen's numerous frictions with his fellow-authors may have owed much to his isolated position as a professional novelist.

His first works were translations from the French, but he soon commenced to write romances which were independent of foreign sources, and his best-known works are *The Adriatic Rosemund* (1645), *Assenat* (1670) and *Simson* (1679). They are all of reasonable length but filled with irrelevant exhibitions of the author's extremely varied knowledge, though he did make some attempt to deal with psychological problems. Zesen naturalised the heroic-gallant novel in Germany, and it was not very long before the original works of this type were more numerous than the translations and adaptations. Andreas Heinrich Bucholtz published his *Herkules and Valiska* in 1660, following it five years later with *Herkuliskus and Herkuladisla*, and the most distinguished of the fashionable novelists in point of rank was the Duke Anton Ulrich of Brunswick-Lüneburg, whose *The Syrian Aramena* appeared in 1669–73 and *The Roman Octavia* in 1677. The heroic-gallant novel attained its highest development in the last quarter of the century with Heinrich Anshelm von Ziegler's *The Asiatic Banise* (1688) and Casper von Lohenstein's *Arminius and Thusnelda* (1689). Arminius, or Hermann, is the ancient hero of the Teutons, and Lohenstein is entitled to credit for choosing a protagonist from his country's past. In these last two novels the type of the heroic romance is seen in its most characteristic form, and *The Asiatic Banise* was the most popular of all the fashionable novels of the seventeenth century. Perhaps the most striking evidence of the kind of public to which the novelists of the period wished to appeal is afforded by the dedications, which are mostly to dukes and duchesses, kings and queens, emperors and empresses, and one novel is even dedicated to "all the princesses of the Holy Roman Empire."

In spite of all the pedantry and wearisome length of the seventeenth-century novel, one can yet divine the tortuous attempts to hammer out a new form of literary art. It has always been characteristic of the Germans to precede practice by theory. The theory and formalism of the first decades of the century demonstrate their anxiety to have a firm basis of rules on which to raise the literary edifice, but though it was during this period that the prose medium consolidated its hold in German literature, the main desire of the reading public was for entertainment, and interest was centred almost solely on the subject-matter. The form was unimportant, and since the supply of original works was not sufficient to satisfy the prevalent reading mania, there was all the time a continuous output of translations of heroic-gallant novels from the French.

Even in the previous century, however, there had already arisen in Spain a reaction against the exaggerated, marvellous adventures of impossibly ideal heroes and heroines. It was the Spaniards who gave Europe the original *Amadis*, but they redeemed their literary reputation by the invention of the picaresque novel, which soon became popular in Italy, France and Germany. In the year 1615 there appeared in Munich a translation of Mateo Aleman's *Guzman de Alfarache*, the original of which had been published at Madrid in 1599. The translation, or rather free adaptation, was by Aegidius Albertinus, the secretary of the Duke Maximilian of Bavaria, and about ten years later it was followed by a continuation from another hand, which had no connection whatever with the original, except the name. The alterations made by Aegidius Albertinus were not to the advantage of the book, for he left out parts of the narrative, in order to introduce tedious "discourses." The next Spanish picaresque novel to be introduced into Germany was *La vida de Lazarillo de Tormes* (1554), which, together with Cervantes' short story, *Rinconete y Cortadillo*, was translated and adapted by Nicolaus Ulenhart and published at Augsburg in 1617. Both the novel and the short story appeared in one volume. The *Justina* of Úbeda, which describes the career of a female vagabond, was translated from Spanish into Italian and, in 1626, from the Italian into German. There was also published in 1621 a translation of a part of *Dox Quixote*, which is a satire on the absurd exaggerations of the romance of chivalry. A single episode had already been translated in 1617, but a complete version did not appear till much later. These translations and adaptations were soon followed by a mass of German romances of the same type.

In the picaresque novel, the adventures are transferred to a more probable plane. The knights and shepherds have given place to the rogue, who has to make his way through life by means of his wits, and the atmosphere is realistic. We descend among the people, and there is a connection between the heroes of the picaresque novel and those of the German popular literature. During the fifteenth and sixteenth centuries there appeared the folk-book of *Till Owlglass*, the rogue who lives by pretending to be a fool. Other popular figures were Doctor Faust, the Wandering Jew, and the people of Schilda, who were as stupid as our Wise Men of Gotham. These creations were, for the most part, genuinely German, and rooted in popular legend, so when the *picaro* was introduced from Spain, there was little difficulty in naturalising him in Germany. Johann Fischart had already adapted Rabelais' *Gargantua and Pantagruel* freely to the German genius and German conditions in his *Geschichtklitterung*. When Ulenhart translated Cervantes' *Rinconete*, he transferred the scene to Prague, and the chief of the band of rogues was the Zuckerbastel, of whom Grimmelshausen speaks at the beginning of *Simplicissimus*. Neither Wickram's attempt to found a national novel, nor the continued popularity of the folk-books, was able to stem the tide of foreign literature, and even the German picaresque novel did not owe its origin to the German national spirit. The Thirty Years War, however, familiarised people with the living prototypes of the vagabond who was now finding his way into literature, and it remained for Grimmelshausen to transform this novel of adventure into a truly national novel. Of the mass of translations and imitations of the Spanish models which appeared during the seventeenth century, there is nothing to compare even remotely with *Simplicissimus*, which is the only German novel of the century that can be said to spring directly from the actual experience of the author, and to give a true and original picture of social conditions at the time of the Thirty Years War.

There remains another form of literature to be mentioned, which is connected with one aspect of the picaresque novel. The *Sueños* of the Spaniard Francisco de Quevedo are satires in the form of dream-pictures, and they were translated into many languages, to be followed inevitably by adaptations and imitations. The satirist Hans Michael Moscherosch began to publish in Strassburg about the year 1640 *The Visions of Philander von Sittewald*, which is an attempt to adapt Quevedo's *Sueños* to German conditions. Moscherosch substituted for the Spanish conditions satirised by Quevedo the even more undesirable and degenerate conditions of his own country, and it is perhaps significant that he is entirely lacking in the humour which is to be found in his Spanish model.

The title-page of *Simplicissimus* states that the story is by German Schleifheim von Sulsfort, but an advertisement to the reader, which was appended to the sixth book, says that it "is the work of Samuel Greiffenson von Hirschfeld, since I not only found it among his papers after his decease, but he himself also refers in his book to *The Chaste Joseph*, and in his *Satirical Pilgrim* he refers to this his *Simplicissimus*, which he wrote partly in his youth, when he was still a musketeer; but from what cause he altered his name by transposing the letters, and put instead German Schleifheim von Sulsfort on the title, is unknown to me." The consequence of this statement was that for nearly two hundred years the name of Samuel Greiffenson von Hirschfeld appeared in the literary histories as the author of *Simplicissimus* and other works. It was not until nearly the middle of last century that the name of the greatest German prose writer of his time was found to be Hans Jacob Christoffel von Grimmelshausen, who had a peculiar passion for publishing his books under pseudonyms, which are all more or less perfect anagrams of his real name. The complete list of his pseudonyms, in addition to the above two, is as follows; some of them are spelt in a variety of ways :—

> "Melchior Sternfels von Fugshaim,
> Philarchus Grossus von Trommenheim,
> Signeur Messmahl,
> Michael Regulin von Sehmsdorf,
> Erich Stainfels von Grufensholm,
> Simon Lengfrisch von Hartenfels,
> Israel Fromschmidt von Hugenfels,"

and the letters

> "A c eee ff g hh ii ll mm nn oo rr sss t uu."

The reason for this hide-and-seek method of signing his books may have been the contempt in which the literature of the common people was held. In the few cases where Grimmelshausen published under his real name, the book in question was either a heroic-gallant novel of the type then in fashion, or a harmless political pamphlet which was not likely to call down on the head of the author the wrath of the powers that were. At the same time it is to be observed that the custom of writing under pseudonyms was not unusual at that time, and Grimmelshausen may merely have been amusing himself with the game of anonymity. There is a sonnet appended to his novel *Dietwald and Amelinde* which shows that the authorship of *Simplicissimus* and other books was not an absolute secret, and in nearly all his writings he seems to have taken pains to hint in some manner or other at his real name.

The early part of Grimmelshausen's life is somewhat of a mystery. It is even uncertain whether he was born in 1624 or 1625, as is generally assumed, or, according to the latest theory, in 1610. He refers to himself as "Gelnhusanus," a citizen of Gelnhausen, in Hesse, so he was probably born either in that town or in the vicinity. His grandfather is said to have been a baker. It has been suggested that the family originally belonged to the nobility, and became impoverished in the fourteenth century, but there is hardly any evidence to support this view. Until the year 1639, all that we know for certain is that he was for at least four years on active service in the army. About this time he became secretary to Count von Schauenburg, the commandant of Offenburg, in Baden, and he appears to have kept his position until 1647 and perhaps later. In the following year he held a similar position in a regiment, where he saw more fighting, but it was not long before he returned to Offenburg, where he married Katharina Henninger on August 30, 1649, and again became secretary to the commandant. In the following year he went to live in Gaisbach, near Oberkirch, where he was still in the service of the Schauenburg family, for whom he seems to have performed various duties, including that of steward, and he also for a time acted as host to a tavern belonging to them. In the year 1667 he was appointed to the post of mayor in the village of Renchen, in the Black Forest, which belonged to the Bishopric of Strassburg. Among his duties were those of magistrate and tax collector, but he appears to have enjoyed a considerable amount of leisure for his literary work. Seven years later, the district was invaded by the French, and Grimmelshausen's family was scattered. It is probable that he again joined the army, but we know nothing definite about his fate except for the entry in the parochial register at Renchen, which states that he died on August 17, 1676, and that though his sons were dispersed, they all returned to the house. *Anno* 1676, *Augusto* 17. *abiit in Domino Honestus et magno ingenio et eruditione Iohannes Christophorus von Grimmelshausen praetor huius loci, et quamuis ob tumultus belli nomen militiae dederit et pueri hinc inde dispersi fuerint, tamen hic casu omnes convenerunt, et parens Sacramento Eucharistiae pie munitus obiit et sepultus est, cuius anima requiescat in sancta pace.*

Grimmelshausen thus appears to have had a very adventurous youth, succeeded by a long period of sedentary work and leisure, when his duties were not too arduous to permit him to make up for his early lack of education by extensive reading, in addition to which his literary industry was considerable. He was self-taught, but to judge from the varied mass of scientific and literary allusions and quotations, which are scattered so profusely throughout his writings, it would be natural to assume that he had read widely not only in German, but also in French and Latin. He appears to know his Roman authors, and to have much more than a nodding acquaintance with jurisprudence, theology, astronomy and mathematics. He most probably, however, drew a great deal of his knowledge of this type from the collections of miscellaneous information which performed at that time the service of encyclopædias. He certainly possessed an excellent first-hand acquaintance with contemporary German literature, in addition to a vast stock of legendary lore. His works are a mine of information about the superstitions of the people and their social customs, and he must have travelled very extensively. According to the Latin entry by the pastor of Renchen in the parochial register, Grimmelshausen was regarded as a man of great intellect and erudition, and his position as mayor, or *Schultheiss*, naturally made him one of the most distinguished citizens of the place. He is thought in later years to have become converted to Catholicism, and he was certainly in the service of the Catholic Bishop of Strassburg, whose friendly attitude to the French invaders made things more difficult for Grimmelshausen when Renchen was overrun, for the Emperor relieved the Bishop's subjects of their oath of allegiance. Even this theory has little evidence to support it, however, and in spite of the numerous details concerning him which have been discovered in quite recent years, we are as much in the dark as ever with regard to the essential features of what was certainly an extremely varied and adventurous career. A considerable amount can be learned from his writings, because his vitally realistic style enabled him to pour out all the accumulated store of knowledge about countries and people which his wars and travels had instilled into him. He was in touch with the actual world around him, and knew how to communicate his experience in literary form. He cannot be identified completely with his hero Simplicissimus, though there is not the slightest doubt that there is much in the novel which is of an autobiographical nature.

Grimmelshausen's first literary effort, a translation from the French, was followed within a period of about eighteen years by a score or so of other books in quick succession. The following is a detailed list, which is all the more important, as our knowledge of the actual facts of the author's life is so scanty:—

1659 *Der fliegende Wandersmann nach dem Mond* [*The Flying Traveller in the Moon*]. This is a translation of F. Baudoin's *L'homme dans la Lune*, which appeared in Paris in 1648. The French book is itself a translation of Francis Godwin's *The Man in the Moon, or a Discourse of a Voyage thither, by Domingo Gonsales*, published in London in 1638. The title sufficiently explains the contents of the volume. Among other peculiarities, the inhabitants of the moon have a habit of exchanging any moon-child, who exhibits a tendency to vice, for an earth-child, and that is supposed to have been the origin of the inhabitants of America. Some details of Godwin's book were imitated by Cyrano de Bergerac, from whom Swift derived valuable hints for Gulliver's voyage to Laputa.

1660 *Traumgeschicht von Dir und Mir* [*Dream-story of You and Me*], and *Reise in die neue Oberwelt des Monds* [*Journey to the New Upper-world of the Moon*]. These are both satirical dream-pictures. In the former, Oliver Cromwell is mentioned as

97

being still alive, so the story must have been written before 3rd September, 1658.

1666 *Der satyrische Pilgram* [*The Satirical Pilgrim*]. A satirical treatise in popular form, dealing among other things with God, money, dancing, women, wine, beauty, priests, poetry, love, tobacco, philosophy, beggars and war.

1667 *Der keusche Joseph* [*The Chaste Joseph*]. Deals with the Biblical story of Joseph and Potiphar's wife. The later editions of this book contain the story of Joseph's servant, Musai, who is a sort of *picaro*.

1668 *Der abenteuerliche Simplicissimus* [*The Adventurous Simplicissimus*]. It is most probable that the first edition appeared in this year, though the earliest edition in existence bears the date 1669. The first edition contained five books, but as its popularity was very great, Grimmelshausen hurriedly wrote a sixth book, which appeared at first separately, in 1669, as *Continuation of the Adventurous Simplicissimus, or Conclusion of the Same*, and was then included in the same volume as the original work. This extra book is now included in all the editions, but it only disturbs the cohesion of the story by providing a new beginning and a new conclusion, and has no intrinsic merit in itself. It is interesting solely because it presents a picture of Simplicissimus cast away on a desert island, and is therefore an example of a "Robinsonade" some fifty years before the publication of Defoe's *Robinson Crusoe*, a book which called forth great enthusiasm and a correspondingly large number of imitations in Germany.

Two years later there appeared a first, second and third *Continuatio*, which are equally, if not even more worthless than the so-called sixth book; they were most probably first printed in various almanacs published by Grimmelshausen.

Between 1670 and 1674 there appeared four more sequels, which, together with *Simplicissimus* and the *Continuations*, form what are known as the *Simplician Writings*. These sequels are *Trutz-Simplex: oder Lebensbeschreibung der Erzbetrügerin und Landstörzerin Courage* [*Trutz-Simplex, or the Life of the Arch-Impostor and Adventuress Courage*], *Der seltsame Springinsfeld* [*The Rare Jump-in-the-Field*], *Das wunderbarliche Vogelnest* [*The Magic Bird's Nest*] and *Der ewigwährende Kalender* [*The Everlasting Almanac*].[1]

---

[1] For contents of these sequels, see below, p. 105.

1670 *Simplicissimi wunderliche Gaukeltasche* [*Simplicissimus' Singular Juggler's-Bag*]. A puzzle picture-book.

1670 *Der erste Bärenhäuter* [*The first Sluggard* or *Malingerer*]. This story gives the origin of the word *Bärenhäuter*. In the year 1396 a German soldier lost his way in a wood, when an evil spirit appeared to him and offered him a rich reward if he would enter his service. The soldier was first ordered to shoot a bear which just then came in sight, and then to promise to stand sentry for an hour at midnight during a period of seven years. During this time he was not to comb or cut either hair or beard, cut his nails, blow his nose, wash his hands, face or other part of his body; he was to wear the skin of the bear he had just shot, instead of a cloak, use it instead of a bed and never say the Lord's Prayer. On account of this bear's skin (*Bärenhaut*), he was to be called Bärenhäuter. The soldier faithfully carried out his master's orders, and was rewarded eventually with a beautiful wife.

1670 *Dietwald und Amelinde.* A romance, in the heroic-gallant manner, of two royal and virtuous lovers.

1670 *Simplicianischer Zweiköpfiger Ratio status* [*Simplician Two-headed Ratio Status*]. Disquisitions on the origin and meaning of sovereignty. The idea is that the people should choose their own ruler, but the book is merely a compilation, based on other sources.

1672 *Das Ratstübel Plutonis, oder Kunst, reich zu werden* [*The Council Chamber of Pluto*,[1] *or the Art of becoming rich*]. Simplicissimus, his father and mother, Courage, Springinsfeld and various other characters discuss the art of becoming rich.

1672 *Proximus und Lympida.* An historical novel of a similar type to *Dietwald and Amelinde*.

1672 *Die Verkehrte Welt* [*The World turned topsy-turvy*]. The author descends to Hell, converses with the damned, and describes the conditions in the upper world ironically as being beyond reproach. A satire on Court life. The author had already employed the same idea in the Mummelsee episode in *Simplicissimus*.

1673 *Der deutsche Michel* [*The German Michael*]. This is a nickname for the typical German, like the English "John Bull." The book deals in a popular manner with current abuses in the German language.

---

[1] Grimmelshausen exhibits his weakness in Latin by confusing *Pluto* with *Plutus*, and making *ratio* a masculine noun.

1673 *Simplicissimi Galgenmännlein* [*Simplicissimus' Mandrake*]. Deals with the superstition concerning the root of the mandragora which often has human shape, and is dug up at midnight at the foot of the gallows. It is engendered from the semen of a man who has been hanged, and possesses magic virtues.

1673 *Der Stolze Melcher* [*Proud Melcher*]. The story of a peasant's son who goes to the war of 1672–78 between France and Holland and returns home in humble circumstances, thus giving his relations and neighbours an opportunity of expressing their views on the foolishness and frivolity of the younger generation.

Grimmelshausen's writings have been likened to an oasis in the desert. "The agony which I have had to endure in reading the works of Lohenstein, Ziegler, and their contemporaries, in order to be able conscientiously to judge Grimmelshausen's relationship to the other German novelists of the seventeenth century, entitles me to employ such a strong expression. I know of no novelist of the seventeenth century in Germany who can bear the remotest comparison with Grimmelshausen, and of all the literary romances of the seventeenth century there is none which is so deeply rooted in the life of the people as the *Simplician Writings*."[1] The heroic-gallant novelists scorned to draw their material from contemporary life, and believed that distance of time and place lent the enchantment which the educated reader of the period found so necessary as an anodyne. In consequence, they have sunk into obscurity, and the one enduring prose-work of the century, the first five books of *Simplicissimus*, on which the fame of Grimmelshausen rests, is an unique contribution to contemporary sociological history.

The discursive title is at the same time a programme. The story is to tell the life and adventures of an individual who has seen, learned and done many strange things, and has eventually decided voluntarily to quit the world of action and experience for the tranquillity of a hermit's cell. It is

[1] F. Bobertag: *Über Grimmelshausens Simplicianische Schriften* [Breslau, 1874].

a novel of development, and although the attitude of the hero is on the whole fairly passive, since he is influenced by the situations in which he is placed, instead of moulding them to his own ends, there is yet a satisfying external unity, and there is sufficient of a psychological problem for the novel to bear some slight comparison with the medieval epic of *Parzival* by Wolfram von Eschenbach and the *Wilhelm Meister* of Goethe. Parzival goes out into the world as an innocent youth, a "guileless fool," who on his journey through life has to solve the problem of adapting himself to his worldly environment, without losing his vision of the higher life and those spiritual ideals which are so hard to reconcile with the practical necessities of material surroundings. Wilhelm Meister also goes through a period of apprenticeship and wandering, and succeeds eventually in combining poetry and life, in reconciling the two aspects of his double nature, the poet and the man of the world. Simplicius starts life as an ignorant peasant lad, receives a rather narrow, one-sided and superficial education from the hermit, and knows nothing of the realities of life until he leaves his forest and arrives in Hanau. Before long, however, he develops the ready, practical sense and adaptability which bring him fame and fortune as the huntsman of Soest. After he has bought his farm in the Black Forest, his adventures cease to be actual, and read more like those of Baron Munchausen. The extraordinary episode of the Mummelsee, and his journey to Russia and back via Asia, are utterly out of harmony with the remainder of the story, and the final retreat to a hermit's cell, preceded by a lengthy farewell to the world, taken bodily from a work of the Spanish ascetic Antonius de Guevara, does not come as a natural consummation.

The most congenial feature in the character of Simplicius is the firm, enduring friendship that subsists between him and the younger Herzbruder. This friendship deserves to be cited as that of a new Damon and Pythias, for it could not be exceeded in disinterestedness on either side. In his affairs with women he is light-hearted in the extreme. He even seems to feel no compunction at leaving his wife in Lippstadt for so long, while he stays at Cologne, goes to Paris and later travels about with Herzbruder. The death of his wife is recorded without comment, except that he rejoices a little later in the thought of his freedom, and on the decease of his second wife, he "well-nigh laughed himself into a sickness," though in the second case there was certainly good cause for relief. Towards the end, after he leaves Paris and falls in with Oliver, he begins to feel remorse at needless killing, though as the huntsman of Soest he had appeared as a sufficiently bloodthirsty person; even then, however, he has let the impostor huntsman of Wesel off very lightly. The eventual resolve to quit the world, insufficiently motivated as it is, yet provides a satisfactory conclusion to a life of action such as that of Simplicius, and there can therefore be no hesitation in regarding *Simplicissimus* as a novel of development. It is just this element which is missing in the picaresque novels, where the reader is interested in the external incident, but is unable to perceive any psychological development in the character of the hero. Grimmelshausen is indebted to the picaresque novel for the use of the "I" form, which he employs in all the *Simplician Writings*, and also for the general biographical framework, beginning with a description of the parental house and the circumstances which force the hero out into the world at a tender age. Otherwise he owes nothing essential to literary sources, though an example of his wide reading is seen in the episode of Simplicius and the love-sick ladies of high degree in Paris, which is borrowed, though probably not directly, from Bandello.

The universal belief in witchcraft and magic is seen in the frequency with which Simplicius is taken for a magician. The Witches' Sabbath is described as though it were an actual occurrence, witnessed by the hero himself, and the reputation for being "frozen," i.e. invulnerable, was possessed by numerous individuals at the time of the Thirty

Years War. Oliver and the Provost-Marshal could not be killed by bullets, and Simplicius, as the huntsman of Soest, was believed by his enemies to be similarly protected. Great play is made with the prophecies of the elder Herzbruder and the conjuring tricks of the Provost, and there are frequent allusions to the prevalent superstitions. When the huntsman of Wesel goes sheep-stealing, his servant tells him that he must first of all see "if Bläsy is at home or not," that is to say, St. Blasius, the patron-saint of domestic animals. It was only necessary for a man to be a prominent scholar, to have performed some conspicuous and difficult feat, or even merely to be cleverer or more cunning than his fellows, in order to arouse the suspicion that he was in possession of supernatural powers, purchased from the devil at the price of his soul.

None of the great historical figures of the Thirty Years War appears in *Simplicissimus*, for by the time the hero leaves the forest for Hanau, Gustavus Adolphus has already been killed at the battle of Lützen and Wallenstein murdered at Eger. Prince Bernhard of Weimar and Johann von Werth are barely mentioned. James Ramsay, the Scotch colonel in the Swedish Army, commandant of Hanau, who is supposed to be the brother of Simplicius' mother, is well known for his defence of that town, but his connection with the hero of Grimmelshausen is, of course, fictitious, and the name Melchior Sternfels von Fugshaim, as it is sometimes spelt, is an anagram of "Christoffel von Grimmelshausen." If the course of Simplicius' career is compared with the actual dates of the various incidents of the war mentioned by the author, we discover some curious discrepancies. Simplicius was born just after the battle of Höchst, which took place on June 10, 1622, when his father and mother were separated, so that the former resolved to become a hermit. He was ten years old when he came to the hermit, with whom he stayed for two years, and after the battle of Nördlingen, September 6, 1634, he left the forest, his first real step out into the world, and arrived in Hanau, where he spent the winter of 1634–35, which was noted for being extraordinarily cold. In the early part of 1635 he was captured by Croats. During the siege of Magdeburg in 1636 he became acquainted with Herzbruder and Oliver. He took part in the battle of Wittstock, September 24, 1636, and during the summer of 1637 he was active as the huntsman of Soest. Then came his capture and internment at Lippstadt, during the winter of 1637–38. He was invited to dinner by the commandant on Twelfth Night, 1638, and soon after that married and set out on his journey to Cologne. Then came the trip to Paris and the return to Germany, when he was compelled to serve as a musketeer in Philippsburg. On July 30th, of the same year, there took place the battle of Wittenweier, during August he was with the hangers-on of the army as a "Merode brother," and in December he was acting as a highwayman in company with Oliver. The meeting with Herzbruder, the pilgrimage to Switzerland and the journey to Vienna took place in the following spring. In March, 1645, both Herzbruder and Simplicius took part in the battle of Jankau, and this is the last exact chronological reference we find.

It thus appears that the huntsman of Soest was only fifteen years of age, and that he married before he was sixteen, at which tender age he experienced his amorous adventure with the Parisian ladies. It may be, of course, that the author intended to emphasise the youth of his hero, since he expressly refers (Bk. III, Ch. xi) to the fact that during his activities at Soest he was unpopular with women, since he was like "a wooden statue, without strength or sap," but it would be better to take it as a poetic licence, since it is only apparent after careful correlation of Simplicius' adventures with the fixed historical references.

The so-called sixth book introduces Simplicissimus to us once more, leaving his hermit's retreat and setting off again on his travels. He wanders as far as Loretto, Rome, and

Alexandria, is captured by robbers in Egypt, and is eventually shipwrecked on an island, which he resolves never to leave.

The first Continuation describes how Simplicissimus after his return to Europe acted as a writer of newspapers and almanacs, the second Continuation tells how he left his island, and the third relates some anecdotes of the period after his return.

The story of *The Adventuress Courage* introduces the lady with whom Simplicissimus had a *liaison* at the Spa in the Black Forest. She declares that the child she had left at his door was not his at all, and that she had pretended that Simplicissimus was the father in order to spite him, hence the title, *Trutz-Simplex*. She unfolds a terrible tale, beginning with her service, disguised in boy's clothes, as page to a young captain, whose mistress she becomes when it is no longer possible to conceal her sex. She marries him on his death-bed, but becomes subsequently the mistress first of a count and then of an ambassador. She marries a captain of dragoons, and takes part in various battles until her husband is killed, when she accepts the wooing of a lieutenant, who first tries to whip her into obedience and then deserts her, after which she continues to take part in battles and succeeds on one occasion in capturing a major. She abandons the army and returns to her former nurse, learns that she is of noble birth, marries another captain and goes to the Danish War, where she loses her husband, after having by her courage captured three of the enemy. Unfortunately, she is recognised by the major whom she had captured some time previously, and he takes his revenge by treating her in an unspeakably vile manner, until she is rescued by a Danish captain, who takes her to his castle in Denmark, where she is treated like a countess, but through the treachery of her host's relations soon finds herself back in Germany in misery. Another love-affair comes to an unhappy ending, for her lover is executed for killing his corporal, who had cast eyes on Courage. She makes the acquaintance of a musketeer, whom she calls Jump-in-the-Field, and goes with his regiment to Italy, where she finds occupation as a *vivandière*. Eventually the army returns to Germany, where Courage leaves her companion and marries yet another captain, who is also soon killed, and it is while on a recuperative visit to the Spa that she meets Simplicissimus, with the result already related in the earlier book. Her last husband is a gipsy chief, and she ends her days as queen of the troupe.

The Rare Jump-in-the-Field relates the life-story of the friend of Simplicissimus, who has already appeared as the latter's comrade during the adventures at Soest, and as the companion of Courage. The narrator of the story is a young unemployed secretary, who meets both Simplicissimus and Jump-in-the-Field, the latter now an old wooden-legged fiddler, in the guest-room of an inn. He describes a former meeting with Courage and the gipsies, and his adventures with them, and then Jump-in-the-Field tells his own story, which the secretary writes down. The last chapters relate the discovery of a magic bird's-nest, which has the power of making its owner invisible, and this leads to the third sequel, *The Magic Bird's Nest*, which is in two parts. This unique object enables its possessor to pry into the intimacies of family life, as does Le Sage's *Diable Boiteux*. The most amusing incident is when one of the owners of the nest becomes enamoured of the daughter of a Portuguese Jew, whose acquaintance he has sought for the purpose of robbing him. He persuades her parents that the prophet Elias is present but invisible, and will with the young Jewess beget the Messiah, for whom the Jews are waiting. He plays himself the part of the prophet, and thus attains his object, but unfortunately the child turns out to be a girl. The nest is eventually thrown into the Rhine, and the owner turns his thoughts to repentance.

The Everlasting Almanac has only a nominal connection with Simplicissimus. It is a conglomeration of recipes, weather prophecies, lists of historical events, dialogues on astronomy and astrology, and a series of anecdotes having little or no real connection with Simplicissimus, but whose object seems to be to render him more adaptable to the popular taste. Much of the material is borrowed from other almanacs.

In *Courage* and *Jump-in-the-Field*, Grimmelshausen enlarged his picture of the Thirty Years War by presenting two counterparts to Simplicissimus, and in *The Magic Bird's Nest* he rounded off the picture by depicting social life after the declaration of peace. The *Simplician Writings* present, therefore, an incomparable picture of a period of which Grimmelshausen was the only German writer of the century to appreciate the literary value.

BARON MUNCHAUSEN

IN *The Critical Review* for December, 1785, there appeared the following notice:—

Baron Munchausen's Narrative of his Marvellous Travels and Campaigns in Russia. Small 8vo. 1s. Smith.

"This is a satirical production, calculated to throw ridicule on the bold assertions of some parliamentary declaimers. If rant may be best foiled at its own weapons, the author's design is not ill-founded; for the marvellous has never been carried to a more whimsical and ludicrous extent."

There is a copy of this edition in the British Museum, and the title-page runs as follows:

"Baron Munchausen's Narrative of his Marvellous Travels and Campaigns in Russia. Humbly dedicated and recommended to Country Gentlemen, and, if they please, to be repeated as their own, after a hunt, at horse races, in wateringplaces, and other such polite assemblies; round the bottle and fire-side. Oxford: Printed for the Editor, and sold by the Booksellers there and at Cambridge, also in London by the Booksellers of Piccadilly, the Royal Exchange, and M. Smith, at No. 46, in Fleet-street. 1786. Price one-shilling."

It will be noticed that the year of publication is given as 1786, and this has given rise to the supposition that the British Museum copy is the 2nd edition. In the University Library at Göttingen, however, there is a volume entitled:

"The Singular Travels, Campaigns, Voyages and Sporting Adventures of Baron Munnikhouson, commonly pronounced Munchausen: As he relates them over a Bottle, when surrounded by his Friends. A new Edition, considerably enlarged, and ornamented with four views, engraved from the Baron's Drawings. Oxford: Printed and sold by the Booksellers of that University, and at Cambridge, Bath and Bristol; in London by M. Smith, at No. 46 Fleet-street; and by the Booksellers in Paternoster-Row. 1786."

The preface to the first edition is repeated, and there is also an "Advertisement to the second edition," dated April 20th, 1786, which contains the following statement: "The rapid demand for the first ed. of this little pamphlet is a proof that the Public have seen its moral tendency in a proper light . . . this little collection, which is considerably enriched by his Naval or Sea Adventures, and also embellished with four views from his own pencil."

This is obviously the second edition, and whereas the British Museum copy is a pamphlet of 49 pages, containing only Chaps. II–VI of the modern editions, the Göttingen copy contains in addition Chaps. VII–XIV.

The publisher of the first two editions, M. Smith, then appears to have disposed of the work to G. Kearsley, who published in the same year, 1786, a third considerably enlarged and illustrated edition at the increased price of 2s., under the new title:

"Gulliver revived; or the singular Travels, Campaigns, Voyages and Adventures of Baron Munikhousen, commonly called Munckhausen. 12mo. 3rd Edit. Considerable enlarged, and ornamented with a Number of Views, engraved from the original Designs."

As there is no copy of either the third or fourth editions in the British Museum, the following contemporary reviews of the third edition may be of interest. *The Critical Review* for July, 1786, says: "In our Sixtieth Volume, p. 479, we reviewed the first edition of this whimsical and humorous work. It is now much enlarged, and adorned with characteristic plates. . . . But why should he call it Gulliver revived? The baron is the genuine descendant of Lucian, whose *True History* contains similar wonders, related in the same grave, artless style. If the work arrives at a fourth edition, we would recommend the following title: *Lucian revived; or, Gulliver beat with his own Bow*."

The Gentleman's Magazine for the same month shows a singular lack of humour on the part of the reviewer, who evidently attributes a didactic aim to the story:

"That this performance is suited to the taste of the publick is evident from its having rapidly passed through two editions; and it is indeed well calculated to repress and expose a very pernicious and disgusting practice, which is the pest of society. Few, even of the smallest circles, are without a Baron Munchausen—without some ridiculous liar, who is alone the dupe of his own folly, in supposing that his idle and improbable tales can obtain credit, or entertain and astonish any, except fools and children.

"We cannot, however, compliment the Baron with bearing any resemblance to his celebrated predecessor, the well-known Mr. Lemuel Gulliver."

In June of the same year *The Monthly Review* says it is "Intended to ridicule the extravagant stories of those witless lyars, who are eternally plaguing (or *boreing*, as the modern cant runs) their hearers with improbable rhodomontades and absurd *bouncers*: the most notorious of whom are here outdone, by Baron Munckhausen. Some of these marvellous fibs, though utter impossibilities . . . are very laughable. . . . In short Joe Miller, with the whole tribe of worn-out jest-books, must now give way to the Lyar's Monitor: a title which, as the editor suggests, might, with no impropriety, have been given to this matchless little volume of *wonderful wonders*, had not *Gulliver revived* been preferred."

In 1787 appeared a fifth edition:

> "Gulliver Revived; containing singular Travels, Campaigns, Voyages, and Adventures in Russia, The Caspian Sea, Iceland, Turkey, Egypt, Gibraltar, up the Mediterranean, on the Atlantic Ocean, and through the centre of Mount Etna into the South Sea: also An Account of a Voyage into the Moon and Dog-star, with many extraordinary Particulars relative to the Cooking Animal in those Planets, which we here call the Human Species,

> by

> BARON MUNCHAUSEN.

> The fifth edition, Considerably enlarged, and ornamented with a variety of explanatory Views, engraved from Original Designs.
> London: Printed for G. Kearsley in Fleet-street. 1787."

Since the publication of the second edition, the following additions have been made: Chap. I; the parenthesis "some travellers . . . already related" at the end of Chap. VI; and Chaps. XV–XX (down to the words "the great quadrangle"). And the preface runs as follows:—

"The sudden estimation which this work is grown into (having passed four editions within a few months) is a strong proof that the public have seen its moral tendency in a proper light; it might have been entitled, with great propriety, THE LIAR'S MONITOR: Surely no vice is more contemptible than a habit of abusing the ears of our friends with falsehoods.

"The first edition, for want of more matter, was comparatively slow in sale, but the whole of the second, third, and fourth impressions were purchased within a few days after they were printed. This fifth edition contains such considerable additions, that it may fairly be considered as a new work."

The sixth edition was the same as the fifth, but in 1792 appeared a *Sequel* containing (as Chaps. I–XIV) the Chaps. XXI–XXXIV, and also the Preface to the second volume. On the Portrait of the Baron at the beginning are printed the words "Frontispiece to Munchausen's Travels. Vol. II^d," and on the page facing the preface, there is the announcement: Of the Publishers of this Volume may be had the former Volume, containing The Adventures of Baron Munchausen in Russia, etc., The Seventh Edition." The title-page runs as follows:—

"(With Twenty capital Copper-Plates, including the Baron's Portrait.) A Sequel to the Adventures of Baron Munchausen. . . . Humbly dedicated to Mr. Bruce, the Abyssinian Traveller, as the Baron conceives that it may be of some service to him, previous to his making another expedition into Abyssinia. But if this advice does not delight Mr. Bruce, the Baron is willing to fight him on any terms he pleases. London. Printed for H. D. Symonds, Paternoster Row; and J. Owen, opposite Bond Street, Piccadilly. 1792."

Finally, in 1793 there appeared "The 7th Edition, Considerably enlarged, and ornamented with Twenty Explanatory Engravings, from Original Designs," printed for C. & G. Kearsley, Fleet Street. The title is the same as that of the fifth edition, except that the words "or, the Vice of Lying properly exposed" appear after "Gulliver Revived." The contents are the same as those of the fifth edition, with the addition of the final paragraph ("He has also obtained from Mr. Pitt," etc.) at the end of Chap. XX, and the Supplement which now completes Vol. I. Instead of the words "The End," the Seventh Edition has "End of Volume the First."

The Seventh Edition and the Sequel make up the two volumes which are printed together in the standard modern editions. It must be pointed out that these later editions all retain a number of misprints which do not occur in the first edition of 1785. The beginning of Chapter II (originally the first chapter), for example, should read, "I set off from home," not "I set off from *Rome*."

. . . . . .

For many years the authorship of *Baron Munchausen* remained in doubt. In 1786 the German poet Gottfried August Bürger published a German translation from the second English edition, and in 1788 there appeared a second German edition, enlarged according to the fifth English edition.[1] Both German editions bear the imprint *London*, but as a matter of fact they were printed by the firm of Dieterich in Göttingen. Although Bürger expressly stated that his work was a translation from the English, he was long held to be the original author. One of the theories was that the stories had their origin in the table-talk of the three friends, Bürger, Lichtenberg, and Kästner at the University of Göttingen, while endeavouring to outvie each other in telling tall stories over their wine, and the announcement that the work had been translated from the English was supposed to be an attempt to mystify the public. Another suggestion was that Bürger had met the Baron Hieronymus von Münchhausen at Pyrmont, a well-known watering-

[1] Both the *Encyclopædia Britannica* and Thomas Seccombe [in his introduction to the edition published by Messrs. Lawrence & Bullen in 1895] state that Bürger translated first of all from the fifth edition. This is erroneous, as the first German edition appeared in 1786, and the fifth English edition did not appear until 1787. The second German [enlarged] edition was published in 1788, and in the preface the translator says: "This small collection has been successful in both countries. As the English original went through five editions, we were also impelled to produce a new edition of the German translation, and we have made use of the additions to the latest English Edition." It is therefore clear that Bürger only made use of the fifth English edition for his own second edition (sixty-two pages more than his first), and a comparison of the text shows that he translated in the first place from the second English edition, perhaps from the Göttingen Library copy. A reprint of Bürger's first translation of 1786 was edited in 1925 by Dr. Erich Ebstein for the members of the *Gesellschaft der Bibliophilen*.

place, and had there heard the latter's stories. On the other hand, some people refused to believe that the real Baron had ever existed.

The question of authorship was set at rest by a friend of Bürger named Karl von Reinhard, who, in order to refute the assertion that the poet had published the book simultaneously in English and German in order to pay his debts, made the following statement in the periodical the *Gesellschafter*, for November, 1824: "The collection has for author the late Professor Raspe, who published it after his flight from Kassel to England, where it was very well received and repeatedly reprinted. Bürger translated it from the 5th edition from English into German without mentioning his name." Although Reinhard made a slip in mentioning the *fifth* edition as the original basis for the translation, there is no need to doubt the accuracy of the remainder of his assertion. He had been an intimate friend of Bürger and was the editor of the poet's works, so it is hardly likely that he would have made such an important statement unless he had had the assurance of its veracity from Bürger himself. J. G. Meusel in vol. xi. of his *Lexikon der vom Jahre 1750 bis 1800 verstorbenen teutschen Schriftsteller*, which was published at Leipzig in 1811, appears to have been aware that Raspe had something to do with the book, for he says that the latter "translated the well-known 'Münchhausen Lies' into English." That is impossible, if referring to Bürger's edition, since the first English edition appeared a year before the German. Although the old legend still found credence long after von Reinhard published the true facts, there is little doubt that the first man to publish, in a separate volume, the collection of stories which became the nucleus of the now famous folk-book was the whilom German Professor Rudolph Erich Raspe.

Raspe was born in Hanover in 1737, and studied philology and the natural sciences at the Universities of Göttingen and Leipzig. In 1762 he became a clerk in the University library at Hanover, was appointed secretary two years later, and in 1767 he was called to Kassel as Professor of Archæology at the "Carolinum." He held at the same time the appointment of Inspector of the Landgrave's collections of coins and antiquities, and in 1771 he was given the additional post of second librarian. On account of his numerous writings on literary, mineralogical, geological, and other scientific subjects, including a zoological paper in the fifty-ninth volume of the *Philosophical Transactions* and reviews in both German and English periodicals, he was made an honorary member of the Royal Society in London. He married in 1771, and two years later he travelled through Westphalia, at the expense of the Landgrave of Hesse, in search of old manuscripts. In 1775 it was intended to send him for some years to Italy to purchase coins and antiquities for the Landgrave's collections, but before the plan came to fruition it was discovered that among other delinquencies he had stolen valuables from a cabinet of medals entrusted to him. He was arrested, but escaped to England, with the object, it is said, of going to America. He remained in these islands for the rest of his life, however. His name was removed from the lists of the learned societies to which he belonged, including the Royal Society, but he succeeded in making a name for himself in England as a writer and mine expert. He does not seem to have been able to settle down to any permanent appointment. He was chosen to arrange Mr. James Tassie's famous collection of pastes and impressions from gems, and as a result of his labours he issued a catalogue in English and French which is still regarded as being of some value. In 1782 he went to Cornwall, and for six years was assaymaster and storekeeper at the Dolcoath mine. He then went to Scotland and swindled his employer, Sir John Sinclair of Ulbster, by pretending to discover minerals in ground that he had prepared himself beforehand. He disappeared to escape the consequences, and was next heard of in Ireland, where he went for mineralogical purposes. He stayed at Muckross in order to open a new mine, but died there of spotted fever towards the end of 1794.

While still in Germany he had written a poetic romance of the days of chivalry entitled "Hermin and Gunilde," which excited sufficient interest to call forth a parody. Among his other literary efforts were an original comedy, poems, a translation of a French comedy, and the publication of a periodical called *Der Casselische Zuschauer* ("The Kassel Spectator"), in addition to various scientific treatises. In England he published translations of scientific works, a translation into English of a German poem *Tabby in Elysium*, a translation into English of Lessing's drama *Nathan the Wise*, and *A Critical Essay on Oil-Painting* in English, which Horace Walpole, who appears to have thought highly of him, helped him to publish. Raspe appears to have had an expert knowledge of both English and French, since he not only translated from his native tongue into English, a sufficiently difficult task, but he also wrote original works in English and French. He also wrote in Latin and translated from Italian into German. In the *Catalogue of 500 Celebrated Authors of Great Britain* (London, 1788) he is mentioned as a foreigner of some reputation.

Such was the astounding many-sidedness of this queer mixture of scholar and rogue, who by the publication of his 49-page pamphlet obtained a small niche in the literary hall of fame of both England and Germany. His unfavourable reputation in the latter country at that time may have been one of the reasons why Bürger did not divulge his name, as it certainly would not have helped the circulation of the latter's book.

It was while he was employed at the Dolcoath mine that Raspe published anonymously at Oxford, in the year 1785, *Baron Munchausen's Narrative of his Marvellous Travels and Campaigns in Russia*; but though he showed a certain amount of originality in co-ordinating the stories and casting them into the form of a more or less connected narrative, they had all appeared previously in the pages of a periodical publication in Berlin. In the year 1781 there were printed in the 8th vol. of the *Vade Mecum für lustige Leute*, sixteen anecdotes under the heading *M-h-s-nsche Geschichten*, followed by *Noch zwey M——Lügen* in the 9th vol. in 1783.[1] All the adventures of the 1st edition are to be found in these two volumes, for Raspe translated them all with the exception of one relating to a famous singer whom the Baron met in Petersburg. He gave her a hundred *louis d'or* for one of her most beautiful trills, which he preserved in spirits. Meusel was therefore right when he said that Raspe translated the Münchhausen Lies into English. Even before their appearance in the *Vade Mecum*, however, these stories were already well known in the neighbourhood of Hanover as having been related to a circle of friends by a retired cavalry officer named Karl Friedrich Hieronymus, Baron von Münchhausen.

Baron von Münchhausen was born in 1720 at Bodenwerder in Hanover, and after serving for some years as a cavalry officer in the Russian Army, during which period he took part in the campaigns of 1740 and 1741 against the Turks, he retired in 1760 to his family estate, where he became famous for his marvellous and incredible stories of war experiences and adventures while travelling or out hunting. He used to relate these stories as having actually happened to himself, and his reputation soon extended beyond the narrow circle of friends, who were gathered round his table smoking and drinking punch, to the whole neighbourhood. His fame in this respect is even preserved in the family archives. He appears to have lived happily until the year 1790, when his wife, who had borne him no children, died. He married again four years later, but his second wife only brought misery into the home, and the jovial squire's last years were unhappy. He died in 1797.

The editor of the sixth German edition[2] relates in his introduction how his father visited old Münchhausen a couple of years before the latter's death. He interviewed him in his garden at Bodenwerder and saw a dull old man,

---

[1] These are reprinted by Ebstein *op. cit.*
[2] Adolf Ellissen: Sixth German edition [Göttingen and Berlin, 1849].

who had become distrustful and taciturn in consequence of the publicity caused by Raspe's book. The pastor Cludius, however, confirmed the reports of the Baron's former talent as a *raconteur*. It had been stated in print that in the excitement of the story the Baron's eyes would flash and start out of his head, while his face became redder and redder, beads of perspiration started out on his forehead, and he threw his arms about violently in the air. Cludius denied this and declared that the Baron certainly lent military emphasis to his stories, but that he related them quite as a matter of course, without bombast, and in the easy vein of a man of the world.

After having ascertained that Raspe composed his book on the basis of the stories related by the real Münchhausen, the question arises whether the Baron invented his anecdotes or whether he drew upon memories of what he had heard or read.

It has been proved that there is hardly one of the stories which cannot be traced to one source or another.[1] Some of them appear in various forms not only in Germany but also in other European countries, in classical literature and in the Orient. There are in German literature a large number of *Lügendichtungen*, or mendacious stories, which appear as poems, carnival plays, folk-songs, fairy-tales and fables. The majority of these have come down to us from the fourteenth and fifteenth centuries, though in many cases the origins go back to prehistoric times, and there are traces to be found even to-day in folk-songs and nursery rhymes. Hans Sachs, the famous Mastersinger, classifies the various kinds of liars in his *Schwank von dem Lügenberg*. Among the best-known aspects of the *Lügendichtungen* are the folk-book of the people of Schilda, who, like the inhabitants of Gotham, in England, do all sorts of stupid things, such as cutting a notch in the boat to mark the place where they have dropped their valuables into a

---

[1] V. Carl Müller-Fraureuth, *Die deutschen Lügendichtungen bis auf Münchhausen* [Halle, 1881].

lake in order to keep them safe during a time of war, and the legend of "Schlaraffenland," the land flowing with milk and honey, where roast pigs run along, bidding people come and eat them. Schlaraffenland is also the country where he who tells the biggest lie is chosen king. In 1559 there appeared *Der Finkenritter*, for the most part a compilation of current mendacious stories, which are, like those in *Munchausen*, strung on a very loose thread. A more coherent narrative in the same *genre* is Christian Reuter's *Schelmuffsky* (1696). The hero is citizen of a small provincial town which he has hardly ever quitted, but he relates the most astounding imaginary experiences; he has had love-affairs with noble ladies and been on terms of friendship with distinguished knights; he thinks that wagons come by road from London to Hamburg, and that the inhabitants of Venice suffer from drought on account of the city's being situated on a high rock.

The story of the cherry-tree growing out of the stag's head (Chap. IV) is in a book of anecdotes called *Der lustige Teutsche* (1729), where, however, the cherry-stones are replaced by plum-stones. When the Baron climbs up the bean-stalk to the moon (Chap. VI) there is an obvious connection with the English fairy-tale of *Jack and the Bean-stalk*. The latter was not at that time in print in Germany, so the real Baron must have heard some analogous tale while on his travels. Similarly with the story of the keeping of the bees (Chap. VI). There is a Serbian fairy-tale which relates how a man sinks into the ground and is only able to extricate himself by going home for a spade and then digging himself out; in like manner the Finkenritter crawls into an oak-tree through a hole which is used by bees, which have a hive there, and when he tries to retreat he finds the hole too small, so he runs home, procures an axe, chops down the tree and crawls out through the bottom. This motive also occurs in the first two editions of *Munchausen* where, after falling from the moon into a deep hole, he says, "There was no other way than to go home for a spade and to dig me out by slopes, which I fortunately accomplished, before I had been so much as missed by the steward." This was altered in later editions, and the Baron now digs himself out with his finger-nails (Chap. VI). The story of the wolf, which is turned inside-out (Chap. IV), has many sources, and nearly every other adventure can be traced to some earlier authority. It is hardly likely, however, that the Baron discovered much of his material in books; he most probably stored up in his memory anecdotes that he had heard during his active career. Some of them may not have been related by him at all, but only attributed to him by the Hanoverians to whom he was so well known by repute, and it is possible that the anonymous contributor to the *Vade Mecum* added some on his own account. However that may be, the adventures of Baron Munchausen have become a folk-book both in England and Germany, though there is no doubt that the latter country has the chief claim to them. As Bürger himself said, he simply reintroduced into Germany a German product.

This applies to the nucleus of the book, the Chapters II–VI of the modern editions, which describe the adventures in Russia. The remainder was added by other hands, is purely English, and has nothing to do either with Raspe or the Baron Hieronymus. It is very inferior in humour and invention, and the artistic smoothness is disturbed by the didactic and satirical tendency of the additions.

The text of the first edition varies in a few unimportant details from that of the subsequent editions. The most curious variation is in the second chapter, where, after the Baron has thrown his mantle over the poor old man whom he sees lying on the road, a voice from the heavens blesses him with the words, "You will be rewarded, my son, for this in time." The first and second editions make the voice remark, "I'll be damned, my son, if I do not reward it in time." The alteration in the means by which the Baron escapes from the hole into which he has fallen from the moon has already been mentioned above. Instead of jumping over the hedge with the coach and horses, as in Chap. VI, he takes the carriages to pieces and reassembles them in the required positions. A few errata, which had been noted in a list at the beginning of the first edition, were corrected, as, for example, in Chap. II, where the term of address "you gentlemen" was substituted for the form in the third person, "my readers." There are many cases of slight alterations in the wording, such as at the end of Chap. II, where "French wits or hair dressers" became "French wits or petite [sic] maîtres." The notes about the Baron forgetting his feelings in not feeding his horse, his eyes retaining their fire after he struck his face against the door-post, the port-cullis which cut his horse in two, and his being in favour with the Grand Seignior are not in the earlier edition, and the story runs straight on without chapter headings, con-cluding with the words, "God bless Great George our King."

. . . . . .

In the preface to the seventh edition it is stated that that which was added subsequent to the second edition was not by the original author. The supplementary chapters to the second and third editions, containing the sea adventures, owe much to the "Vera Historia" of Lucian, so that a contemporary critic suggested the title "Lucian revived." There are satirical allusions to Baron Tott's *Mémoires sur les Turcs et les Tartares*, of which an English translation had appeared in the previous year, and the French balloonists Blanchard and Montgolfier. Among other topical references which were familiar to English readers at that time are the birthday of George III, the famous defence of Gibraltar, according to Captain John Drinkwater's *History of the Siege of Gibraltar* (completed 1783), C. J. Phipps' *A Voyage towards the North Pole* (1774), and P. Brydone's *Tour through Sicily and Malta*.

Many of the stories have their source in Bebel's *Facetiae ebelianae* (Strassburg, 1508), the *Utopia Didaci Bemardini*

(1644) of the Jesuit Jacob Bidermann, the *Mendacia Ridicula* in vol. iii. of J. P. Lange's *Deliciae Academicae* (Heilbronn, 1665), and Castiglione's *Cortegiano* (1528). The story, for example, of a man swallowed by a fish is not only reminiscent of the Biblical story of Jonah, but is also to be found in both Lucian and Bebel.

The *Sequel*, published in 1792, with a humorous dedication to Bruce, the Abyssinian Traveller, is mainly a satire on James Bruce's *Travels to Discover the Sources of the Nile* which appeared in 1790, but there are also a great many references to current topics, which the reader can easily discover for himself. It is the least interesting part of the book, and to modern taste it becomes at times somewhat tedious. The most enjoyable and enduring section is that which the refugee German professor elaborated from the already-published German version of the anecdotes of Baron Hieronymus of Bodenwerder.

THE HISTORICAL BACKGROUND OF
GOETHE'S *WERTHER*

TO set *Werther* against its natural background would entail writing a history of the Sentimental Age in Germany, with an exposition of the English and French influences which helped to form it. The tremendous effect of the book was due to its opportune appearance, for, as the author himself says in his Autobiography, "only a slight quantity of powder is required to blow up a powerful mine, and the explosion which took place among the public was so violent because the young generation had already undermined itself, while the convulsion was so great because everyone burst forth with his exaggerated claims, unsatisfied passions and imaginary sufferings." This paper must therefore touch upon the mood of the generation, in addition to discussing the various incidents in Goethe's life which contributed to the shaping of the work. The celebrated account of the period in *Dichtung und Wahrheit* was written some forty years afterwards, when Goethe, no doubt unconsciously, presented some elements of the real situation in an altered light, and it must be corrected in view of what is known of the facts from other sources.

TRUTH AND FICTION

After Goethe had taken his licentiate of laws at the University of Strassburg, which gave him the right to the title of doctor, he returned to Frankfort in August, 1771, where he applied himself to the practice of law to please his father —and of literature to please himself. He did not stay long in his native town, however, for his father wanted him to go to Wetzlar to continue his legal training. Wetzlar was the seat of the *Reichskammergericht*, the supreme court of judicature of the Holy Roman Empire, which, besides acting as the highest court of appeal in civil suits, settled legal disputes between the various states and between the states and their subjects. The sluggishness of the law is illustrated by the fact that there were about sixteen thousand cases awaiting decision in the year Goethe was there. As no more than two hundred could be settled every year, while the annual increase exceeded that number, there must have been many German parallels to the celebrated English case of *Jarndyce v. Jarndyce*. The files of some cases, still unsettled, are said to have accumulated the dust of a hundred years and more. A commission of inspection, which had been sent to enquire into grave abuses, remained for some years and was still there when Goethe arrived. Its main effect was to slow down procedure to an even greater degree, so that business was almost at a standstill, and even if Goethe had been inclined to take advantage of such experience as was available to. him, the professional gain would have been infinitesimal. It was, however, the custom for young lawyers to spend a few months in Wetzlar in order to study the system, and Goethe duly entered his name upon the roll of the *Reichskammergericht* on the 25th of May, 1772.

Wetzlar was at this time a town of over five thousand inhabitants, of whom nearly a quarter were there in connection with the supreme court. Goethe expected to find his new environment little to his liking, but he discovered at the inn where he took his midday meal that the young legation officials had grouped themselves into a sort of lively Round Table, with romantic customs and conventions, each member being known by a pseudonym. He joined them and was dubbed "Götz von Berlichingen," on account of his enthusiastic interest in the knight of that name, about whom he had a manuscript drama in his pocket, which was published in the following year. Bound up with this society was a mystico-philosophic order which had no particular name, but of which the first degree was known as "the transition," and the second as "the transition of the transition," while there were two further degrees called respectively "the transition's transition to the transition" and "the transition's transition to the transition of the transition." The initiates were called upon to expound and amplify the exalted significance of this gradation, by which means time was successfully and entertainingly wasted. Goethe adds, somewhat unnecessarily, that there did not appear to be a vestige of purpose in the proceedings.

One of the members of the Round Table with whom Goethe became more closely acquainted was Johann Christian Kestner of Hanover, who occupied himself conscientiously with his duties as a Secretary of Legation and was but rarely seen at the noisy gatherings. Kestner had been unofficially engaged for about four years to a young girl, some eleven years his junior, named Charlotte Buff, the daughter of the bailiff who managed the estates of the Teutonic Order. Although Charlotte had an elder sister, it was she who managed the household and looked after the numerous younger children of her widowed father. Before he knew that she was betrothed Goethe made her acquaintance on the occasion of a ball on the 9th of June at the village of Volpertshausen, some way out of Wetzlar. Kestner was unable to turn up until later, and Lotte joined Goethe's party, it being arranged that he should call for her in a carriage with his dancing partner and one or more of his female relations who lived at Wetzlar. Kestner refers to this incident in the draft of a letter which was found among his papers. "Dr. Goethe was also in the carriage and this was his first meeting with Lottchen. . . . He did not know that she was no longer free. I came a couple of hours later, and it has never been our custom to give evidence of anything more than friendship in public places. He was on that day excessively merry (as he often is, though on the other hand he is at times melancholy), and Lottchen completely conquered him, all the more as she did not endeavour to do so but only gave herself up to enjoyment. On the following day Goethe called, as a matter of course, to ask after Lottchen's health. He had hitherto known her as a jolly girl who likes dancing and is fond of pleasure. Now he

127

learned to know her from the aspect in which she shows up best, the domestic aspect." Goethe soon became a frequent and welcome visitor, and Lotte's constant companion, Kestner sometimes joining them when his official duties permitted. It is interesting to see what Goethe himself says on this subject. "Her *fiancé*, who was of a thoroughly upright and trusting disposition, soon introduced to her everyone he liked, and since he was busily engaged for the greater part of the day, approved of her seeking distraction after her domestic toil was over, and enjoying herself in the society of men and women friends by indulging in walks or picnics."

Goethe found that he could not do without Lotte. "The new arrival [i.e. himself] was entirely without ties and carefree in the presence of a girl who was already promised to another and would not interpret the most devoted action as that of a suitor, thereby finding all the greater pleasure in it. He thus went on unthinkingly but was before long so entangled and captivated, and the attitude of the young couple was at the same time so trustful and friendly, that he no longer understood his own feelings. She liked having him as an escort, and he was unable to bear being away from her, for she acted as an intermediary between him and the everyday world, and so they soon became inseparable companions. When her *fiancé's* duties allowed him to do so, he joined them; they had all three got used to one another, without an effort of will, and they were unaware how it had happened that they had grown mutually indispensable. And so throughout the whole glorious summer they lived a genuine German idyll, for which the fruitful countryside provided the prose and a pure affection the poetry. . . . One day absorbed another and they all appeared to be days of festival; the whole calendar ought to have been printed in red."

Though they were thus all three the best of comrades, Kestner was fully aware of the dangers of the situation. He says in a letter to a friend with reference to Goethe, "Although he had to give up all hope with respect to Lotte, and did give it up, yet with all his philosophy and natural pride he was unable entirely to overcome his inclination. He has qualities which can make him dangerous to a woman, especially to one of taste and feeling, but Lottchen knew so well how to treat him and keep him in check that he could have no grounds for hope and even had to admire the way she acted. His peace of mind was very much disturbed by this; there were various odd scenes which made Lottchen all the dearer to me and caused me to esteem him even more as a friend, though I was often led to marvel what very queer creatures love can make of even the strongest and usually most independent of men. I was generally sorry for him and my mind was torn two ways, since on the one hand I thought that I might not be able to make Lottchen as happy as he would, and on the other hand I could not tolerate the thought of losing her. The latter motive gained the mastery, and I have never even noticed a suspicion of similar considerations on the part of Lottchen." And in his diary towards the end of June he records that when he called at Lotte's house after his day's work was over he found Goethe there. "He is in love with her and though he is a philosopher and absolutely good-hearted, yet he does not like it when I come and am happy with my girl. And I, though I am very fond of him, yet I do not like either that he should be alone with my girl and entertain her."

On the 13th of August we have the following interesting entry: "In the evening the confession of a kiss. A little *brouillerie* with Lottchen, which was forgotten the next day." But when Goethe called in the evening of the following day, he was received coldly and did not stay long. On the 15th they sent him to a neighbouring village to take some fruit to a friend who was lying sick. He returned at ten o'clock in the evening and found Lotte and Kestner sitting outside the house. The flowers he brought were left unheeded, and realising he was out of favour he threw them away. He and Kestner went for a walk through the streets till midnight, Goethe being in a very ill humour and giving vent to all sorts of fantastic remarks until at last they both leaned against a wall in the moonlight and burst out laughing. On the next day Goethe had to listen to a sermon from Lotte, in which she told him that he could hope for nothing but friendship, whereupon he grew pale and was very depressed.

At the end of August Kestner wrote a letter to Lotte in which he offered to release her from their engagement, averring that he could not do without her, but that if she would be happier without him he would prefer her happiness to his own. "My mind repeats this statement, but my heart, my feeling contradicts it. Even when I made the resolution I felt that it was beyond my powers. I felt it again in full force recently, when I was faced with the danger, or at least the possibility, of losing you, and I still cannot overcome the fear which this has caused to spring up in me. Yet I have still sufficient control over myself, at least in my moments of reflection, at least in my imagination, to perceive how unjust it would be to sacrifice your happier fate to my own desires and happiness. My future is still too unsettled for me as an honourable man, as one who should be able to control his passion, to demand that yours should be dependent on mine. In moments of reflection I still believe myself capable of giving up my claims when your happier fate demands it. I believe this because I ought to do it. What it would cost me I can only feel, not describe." He then advises her that all is not gold that glitters (this referring palpably to Goethe), that one cannot rely on words that have been culled, perhaps, from a book or are only uttered because they sound clever; that it is not difficult for a man to be bright and amusing when he is his own master and not compelled to engage in a profession which may be little to his taste. This poignant letter, which he asks Lotte to burn as soon as she has read it, tells us all we need to know of the sincerity and integrity of Kestner. Working hard in an office all day and calling in the evening for a carefree hour or two with the girl to whom he was betrothed, and whom he could not marry because his

professional prospects were still uncertain, he always found
a romantic young man there, eight years younger than
himself, well-to-do and idle, and obviously in love with
Lotte. Yet he did not complain, but only warned her against
returning a love which might be unworthy. The extraordinary thing is that he and Goethe remained such good
friends. Except for the above reference, he has only the
warmest words of admiration for Goethe's mind and
character, an appreciation which Goethe wholly recipro-
cated. Kestner at this time was 31 years of age, Goethe was
23, and Lotte 19.

The situation was evidently growing difficult, and a
severe reproof from his friend and mentor Merck strengthened Goethe's resolution to go away from Wetzlar. He spent
the evening of the 10th of September with Kestner and
Lotte, and there was what Kestner in his diary calls a
"strange conversation" concerning what happens after this
life and about departing and returning, which was started
not by Goethe but by Lotte. They made a pact that which-
ever of them died first should communicate to the others,
if possible, information about the state in which he found
himself. Goethe was very depressed, for he intended to go
away on the morrow, though neither of his friends knew of
this. The last letter of the first part of *Werther* bears the same
date, the 10th of September, and the memory of that last
evening must have been strong in Goethe's mind when he
wrote it. On the following day he left Wetzlar without
having said good-bye, only leaving behind him a letter for
Kestner with two enclosures for Lotte. The letter is dated
the 10th, and must have been written just after he had left
them:—

"He will be gone, Kestner, when you receive this note;
he will be gone. Give Lotte the enclosed note. I was very
composed, but your conversation has broken me down
completely. I can say nothing for the moment but good-bye.
If I had remained a moment longer I should not have been

able to contain myself. Now I am alone, and to-morrow I go. Oh, my poor head!"

The enclosure for Lotte, which is rather incoherent, runs as follows:—

"I hope to return, but God knows when! Lotte, how did I feel when you were speaking, knowing that it was the last time I should see you! Not the last, and yet to-morrow I go away. He has gone. What spirit led you to talk as you did? When I could say all I felt, oh, I was concerned with here below, with your hand that I kissed for the last time. The room to which I shall never return, and your dear father who accompanied me for the last time. I am now alone, and may weep, I leave you happy, and do not go out of your hearts. And shall see you again, but not to-morrow is never. Tell my youngsters he has gone. I can write no more."

On the following morning, just before his departure, he added another enclosure for Lotte:—

"I have packed, Lotte, and day is breaking, another quarter of an hour and I shall be gone. Let the pictures, which I forgot and which I beg you to share among the children, be my excuse for writing, Lotte, since I have nothing to write about. For you know everything, you know how happy I have been during these days, and I am going, to the dearest, best of people, but why from you? It is thus, and my fate that I cannot add to to-day to-morrow, and the day after to-morrow—which I often did in jest. Be ever cheerful, dear Lotte, you are happier than a hundred others, only do not be indifferent and I, dear Lotte, shall be happy to read in your eyes that you believe I shall never change. Adieu, a thousand times adieu!"

The feelings of Kestner and Lotte on receipt of these letters can be gathered from an entry in the former's diary on the 11th of September:—

"Goethe left at 7 o'clock this morning without taking leave. He sent me a note together with some books. He had long ago said that he would make a journey to Coblenz about this time, where Merck was expecting him, and that he would not say good-bye, but would go off suddenly. I had thus expected it. But that I was nevertheless not prepared for it—that I felt, felt deep in my soul. . . . In the afternoon I brought Goethe's notes to Lottchen. She was sad at his departure; the tears came into her eyes as she read. But she was glad that he had gone, since she could not give him what he wished. For he was very much in love with her, to the verge of frenzy. She had, however, always kept this at a distance and conceded him nothing but friendship, had even formally told him so. We spoke only of him; I could do nothing but think of him, and I defended the manner of his departure when some undiscerning person blamed him for it; this I did with considerable heat. I wrote to him afterwards what had happened after he left."

A few days later Kestner was in Frankfort and saw Goethe, when, he says, "it was an indescribable joy to me; he fell on my neck and almost suffocated me."

Goethe went from Wetzlar down the Rhine in order to pay a visit to the house of Frau von La Roche at Ehrenbreitstein, where he stayed for a few days. A sentimental congress was being held there, part of the entertainment being the reading to one another by members of the group of sentimental letters they had received from their friends. One of the party had brought with him a number of caskets full. Frau von La Roche had a handsome black-eyed daughter, named Maximiliane, to whom Goethe soon became attracted. As he puts it rather complacently in his Autobiography, "It is a very pleasant sensation when a new passion begins to stir in us before the old one has quite died away. When the sun is setting one likes to see the moon rising on the other side and rejoices in the dual brilliance of both luminaries." Frau von La Roche afterwards married

Maximiliane to an elderly merchant named Brentano, a widower with five children. Happily for Goethe, Brentano lived in Frankfort, whither Maximiliane came in January, 1774. He became a regular visitor to the house and accompanied her on the 'cello while she played the harpsichord, her husband being otherwise engaged in the wholesale grocery business downstairs. Brentano at first welcomed the young man, but after a time he grew jealous and made a scene, so that Goethe found it advisable to keep away from the house. His description of the episode in his Autobiography does not seem to give all the facts. "My former relations with the young wife, which were really of a brotherly nature, were continued after her marriage. We were matched in age, and I was the only one in the whole circle in whom she found a reminder of that intellectual atmosphere to which she had been accustomed since youth. We continued to live on a footing of childlike intimacy, and, although there was nothing of a passionate nature in our intercourse, yet it was painful enough since she could not get on in her new environment either. Although well endowed with worldly goods, she had been transferred from the cheerful vale of Ehrenbreitstein and a happy youth to a gloomily situated business house, and had to conduct herself as the mother of a number of stepchildren. It was in such novel social conditions that I found myself cramped, without any real participation or collaboration. This was only natural when the members of the family got on well together; but most of them turned to me when things became difficult, and my active interest used to make them worse instead of better. It was not long before the situation became quite intolerable; all the weariness with life which usually springs from such unsatisfactory relations seemed to weigh doubly and trebly upon me, and a new and forcible resolve was necessary to give me my freedom."

The idyll with Maximiliane came to an end about a year and a half after Goethe had last seen Lotte, but soon after his leaving Wetzlar something had occurred but for which

Werther would probably have never been written. This was the suicide of Karl Wilhelm Jerusalem, a young Secretary of Legation with whom Goethe had been slightly acquainted. Jerusalem had long been noted for his depression, which was traceable to two or three causes. He was very badly treated by his superior, the head of the legation, named Hoefler; he had been subjected to a snub at an aristocratic gathering at the house of the President of the *Kammergericht*, Count von Bassenheim, and he was in love with Frau Herd, the wife of one of his colleagues. Herd eventually forbade him the house, and he sent a note to Kestner asking for the loan of his pistols as he intended to go on a journey. Kestner complied with this request, and about one o'clock in the morning Jerusalem shot himself in the head over the right eye. He was found in the morning lying on the floor and died towards noon. This was on the 30th of October, and within a few days Goethe had received from Kestner a circumstantial account of the whole affair.

The first part of *Werther* is based on Goethe's relations with Lotte and Kestner. The second part is based on the unhappy experiences and fate of Jerusalem. A comparison of the novel with the above recorded facts will show how much there is in it of truth and how much fiction. The account of Werther's death and burial is, in part, taken word for word from Kestner's letter.

In his Autobiography, Goethe makes it seem as though he had heard of Jerusalem's death while he was still smarting under the hostility shown to him by Maximiliane's husband, but that is obviously impossible, since there was an interval of over a year between the two incidents. After discussing the reasons why the age was ripe for an epidemic of suicides, he describes his own somewhat half-hearted attempt to quit this life: "In my collection of weapons, which was pretty considerable, I possessed a valuable and well-sharpened dagger. I always laid it next to my bed, and before I put out the light I tried whether I could not sink the sharp point a couple of inches into my breast. As I was never able to do so, I at last ridiculed myself, cast off all my hypochondriac caprices, and decided to continue living. In order to be able to do this calmly, however, I had to carry into effect some poetic task, in which everything that I had felt, thought, and imagined about this important matter should find verbal expression. For this purpose I collected all the elements which had been fermenting in me for a couple of years, I visualised to myself the situations that had caused me most affliction and anguish—but I could not give them shape, there was lacking some incident, some plot in which to incorporate them.

"Suddenly I learned of the death of Jerusalem. Immediately after the general rumour there reached me the most exact and detailed description of the occurrence—and at that moment the plan for *Werther* was in being. The whole shot together from all sides and became a solid mass, like water in a container which is just at freezing-point and is immediately turned to firm ice by the slightest shake. It was all the more opportune that I should hold fast to this advantageous framework that had come to me so strangely, and that I should picture to myself and execute in every detail a work of such significant and varied content, since I already found myself in another painful situation which afforded even less hope than the others and prophesied nothing but renewed depression, to say nothing of actual annoyance."

The "painful situation" is the Brentano affair. If Goethe really conceived the complete plan for *Werther* as soon as he heard of Jerusalem's suicide, then he must have waited until the early part of 1774 before writing it, for the Lotte and Albert of the novel are to some extent based on Maximiliane and Brentano. In any case the chronological order of events shows him to be definitely misleading, when he says that the shock of the news made him realise the similarity of his own situation with that of the unfortunate youth. The first sentence in the following passage refers to his relations with Maximiliane and not to his relations with

Lotte: "The death of Jerusalem, which had been caused by an unhappy love for the wife of a friend, shook me out of my dream, and, since I not only saw clearly what had happened to him and to me, but the similarity of my own experience at the moment also aroused in me a passionate activity, I could not fail to breathe into the work which I then undertook all the ardour which prevents any distinction between the poetic and the real. I had completely isolated myself from the outside world, I had even asked my friends not to visit me, and so I also inwardly laid aside everything which did not belong directly to the matter in hand. On the other hand I collected everything that had any bearing on my purpose, and I recapitulated my immediate experiences, of which I had not yet made any poetic use. It was in such circumstances, after such protracted and secret preparations, that I wrote *Werther* in four weeks, without a plan of the whole work or the treatment of any portion of it having previously been put to paper. . . . Since I had composed the work more or less unconsciously, like a somnambulist, I was myself surprised when I went through it to make emendations or improvements. Expecting, however, that after a time, when I was able to look at it from a certain distance, many things would occur to me which would be to its advantage, I gave it to my younger friends to read; but the effect it had on them was all the greater since, contrary to my usual custom, I had not previously told anyone about it or revealed my purpose. To be sure, it was the theme which really produced the effect in this case also, and therefore their mood was the antithesis of my own, for I had, in composing this work, rescued myself more successfully than by any other of my writings from a turbulent element on which I had been most violently tossed about through my own fault and that of others, through a manner of living which was partly accidental, partly of my own choice, through design and rashness, through obstinacy and weakness. I again felt free and cheerful, as though after a general confession, and justified in entering upon a new life. My old remedy had served me excellently well this time. But just as I felt eased and clearer in mind at having transformed reality into poetry, my friends became bewildered, since they thought that they must transform poetry into reality, imitate a novel like this in real life and, in any case, shoot themselves; and what occurred at first among a few took place later among the general public, so that this book, which had done me so much good, was condemned as being highly dangerous."

It is thus clear that we have in the story of *Werther* a combination of three different elements. The Lotte, Albert and Werther of the first part are on the whole the Lotte, Kestner and Goethe of real life. The Lotte of the second part contains an admixture of the qualities of Maximiliane, Albert becomes more like Brentano and possibly Herd, and most of Werther's concrete experiences are those of Jerusalem, though he shows what Goethe himself might have become had he not possessed the power to "say what he suffered" and purge his soul of its morbid matter. Jerusalem's *character* is not to be identified with that of Werther. Jerusalem's superior, Hoefler, appears as "the ambassador," the Count von Bassenheim as the Count C., and a number of minor characters are also recognisable. Garbenheim, a favourite spot both of Goethe and Jerusalem, appears as "Wahlheim." Lotte is turned into the eldest daughter and is given eight brothers and sisters instead of eleven, and she has the black eyes of Maximiliane, while Lotte Buff's eyes were blue. Goethe was only at Wetzlar for less than four months in 1772, and he never returned except for four days at the beginning of November when he took the opportunity of going to see Jerusalem's grave; but Werther goes back after the marriage of Lotte and Albert, and the whole action extends over about twenty months, from May, 1771, until Christmas, 1772, though the book is so skilfully composed that there seems to be only a single rotation of the seasons from Spring through Summer and Autumn to Winter. The famous "Werther costume" of a blue coat with yellow waistcoat and breeches, and high boots with brown tops, was that worn by Jerusalem. It had become fashionable in North Germany, being an imitation of the English mode.

Goethe kept up a frequent correspondence with his friends at Wetzlar after his departure. He told Kestner when he dreamed of Lotte, begged Lotte's brother to keep him supplied with news of the family, and especially of his sister, and insisted on being allowed to order the wedding-rings. Lotte's silhouette was pinned on the wall of his study, and as he was always losing his pins he "borrowed them from Lotte," first asking permission. This silhouette appears to have meant a great deal to him, for he asserted his intention of taking it down on her wedding day and not putting it up again until he heard that she was about to become a mother, for that would be the beginning of a new epoch when his love for her would be transferred to her children. "When you ask me to be godfather," he wrote to Kestner, "my spirit shall hover in a twofold way over the boy, and he shall go crazy over girls who resemble his mother." They were married on the 4th of April, 1773, at Wetzlar, and Lotte sent Goethe her bridal bouquet, which he affixed to his hat and wore in the street. He expressed the fervent hope that they would call their first-born Wolfgang after him—which they did—and he followed with sympathetic interest the frequent additions to their nursery. In a number of letters he made dark references to the fact that he was engaged in writing a book which should embody their relations at Wetzlar. On the 23rd of September, 1774, he sent them a preliminary copy, accompanied by a letter to each of them, and was evidently looking forward with eagerness to their praise. In the note to Lotte he said, "How dear the little book is to me, Lotte, you may feel in reading, and this copy is as precious to me as though it were the only one in the world. It is for you, Lotte, I kissed it a hundred times, and locked it away so that nobody should touch it." He asked each of them to read it alone and each of them to drop him a line about it.

Kestner's reply must have come as a shock. "You have, to be sure, woven into each character something that was foreign to it, or have fused several characters into one. There would be no objection to that. But if you had let your heart have a little to say in the matter during this process of weaving and fusing, you would not have so prostituted the actual persons from whom you borrowed certain features. . . . The real Lotte, whose friend, after all, you pretend to be, appears in your representation, which contains too much of her not to point strongly in her direction, appears, I say —but no, I will not say it, it pains me too much even to think of it. And Lotte's husband—you called him your friend—and, God knows, he was——And that wretched creature of an Albert! Even though he may be an original representation and not a copy, yet he also bears such resemblance to a model (only externally, thank God, only externally) that the public can easily guess who the latter is. If you wanted him like that, was it necessary to make him into such a boor? So that you, I suppose, could step up proudly and say, 'See what a fine fellow *I* am!' "

Kestner got over his bitterness very soon, for we find him writing to his friend Hennings that though he and his wife were very annoyed by the book, and doubly so by its success, he was inclined to forgive the author—without, however, telling him so, in order that he might be more careful in the future. This letter was written with the object of enlightening Hennings as to the background of truth in the story, and he was asked to burn it immediately after perusal, for if it were lost, the sequel might be a second edition of *Werther* with notes, and Kestner vowed that he would never again write anything to an author which he did not mind the whole world reading. We may judge of Kestner's own love for his wife by his admission to Hennings: "If I had had to give her up, I do not guarantee that I would not myself have become Werther."

Werther was published in 1774 at the Michaelmas Fair in Leipzig. Goethe's name was not on the title-page, but the publisher put it in the catalogue and so gave away the secret of his authorship. He continued to correspond with Kestner until shortly before the latter's death, but they did not meet again. He saw Lotte only once, in 1816, when they were both over sixty. She was then a widow with twelve children, and forty years had elapsed since the events at Wetzlar. Kestner died in 1800 and Lotte in 1828, four years before Goethe.

The Sentimental Age

In his Autobiography Goethe discourses at length on the causes of the morbid mood which was prevalent in Germany in the 'sixties and 'seventies of the eighteenth century, tracing it in great measure to the melancholy influence of English literature, especially English poetry, the great merits of which, he says, "are accompanied by a pensive gloom that communicates itself to everybody who occupies himself with it." He goes on to cite specific examples:—

"The most cheerful works have the same purpose as the most serious ones, namely, to moderate both pleasure and grief by means of a successful and ingenious representation. If the majority of English poems, of a mostly moral and didactic nature, are considered in this sense, they will be found to exhibit, as a rule, only a melancholy weariness of life. Not only Young's *Night Thoughts*, where the theme is worked out in a remarkable manner, but also the other poems of contemplation diverge, before one is aware of it, into this dismal sphere, where the intellect is assigned a problem that it is not adequate to solve. . . . Even their tender poems are occupied with dismal matters. Here there expires an abandoned maiden, there a faithful lover is drowned or else devoured by a shark before he can reach his sweetheart; and when a poet like Gray settles down in a village churchyard and again strikes up the well-known airs, he can be sure of collecting round him a number of the friends of melancholy. Milton's 'Allegro' must first disperse his depression in forcible verses before he can attain to a very moderate joy, and even the cheerful Goldsmith loses himself in elegiac feeling when his 'Deserted Village' depicts a lost Paradise, sought again by his 'Traveller' throughout the whole world, as no less sad than lovely. . . . These earnest poems, which undermined human nature, were the favourites that we chose above all others, one seeking the lighter elegiac lament, which accorded with his temper, another the burdensome hopelessness of despair. Strangely enough, our father and teacher Shakespeare, who knows so well how to create a serene atmosphere, himself strengthened this depression. Hamlet and his monologues remained spectres, which worked their uncanny will in the minds of the younger generation. Everyone knew the chief passages by heart and liked to declaim them, and everyone believed he had the right to be as melancholy as the Prince of Denmark, even though he had not seen a ghost and had no royal father to avenge.

"In order that all this gloom should not lack a suitable *milieu*, Ossian had enticed us to the *ultima Thule*, where, on the grey, unending heath, under projecting, moss-covered tombstones, we saw all around the grass waving weirdly in the wind with the dark and clouded sky above. It was only by moonlight that this Caledonian night was turned to day; departed heroes, maidens who had faded into the tomb, hovered round us, until we at last thought we saw the spirit of Loda in his actual and terrible shape.

"In such an element, in such an environment, tortured by unsatisfied passions amidst inclinations and pursuits of such a kind, lacking external incitement to any considerable activity, with the sole prospect of leading a dragging and unintellectual *bourgeois* existence, we accepted with ill-humoured arrogance the idea that we could, in any case, quit this life at will when it no longer had anything to offer us, and thus we were able to put up, meagrely enough, with the iniquity and *ennui* of existence. It was because this state of mind was so general that *Werther* produced the great effect it did, when it took root everywhere and depicted openly and tangibly the manner and nature of a morbid, youthful madness."

In a conversation with Eckermann in 1824, however, he contradicts what he had written previously about the great effect of *Werther* being due to its opportune publication, and he agrees with his secretary that the book would have created a sensation in any age. He says, further, that it was hardly necessary for him to trace his own youthful melancholy to the general influences of the time and the reading of certain English authors, for the state of mind in which he wrote *Werther* was to be ascribed to the fact that he had "lived, loved, and suffered a great deal." Goethe is here glossing over the effect of the mood of the generation of his youth, though he shows true psychological insight when he asserts, in the same passage, that every individual passes through a Werther-phase in the process of learning how to adapt his inborn natural tastes to the restricted forms of an antiquated world. "Happiness unattained, ambition unfulfilled, and desires unsatisfied are the defects not of any particular age but of every single individual, and it would be a bad thing if everybody did not, once in his life, pass through a phase when it seemed to him as though *Werther* had been written specially for him."

The words "pathological condition" are used by Goethe himself to characterise his state of mind at the time, and they are, to some extent, applicable to what is known in Germany as *Weltschmerz*, of which Wertherism is only one aspect. An attempt to define *Weltschmerz* was made by the present writer in a book published some years ago,[1] from which he may be permitted to quote:—

"*Weltschmerz* is the psychic state which ensues when there is a sharp contrast between a man's ideals and his material

[1] *From Goethe to Byron* [Routledge, London; Dutton, New York, 1924].

environment, and his temperament is such as to eliminate the possibility of any sort of reconciliation between the two. The result is a nostalgia for the unattainable, whether the latter be symbolised by a person, a country, or a golden age, any of which may or may not exist wholly in the imagination. This definition might, of course, be extended to embrace the dissonance between the ideal and the actual which must necessarily exist in the soul of every artist, whether creative or merely receptive, but it must be limited to those in whom the symptoms of psychic disturbance assume a pathological form. The man who is able to give concrete expression to his longings, or, if these be unattainable, to give them artistic expression, will be less likely to permit his spiritual conflict to obtrude itself unduly into practical life than the man who is sensitive to outward impressions without possessing the power to return them in the shape of artistic production."

That is what Goethe means when he says that his old remedy had served him excellently well and that he felt eased and clearer in mind at having transformed reality into poetry. *Weltschmerz* became prevalent in German literature a couple of decades before the French Revolution, and it was symptomatic of the general unrest that was stirring the mind of Europe. *Hamlet*, *Ossian*, the works of James Thomson, Edward Young, Richardson, Fielding and Sterne, the nature-philosophy of Rousseau[1]—all these exerted a profound influence on a generation which was realising the extent of the intellectual, social and political restrictions to which it was subjected, while introspection and concentration on the emotional life were fostered by the Pietist movement.

It was in *Werther* that the younger generation found the first satisfying expression of its spirtual longings and unrest. In his *Kampagne in Frankreich* Goethe replies to the accusation

[1] A comparison between *Werther* and *La Nouvelle Héloïse* reveals many points of contact, but the question of Goethe's debt to Rousseau opens up problems which lie outside the scope of this paper.

that the novel promoted a fever by asserting that it only revealed a malady which was already latent in the younger generation. "There came . . . a certain sentimentality, in the origin and development of which we cannot fail to recognise the influence of Yorick-Sterne. . . . There arose a kind of tender-passionate asceticism, which, since we lacked the humorous irony of the Briton, was generally bound to degenerate into a distressing form of self-torment. I had tried to free myself personally from this malady and aspired, in accordance with my convictions, to be helpful to others; but this was more difficult than one might think, for it was really a matter of helping each individual against himself." As a matter of fact he did not suggest a remedy until much later, in *Wilhelm Meister* and the second part of *Faust*.

REVERBERATIONS

Werther became for Goethe an old man of the sea, whom he was unable to shake off as long as he lived. The younger generation seemed to be modelling its spiritual and, in many cases, its physical life on that of the hero of his novel, while their elders regarded it mainly as an apology for suicide and fulminated against a pernicious work which led young men and women to "transform poetry into reality." There are numerous references scattered through Goethe's writings which show how the spirit of Werther was haunting him, though a letter from a young Frenchman, which he prints in his *Italienische Reise*, may have consoled him for so much unhappiness being laid at his door. His unknown correspondent thanks him for having restored him to the bosom of his family, and expresses the pious hope that the author of *Werther* has experienced a happier fate than the creature of his imagination. "Je vous dois la meilleure action de ma vie, par conséquent la racine de plusieurs autres, et pour moi votre livre est bon. Si j'avais le bonheur d'habiter le même pays que vous, j'irais vous embrasser et vous dire mon secret, mais malheureusement j'en habite un, où personne ne croirait au motif qui vient de me déterminer à cette démarche. Soyez satisfait, Monsieur, d'avoir pu à 300 lieues de votre demeure ramener le cœur d'un jeune homme à l'honnêteté et à la vertu ; toute une famille va être tranquille, et mon cœur jouit d'une bonne action. Si j'avais des talents, des lumières ou un rang qui me fît influer sur le sort des hommes, je vous dirais mon nom, mais je ne suis rien et je sais ce que je ne voudrais être. Je souhaite, Monsieur, que vous soyez jeune, que vous ayez le goût d'écrire, que vous soyez l'époux d'une Charlotte qui n'avait point vu de Werther, et vous serez le plus heureux des hommes ; car je crois que vous aimez la vertu."

Goethe has related in his Autobiography how he was pestered by well-meaning friends who wanted to know how much truth there was in the book. "I was very annoyed," he says, "and my replies were mostly exceedingly rude. In order to answer this question I should have had to pluck to pieces again the work which had caused me so much thought in giving poetic unity to so many different elements, and I should have destroyed the form, thereby if not demolishing, at least dispersing the real constituent parts. . . . I hoped to be rid after a time of these painful enquiries, but they accompanied me throughout my whole life. I tried to escape by travelling about incognito, but even this expedient was unexpectedly frustrated." Wetzlar became a tourist centre for people, including Englishmen, who asked to have pointed out to them the various places mentioned in the book. In after years the legend got rather mixed up, and when Charlotte Kestner, many years after her marriage, returned to Wetzlar on a visit, she was pointed out as the bailiff's beautiful daughter on whose account Jerusalem had shot himself. The latter was supposed to have been buried in Garbenheim (the Wahlheim of the story) under the lime-tree where he had been fond of sitting, and the landlord of the inn set up near the supposed spot a mound which became a place of pilgrimage for the sentimental, some of whom decorated it with a funeral urn. The schoolmaster's daughter of the letter of the 27th of May, whose two children Werther drew, lived to a ripe old age and became one of the sights of the village, together with the old lime-tree and the spring at Wetzlar, of which Werther was so fond. The tree has fallen and the spring has dried up, while the urn was stolen by a Russian general during the Napoleonic wars and sent to St. Petersburg.

In various countries the authorities took steps to protect the public from what they looked upon as a dangerous influence. The sale of the book was forbidden in Leipzig, and in Copenhagen it was not even allowed to be printed, while in Milan the bishop bought up an edition of the Italian translation and had it destroyed. There was some reason for these measures, for the suicide of a number of young people was undoubtedly influenced, though it may not have been actually inspired, by the reading of *Werther*. The body of a young woman, with a copy of the book on her, was fished out of the river not far from Goethe's house in Weimar. In the year 1784 the subject set for a prize essay by the Theological Faculty in Göttingen was whether suicide could be defended according to the principles of Christian morality, and Werther was referred to by the prizewinner in his dissertation.

The "Werther-fever" (a term which was current within two years of the publication of the novel) nevertheless made headway, and the Werther costume was adopted by enthusiastic young men. Even Goethe himself was attired in a blue coat with yellow waistcoat and breeches when he first appeared at Weimar, and his example was followed by the whole Court, headed by the Duke. It would greatly extend the size of this volume even to give a list of the translations of *Werther* and the imitations, parodies, dramas, ballets, operas and songs which were based on it. Scenes from the story were engraved, or painted on linen, porcelain and fans, while even the Chinese painted the unhappy love-story of Werther and Charlotte on glass. A porcelain breakfast service, decorated with Werther scenes, is now in the Victoria

and Albert Museum in London. An eighteenth-century
traveller has left an account of an elaborate representation
in fireworks, called *Werther's Meeting with Lottchen in Elysium*,
of which he was a spectator. The various scenes depicted
Werther during his happy days, his meeting with Lotte, his
union with her at his graveside, and their sojourn in the
Elysian fields. Young girls were given the name of "Wer-
thérie" and there was even a perfume called "Eau de
Werther."

France and England were no less inflamed than Germany,
and in this country, in fact, the Werther-fever lasted longer
than in either of the others, though Werther's literary
progeny are more numerous in France. There have been
eight English translations hitherto,[1] all of them utterly
inadequate, except the last. The first was not from the
original, but from the French, and the authorship was for
some time attributed to Daniel Malthus, the father of the
celebrated economist, but recent research is inclined to
father it on the Rev. Richard Graves, Rector of Claverton,
near Bath. As there were two French translations in 1776
and one in the following year, it is certain that Werther was
known in England before the English translation. The full
list of these translations is as follows:—

The Sorrows of Werter : a German Story. 1779. There were
two issues in this year, the title-page of the earlier one bearing
the words *Founded on Fact*, and that of the latter the Latin
motto *Taedet coeli convexa tueri*. The text is identical in both,
but the latter has a list of twelve misprints.[2] The translator
says in his preface: "Werter appears to have been strongly
impressed with sentiments of religion: and it is not to be
wondered at, that in his state of mind they should take an
irregular form, and sometimes border upon extravagance.
A few expressions which had this appearance have been

[1] The translation to which this paper was originally an Introduction
is the ninth [The Scholartis Press, 1929].
[2] *Vide* an article by Anton Kippenberg in the fifth volume of the
Jahrbuch der Sammlung Kippenberg [Insel Verlag, 1925].

omitted by the French, and a few more by the English translator, as they might possibly give offence in a work of this nature."

Werter and Charlotte : A German Story. 1786. This was also anonymous, but was translated from the German.

The Sorrows of Werter. A German Story. 1789. This was by John Gifford, and was translated from a French version.

The Letters of Werter. 1799. Anonymous. This and the following translations are from the German.

The Sorrows of Werter. 1801. By William Render, D.D., who prints an Appendix "Containing an Account of a Conversation which the Translator had with Werter, a few days preceding his death." By Werter he means Jerusalem, with whom he pretends to have discussed, among other things, the subject of suicide. He says Werter appeared to be anxious to get back to Charlotte, and concludes by asserting that when he heard of the end of Werter, "The news, indeed, affected me very much, but, I must confess, it did not surprise me."

The Sorrows of Werter. 1802. By Frederick Gotzberg, "assisted by an English literary gentleman." The preface says, "Frederick Gotzberg is a native of Germany, had some knowledge of Werter's family, and ranks foremost among the *literati* of his country." He puts Ossian into verse :—

> "Alone, on the sea-beaten rock,
> My daughter was heard to complain,
> Loud and frequent, alas! were her sighs—
> The father's assistance was vain!
>
> I stood on the shore all the night,
> And by the pale moon saw her plain;
> All the night heard her heart-rending cries,
> Tho' loud was the wind—hard the rain!
>
> 'In pity will none of you speak?'
> Not heeding their father they go—
> I'm sad—very sad, I'm indeed—
> For great is the cause of my woe!"

This is the edition which was reprinted in Cassell's National Library.

The Sorrows of Werter. No date, but not later than 1807. By Dr. Pratt.

The Sorrows of Young Werther. 1854. By R. Dillon Boylan. This appeared in Bohn's Standard Library. Werther had all along been spelled in English without an *h*, and Boylan was the first of the translators to spell the name correctly.

Carlyle, who for some time cherished the plan of writing a novel on the lines of *Werther*, had no good opinion of the English translation with which he was acquainted, for he says: "The English reader ought to understand that our current version of *Werter* is mutilated and inaccurate; it comes to us through the all-subduing medium of the French; shorn of its caustic strength; with its melancholy rendered maudlin; its hero reduced from the stately gloom of a broken-hearted poet to the tearful wrangling of a dyspeptic tailor."

The effect of the book in England seems to have been much the same as in Germany. *Werther*, after all, was bringing back to England in a different form the sentimentality which Germany had imported from her some years previously. It was England which had invented the term "the joy of grief." In 1784 a young lady committed suicide, and a copy of a translation of *Werther* was found under her pillow. An announcement of her death in a journal drew attention to the latter circumstance, "in order, if possible, to defeat the evil tendency of that pernicious work." The English seem to have been renowned on the Continent for the number of their suicides, and possibly *Werther* encouraged a morbid tendency that was already widespread. The moral aspect of the book was, of course, emphasised in England, and both Werther and Charlotte were censured by the critics for their conduct. A certain Lady E. Wallace published a volume in 1787 entitled *A letter to a Friend, with a Poem called the Ghost of Werter.* The lengthy epistle which precedes the poem discusses a number of things, including the sad state of female education, and attacks, in a most uncalled-for manner, the character of Charlotte. It begins: "You have often heard me, my dear Louisa, express my wonder that anyone should pronounce Charlotte an amiable character. —I send you a little Poem, which I have written, called *The Ghost of Werter*; and, since you desire it, I will here express to you those sentiments which lead me to condemn her as an ungenerous, vain, unfeeling character; one the more dangerous to society, because not *actually* criminal. That she was not so, was undoubtedly owing to Werter's honour and respect for her, and the horror he felt at the idea of violating Albert's friendship and hospitality, which led him to repulse her *agaceries*." Lady Wallace then proceeds to mention in detail the sins of poor Charlotte: "The woman of *gallantry* must censure her for coquetting unmeaningly with Werter; and the woman of generosity, benevolence, and delicacy, condemn her for embittering the quiet of both, and even in *appearance* injuring her virtue and her husband. But when we cast our eyes to the indecency of her conduct on the sofa, the last scene she had with him, who can attribute it to Charlotte that Werter did not triumph over the poor remains of her virtue and Albert's peace; and even if they suppose her so unimpassioned, they must find no excuse for her so grossly sacrificing delicacy, and coldly trifling with his distracted passions."

The reproaches are continued in the poem by Werther himself:—

> "Why did you nurse th' enthusiastic fire
> My nature sway'd, to throb with fond desire?
> My mind you saw bewilder'd by my pain,
> When nervous tremours throbb'd in every vein.
> Why, when kind Albert gave thee up his heart,
> And hop'd from thee each joy truth can impart,
> With confidence and honour left thee free,
> To win, seduce, distract a wretch like me,
> Why was thy soul ungenerously vain,
> To find indulgence in bestowing pain?

> To torture Albert with sad discontent,
> And anxious doubts his kindness could not vent;
> To sacrifice the prudence of thy sex,
> And by feign'd tenderness my soul perplex;
> And when you found me mad to curb desire,
> Why by endearments aggravate each fire?"

In 1784 a young Irishman from Tipperary published *Werter to Charlotte: A Poem*, in which he "endeavoured to express, in verse, some of the incidents and sentiments with which he was chiefly struck, in the perusal of that affecting story." It is supposed to be an epistle, "written by Werter, at that period when he was under the most violent agitations of disappointed love, and frantic despair." The following extract will give an idea of the poet's method of treatment:—

> "But lo! the fatal nuptial knot is ty'd,
> The joyful Albert leads his blooming bride:
> For ever Charlotte from these arms is torn,
> And to the bridal bed in triumph borne.
> Oh heav'ns! while Werter bleeds in dire dismay,
> And night renews the torments of the day,
> The happy Albert folds thee in his arms,
> Glues to thy lips, and riots on thy charms;
> He checks thy terrors with an ardent kiss,
> Those virgin terrors that augment the bliss;
> Then, then as closely in his arms thou'rt prest,
> Does no one secret sigh escape thy breast,
> Nor one sad tear for hapless Werter flow!
> For him, who bears for thee a world of woe?
> Ah no! false Fair! thou yield'st him all thy charms,
> And Werter is forgot in Albert's arms."

Werter: a Tragedy in 3 Acts by Frederick Reynolds was performed at Covent Garden about the same time, and as late as 1809 there was a harlequinade called *Werter* at the Royal Circus in London. In the summer of 1785 a predecessor of Madame Tussaud was holding an exhibition in Fleet Street, as we know from one of her handbills:—

CHARLOTTE AND WERTER
AT

Mrs. SALMON's Royal Historical WAX-WORK,
Which has been greatly improved, and received considerable
additions,
Is to be seen the much-admired Group of

The *DEATH* of *WERTER*,

ATTENDED BY

CHARLOTTE and her Family;

No. 189, near St. *Dunstan's* Church, FLEET-STREET

England also had its complement of engravings and caricatures, including some by Rowlandson, and the story attained
the summit of popularity by appearing in the form of a
chap-book. Goethe was little more than a name in this
country during the height of his hero's vogue, and doubts
were even cast on his existence. In Scotland the authorship
was at one time attributed to Macpherson, the famous
"forger" of *Ossian*. The names of Werther and Charlotte
have, perhaps, lived longest in Thackeray's ballad, which
has neither wit nor humour, but is merely facetious.

SECOND THOUGHTS

When Goethe realised what the Kestners felt about *Werther*,
his apologies were immediate and profuse, and though he
insisted that the popularity of the book ought far to outweigh
the hurt to their feelings, he promised to wipe out within a
year any suspicion or misinterpretation that might provide
matter for public gossip. It was not, however, till 1782 that
he took the revision in hand, and we find him writing to
Kestner in the following spring that he was going to try to
"screw Werther up a few degrees," part of his intention
being to make it impossible for the reader to mistake Albert's

153

character, though Werther himself might do so. Kestner expressed his pleasure at the prospect of revision, and offered a few suggestions which he hoped his friend would accept, since his "youthful fires had no doubt cooled somewhat in the course of ten years and would give place to the calmer consideration of the mature man."

The new version did not appear till 1787, and the extraordinary thing about it is that Goethe used as the basis for his revision a pirated and much corrupted edition which had been published in 1779. The changes he wrought were of two kinds. He moderated the typical *Sturm und Drang* vigour of expression and eliminated his youthful peculiarities of spelling and dialect, so that the language and style of the second version approximate more closely to the standard literary norm. More important were the alterations introduced into the context. These were fairly considerable, with the chief object of throwing Werther's morbid state of mind into sharper relief and making it appear that his view of Albert's attitude and conduct is distorted. Lotte's attitude to Werther becomes more objective. There is no longer room for the reader to believe that she returns his love and no suggestion that she is unhappy in her marriage. Albert therefore appears in a more favourable light. The effect of the social snub is weakened and it loses its force as a direct cause of Werther's suicide. In the year 1808 Goethe had an interview with Napoleon, who said he had read *Werther* seven times and found fault with what he regarded as a mixture of motives—hopeless love and wounded pride. He thought it was contrary to human nature that there should be two motives leading to Werther's suicide, and that only one of them could lead to the decisive step. The same criticism had already been made many years before by Herder, who found the combination of motives inartistic. They both based their opinion on the first version, but even so they were wrong, for they failed to see that the immediate causes of Werther's unhappiness sprang from, and were less important than, his supersensitive spiritual condition. All the action of the novel—and it is surprising how much more there is than appears at first sight—has to be considered against the background of his temperament.

An important new feature is the tragic episode of a peasant youth who is in love with the widow by whom he is employed and is driven by hopeless jealousy to murder his rival. Its purpose is to emphasise the possibilities of Werther's condition and to help him to see whither he is drifting. From this point of view it is a parallel to the episodes of the clerk who went mad through love for Lotte and the girl who killed herself on being abandoned by her lover.

Werther appeals to the human spirit, though its significance cannot be fully understood except against the background of Goethe's life and generation. The narrower interest of the book is as a mirror of a generation before the French Revolution, which was filled with an impotent longing to burst the empty forms of an antiquated social structure and saw in Werther the outburst of individualism for which it was waiting. Latent forces were brought into the open and given a powerful impetus, though the time had not yet come for fulfilment. *Werther* would, however, be little more than a version of the eternal triangle if it were not a symbol of the struggle of the human spirit against its material restrictions. Its essential significance is that it pictures the disintegration of a cultured and sensitive mind which is unable to adjust itself to the outer world when compelled to cope with concrete problems. Goethe has given us a psychological novel which, as his biographer Bielschowsky has pointed out, was only possible after the way had been prepared for the mind and individuality of a Werther by centuries of ascetic doctrine and intensive introspection.

GOETHE AND THE JEWS

IN approaching the subject of Goethe's relations with those Germans of the Jewish faith, or of Jewish descent, with whom he came into contact, and in considering his attitude to the Jews as an entity, it is necessary to bear in mind a number of factors which tend to cloud the issue. It must be admitted that the material is scanty. There are, scattered through his writings, numerous references to the Jews, but they are generally very short, and many of them consist merely of *clichés*, in which the term Jew is regarded as being synonymous with usurer, moneylender, or haggler, or in which he is coupled with the Turk and the Heathen. Even in the cases where he is not employing set phrases, it is not always possible to take what he says at its face value. They do not permit us to dogmatise about his attitude to the Jews any more than we can, for example, dogmatise about his attitude to the Christians from his remarkable statement in the 66th Venetian Epigram:—

"Wenige sind mir jedoch wie Gift und Schlange zuwider,
  Viere: Rauch des Tabaks, Wanzen und Knoblauch und Christ."

Considering the importance of the Jews for the intellectual life of Germany, the bibliography on the subject of Goethe and the Jews is extraordinarily small. Three short books, hardly more than pamphlets, and an essay all bear the same title *Goethe und die Juden*, and only the essay is the work of a scholar of the first order—Ludwig Geiger. Of the other three books the most recent is by Julius Bab, but it contains little that is not to be found in the other two. And these two are mainly compilations of relevant passages in the works of Goethe which each author interprets in a far from objective manner. The first is by Max Maurenbrecher, and it appeared in a series, the avowed object of which is to provide evidence that the Jewish mind is a parasitic growth battening on the body politic of Germany and poisoning the pure stream of Nordic culture. Maurenbrecher quotes the sayings and writings of Goethe in order to prove that he was a conscious and deliberate anti-Semite. The author of the second book, Heinrich Teweles, quotes the same passages to show that Goethe found the Jews congenial and regarded them with sympathy.[1] Any new study of the subject must therefore go direct to the sources, that is to say, to Goethe's own writings, and it is only possible to interpret these objectively and without bias if we take into account two things. We must keep in view the social and historical background of the period during which Goethe lived, and we must realise that his mind was deeply coloured by the early literature of the Jews, namely, the Bible.

The treatment of the Jews in Frankfort-on-the-Main at the time when Goethe was born was hardly different from the way they were treated in the Middle Ages. It was, if anything, worse; for it was not until the fifteenth century that they were compelled to live within the confines of a single street bordering on the city wall. Here they were cooped up until the end of the eighteenth century, a period of more than 300 years. They were the leading Jewish community in the Holy Roman Empire, a position which had formerly been held by the Jews of Nuremberg; but only 500 families were permitted to live in the city and, as a rule, only twelve marriages a year were allowed by law. They had to wear a distinctive form of dress and to keep the gates of the Ghetto closed all day long on certain occasions, and in any case they were forbidden to leave it at night, on Sundays and on holy days. They were unable to own land, and trading in specified goods was closed to them. They were not allowed to use the same walks as the Christians, and were restricted for exercise to the lonely part known as the Fischerfeld. In the year 1756, however,

[1] Ludwig Geiger: *Die deutsche Literatur und die Juden*, pp. 81–101 [Berlin, 1910].

Julius Bab: *Goethe und die Juden* [Berlin, 1926].

Max Maurenbrecher: *Goethe und die Juden* [Munich, 1921].

Heinrich Teweles: *Goethe und die Juden* [Hamburg, 1925].

they were given permission to go outside the precincts of the Judengasse on Sundays and holy days if the matter were urgent, such as obtaining the services of a doctor or a barber, or sending a letter, but it was laid down that they must return by the shortest way. A few years later, in 1787, they were permitted to go out after five o'clock in the afternoon on Sundays, but they were required to conduct themselves in a seemly manner and not give any Christian cause for offence. The Jews humbly returned thanks, and promised that they and their descendants would always return praise for this proof of their fellow-citizens' humanity.

The Jews amounted to about one-tenth of the 35,000 inhabitants of Frankfort in the middle of the eighteenth century, and the restriction of space forced them, like the inhabitants of New York to-day, to provide for the teeming population by making their houses more than usually high. In the ancient cemetery the corpses of centuries were piled one on top of the other, since Jewish law forbade the disinterment of the crumbling bones in the lower layers. There was thus sufficient room neither for the living nor the dead. The Napoleonic invasion gave the Jews a temporary respite, for it introduced the French law of equality for all races and creeds; but with the defeat of Buonaparte and the cessation of the French occupation, the City Fathers immediately reimposed the restrictions of the old regime as far as possible.

The sordid, if picturesque, outside of the street did not always correspond to the appearance of the houses inside. Some of the inhabitants had grown rich as purveyors to various princes or as army contractors and they were able to furnish their dwellings with taste and even luxury. But as a general rule each house was occupied by more than one family, and even Meyer Amschel Rothschild, the founder of the fortunes of the international banking family of that name, who was born six years before Goethe, had for many years to put up with cramped quarters in which he both lived with a numerous family and carried on his business.

The Jews were, in short, regarded by their neighbours as a foreign element in the town, and were treated as outcasts who could not be admitted to the common rights of citizenship. It is therefore little wonder that Goethe's early impressions of them were unfavourable. Yet in spite of the fact that he felt repelled by a race whose manner of living was a medieval anomaly, he was sufficiently interested to pay a number of visits to the Ghetto. In his childhood his attention was attracted to a weatherbeaten skull, stuck on an iron spike on the Brückenturm, which had been there since the year 1616. It was a relic of an evil day in the history of the Frankfort Ghetto, when a mob of rioters, headed by a baker of *Lebkuchen* named Vincenz Fettmilch, invaded the Judengasse and sacked and burned the houses. The Jews sent their women and children to take refuge in the cemetery, which was situated at the farther end of the street; but in spite of their defence they were overpowered and the next day, after spending all night in the cemetery, they left the town, at the order of Fettmilch, to the number of 1,380. This was in August, 1614. Fettmilch was eventually arrested at the order of the Emperor. The Jews returned to Frankfort in February, 1616, the year in which Fettmilch and a number of his confederates were hanged and quartered and the heads of four of them stuck on spikes. It was one of these skulls that Goethe saw some hundred and forty years later, and it led him to enquire into the circumstances of the Fettmilch riots. He tells also in his autobiography how, when he went into the Judengasse, he was haunted by the old legends of the cruelties alleged to have been perpetrated by Jews against Christian children, which he had found in a superstitious old book about devils and witches and other marvels, adorned with horrible woodcuts. He says: "Die Enge, der Schmutz, das Gewimmel, der Akzent einer unerfreulichen Sprache, alles zusammen machte den unangenehmsten Eindruck, wenn man auch

nur am Tore vorbeigehend hineinsah." To intensify the
uncanny feeling, he saw on the Brückenturm a picture
which represented the martyrdom of a Christian child by
Jews, and which had been there since the sixteenth century.
The fact that it was there officially, by order of the town
council, seemed to lend weight to the centuries-old blood
accusation.

In spite of all, however, they were, says Goethe, the
living representatives of Biblical antiquity, and to add to
the interest the Jewish girls were pretty and did not object
to the attentions of a Christian boy when they took their
walks on the Fischerfeld on the Sabbath. "Indessen blieben
sie doch das auserwählte Volk Gottes und gingen, wie es
nun mochte gekommen sein, zum Andenken der ältesten
Zeiten umher. Ausserdem waren sie ja auch Menschen,
tätig, gefällig, und selbst dem Eigensinn, womit sie an
ihren Gebräuchen hingen, konnte man seine Achtung nicht
versagen. Überdies waren die Mädchen hübsch und mochten
es wohl leiden, wenn ein Christenknabe, ihnen am Sabbat
auf dem Fischerfelde begegnend, sich freundlich und
aufmerksam bewies." The *Christenknabe* was, no doubt,
Wolfgang himself. He grew intensely curious to see something of their ceremonies, and he paid a number of visits
to the synagogue, while he also attended a wedding, a
circumcision, and a celebration of the Feast of Tabernacles.
He says that he was always well received, hospitably treated,
and invited to come again. On one occasion he helped to
extinguish a fire by organising a chain of buckets, and
stopped some urchins from molesting and insulting the
victims.

Many years later he told a Jewish friend that the abhor-
rence of Jews which he felt in his early youth was mainly
awe of the mysterious and the ugly. The contempt that
stirred in him was more the reflex of that felt by the Christians around him, and it was only later, when he made the
acquaintance of many talented, cultured members of the
race, that his admiration for the people who had produced

the Bible and for the poet of the Song of Songs was combined with respect. It is, however, doubtful whether the report of this conversation is entirely authentic; or perhaps Goethe was merely being polite. He was naturally, in his younger years, affected by the tradition and attitude of his age. The emancipation of the Jews had not yet even begun, and it was characteristic of their position that Goethe, in *Dichtung und Wahrheit*, used the phrase "from the highest to the lowest, from the Emperor down to the Jews." And there is a certain complacency in the fact that this phrase occurs in a passage in which he puts it to the credit of the Holy Roman Empire that its system of social stratification, instead of separating the classes, served rather to bind them together "from the highest to the lowest, from the Emperor down to the Jews." This statement shows an extraordinary insensitiveness on the part of the author of *Götz von Berlichingen* and *Egmont* to the fact that the great majority of the Germans were living in a state of intellectual and material bondage. And it contrasts strangely with the song of the toper in Auerbach's Keller: "Das liebe heil'ge Römische Reich,/Wie hält's nur noch zusammen?"

Goethe was, from a very early age, deeply interested in the Bible. This led him to study Hebrew, in order that he might be able to read the original text; and a further incentive was the fact that he had already been studying Yiddish, and he found a knowledge of Hebrew was necessary if he was to be able to handle Yiddish with assurance. In order to practise his knowledge of languages he began to write a polyglot novel in no less than seven different ones, in the form of letters from six brothers and a sister, who were to write to each other in German, Latin, Greek, English, French, Italian and Yiddish respectively. At this time he was only about fourteen years of age. He also composed a so-called "Judenpredigt," which, unlike the novel, has been preserved; in this sermon, in very inadequate Yiddish, a Jew is supposed to say that in three hundred thousand years the Messiah will come across the Red Sea to summon the Jews to the blast of a trumpet. They will all find room on the Messiah's white horse and will cross the Red Sea in safety, but the Christians, who will sit on the horse's tail and mock them, will be drowned. Goethe took lessons in Hebrew from Albrecht, the Rector of the Frankfort Gymnasium, and lessons in Yiddish from a certain Christamicus, who was entered by Goethe's father in his housekeeping book as having received a fee of 1 gulden, 30 kreuzer for instruction to Wolfgang in *Judendeutsch*. There is no further entry of payment to Christamicus, so presumably the tuition was not of long duration. Goethe's father was in the habit of Latinising names, so the real name of the tutor may have been Christfreund, and it has been suggested that he was a member of a Jewish family that had been converted to Christianity. A book printed in Yiddish, Schudt's *Frankfurter Judenchronik*, was in the library of Goethe's father.

The language and rhythms of the Old Testament had a considerable influence on Goethe's poetry, perhaps the most striking example of Biblical inspiration being the Prologue in Heaven which appears at the beginning of *Faust*, and which was suggested to him by the Book of Job; and there seems little doubt that the end of *Faust*, Part II, was influenced by the Biblical story of the death of Moses. He composed a number of poetic fragments that dealt with episodes in Jewish history, but he threw them in the fire when he was a student at Leipzig. Many years later, in a letter to Zelter on 19th May, 1812, he discussed the question of basing dramas or operas on Biblical themes, and explained why he did not feel attracted to the subject of Samson and Delilah: "Zu dem Simson hätte ich im Augenblick kein Zutrauen; die alte Mythe ist eine der ungeheuersten. Eine ganz bestialische Leidenschaft eines überkräftigen, gottbegabten Helden zu dem verfluchtesten Luder, das die Erde trägt." And in the same letter he adduced, as one of the reasons why he did not draw inspiration from the Bible, the excuse that when the heroes of Jewish antiquity appeared on the stage, people were struck by the fact that they were Jews and were disconcerted and depressed by the contrast between the ancestors and the descendants. Here again he failed to realise the extent to which external forces were responsible for the wretched conditions under which the Jews of his time were living. His only reaction was one of cold disgust, without a hint of pity or desire for the amelioration of their lot. His interest in the Old Testament did nothing to arouse in him any warmer feeling for the Jews. It cannot even be said that its significance for his life and work had much to do with religion, for what drew him to it was chiefly its historical and æsthetic content. The fact that he insisted on the permanent value of the Bible, and that it certainly had an influence on his ethical development, did not prevent him from declaring to Böttiger in 1795[1] that humanity would have taken a healthier turn if Homer had been its Bible instead of the Scriptures. "Beim erneuten Studium Homers empfinde ich erst ganz, welches unnennbare Unheil uns der jüdische Prass zugefügt hat. Hätten wir die Sodomitereien und ägyptisch-babylonischen Grillen nie kennen gelernt und wäre Homer unsere Bibel geblieben, welch eine ganz andere Gestalt würde die Menschheit dadurch gewonnen haben!" In weighing two wholly different cultures, he here gives the preference to Greece.

One of his early projects was an epic on the theme of the Wandering Jew, of which only a few fragments were written, and part of his scheme was to include a visit by Ahasuerus to Spinoza. If he had carried out this plan, we should possess an absorbing document to illustrate the great debt he owed to the thought of the Jewish philosopher, which he acknowledged himself to be inestimable. He discussed Spinoza's ideas with both Herder and Frau von Stein, and he refers to him in a letter dated 1816 as "unser alter Herr und Meister." About the same time he is reported to have said in conversation with Boisserée that he always carried Spinoza's *Ethics* about with him, and in referring to his own

[1] Teweles, *op. cit.*, p. 17.

philosophical development he said that it was Spinoza who first exercised a great and permanent influence over him. Goethe's conviction of the oneness of God and Nature derives from Spinoza, the founder of Pantheism, and a large bulk of his poetry is based on it. In the year 1830, two years before his death, he wrote to Zelter: "Es ist ein grenzenloses Verdienst unseres alten Kant um die Welt und, ich darf sagen, auch um mich, dass er in seiner Kritik der Urteilskraft Kunst und Natur kräftig nebeneinander stellt und beiden das Recht zugesteht: aus grossen Prinzipien zwecklos zu handeln. So hatte mich Spinoza früher schon in dem Hass gegen die absurden Endursachen gegläubiget."

Spinoza's thought was, of course, opposed to Jewish teaching, and he was excommunicated by the community at Amsterdam. And it was indirectly through Spinoza that Goethe fell out with Moses Mendelssohn, though it was not a personal dispute, for the two never met. Goethe, as a young man, had a high opinion of Mendelssohn, though Mendelssohn did not like Goethe's early works; but in 1785 he spoke in derogatory terms of Mendelssohn's book *Morgenstunden*, which contains his system of philosophy and in which he tries to prove the personal existence of God. Goethe, in referring to this book, wrote in a letter to Jacobi: "Was hast Du zu den *Morgenstunden* gesagt? Und zu den jüdischen Pfiffen, mit denen der neue Sokrates zu Werke geht?" When Lessing read Goethe's poem "Prometheus," he told Jacobi in private that he agreed with its Spinozist philosophy. Jacobi printed the poem without Goethe's consent, and also published what Lessing had said in a book called *Über die Lehre des Spinoza in Briefen an Herrn Mendelssohn*. Mendelssohn was very hurt at this, and, in order to clear his friend Lessing, who was then dead, of the accusation of Spinozism, he wrote a book *Moses Mendelssohn an die Freunde Lessings*, but he died before it appeared, and it was said that his death was caused by the aggravation he had felt at Jacobi's book. Goethe refers to this in his Autobiography, when he says that "Prometheus" caused an

explosion and "Der Riss war so gewaltsam, dass wir darüber
. . . einen unserer würdigsten Männer, Mendelssohn, verloren." And elsewhere he says: "Man erinnere sich nur an
die unglückliche Entdeckung von Lessings geheimer Spino-
zistischer Sinnesart durch Friedrich Jacobi, worüber sich
Mendelssohn in buchstäblichem Sinne den Tod holte."
But when he read this last book of Mendelssohn he did not
find it at all to his taste, for he wrote to Herder that he
found it impossible to read "das Jüdische Neue Testament"
to the end, and had sent it to Frau von Stein, with the hope
that she would have more luck. He told Jacobi that though
he had read his book with interest he had found no pleasure
in it; but there is something patronising in the words with
which he sent Frau von Stein some lampoons against Mendelssohn that had come into his hands: "How petty it all is
and how pitiful! Even a poor Jew cannot quit the world
without being exposed to ridicule." He showed later in the
Xenien, however, that he appreciated Mendelssohn's importance for the *Aufklärung*.

Goethe came into contact with a largish number of Jews in
middle and late life, and with a few of them he entered into
closer relations. When he returned to Frankfort to set up as
a lawyer at the end of his University career, he had some
Jews among his clients. Though there were not many
living in Weimar he met a few of them, and it is recorded
that he recommended a *Schutzjude*, i.e. a Jew under official
protection, who was passing through Weimar, to his uncle,
who was then *Schultheiss* of Frankfort. One day in 1782 he
told Frau von Stein that one of the things that had prevented
him from coming to say "Good morning!" to her had been
a visit from a Jew Ephraim. "Bald habe ich das Bedeutende
der Judenheit zusammen und habe grosse Lust, in meinem
Roman auch einen Juden anzubringen." He obviously
thought that he had sufficient acquaintance with the Jewish
character to introduce a Jewish figure into his novel, and
the novel he was referring to was *Wilhelm Meisters Lehrjahre*.

But he never did so, and in all his writings there is not a single Jewish figure, if we except the Wandering Jew in his youthful fragment and Mordecai in the puppet play of *Esther*, which he introduced into the *Jahrmarktsfest zu Plundersweilern*.

The financial affairs of Goethe, and of the Court of Weimar, were handled by the firm of Elkan. The founder of the bank had been originally poor, and Goethe refers to him in his poem "Auf Miedings Tod." The original version of the two lines in which he is mentioned ran :—

> "Der Jude Elkan läuft mit manchem Rest,
> Und diese Gärung deutet auf ein Fest."

The descendants of Elkan must have protested against this reference to the days when their ancestor, among his other activities, supplied properties for the theatre, and Goethe altered the first line, so that the current version now runs : "Der tätige Jude läuft . . ." without any mention of the name.

Riemer says that since Goethe did the social honours at Weimar, visitors of any creed, including "Juden und Judengenossen," were usually invited to dinner. He certainly had a number of Jewish acquaintances with whom he found pleasure in discussing matters of intellectual interest. Among them were David Veit, a physician and writer from Berlin; Salomon Munk, who later became a well-known Orientalist; Eduard Gans, the jurist and philosopher; and Eduard von Simson, who in later years became President of the Frankfort National Assembly of 1848, President of the Prussian Chamber, and eventually first President of the newly established Imperial Court of Justice at Leipzig in 1879. He took an interest in the painter Moritz Oppenheim, for whom he was instrumental in procuring the title of professor, and helped Michael Beer, the brother of the composer Meyerbeer, to get his play *Der Paria* produced, and it was put into the repertory of the theatre at Weimar. He wrote an introduction to this play for the programme, in which he stated that

167

the pariah could be regarded as a symbol of the humiliated, oppressed and despised humanity of all nations; and since such a theme was a matter of general human interest, it was on that account highly poetical. Meyerbeer he thought the only living musician capable of composing music for *Faust*. With the *Aufklärer* David Friedlaender of Berlin and his son Benoni he came into touch through a mutual passion for collecting antiquities, and they exchanged specimens. Among the visits recorded in his later years was one from the two sons of the English Rothschild, Lionel and Anthony, who came in 1827 with their English tutor. The only other Rothschild he appears to have met is recorded in his diary in 1831: "Nachher Frau von Rothschild, ein junges, anmutiges Wesen." There is a reference to the family in *Eckermann*, where Goethe, discussing the length of time it takes for great projects to ripen, says that Dante appears as a great man, but he had a culture of centuries behind him, and the House of Rothschild is rich, but it took more than one generation to achieve its wealth: that these things all lie deeper than is supposed. A further entry in *Eckermann* tells how Goethe entertained his guests before dinner with a few Frankfort stories, especially of the way in which Rothschild and Bethmann, the two leading bankers of that town, put their fingers in each other's pies. He appears to have had a particular fondness for Jewish jokes, to judge by a number of entries in his diaries. He quotes, for example, the Jew who wished that God had placed his calves in front of his legs instead of at the back, so that he would not hurt himself when he barked his shins. Another story that appears to have amused him was the one about an ignorant Jew who had grown rich and liked to gather information about the various branches of knowledge, of which he only knew the names. He once asked what a table is called in geography. A third anecdote tells of the Jews who wanted to return a favour that had been shown them by a certain prince, and offered him fifteen hundred ducats. He refused to accept money from them, but when they urged him to say what he would like, he said he would be very pleased to accept four pounds of tea, which was then a rare commodity. They beat him down to three, and even then did not give them to him.

Goethe's taste for Jewish stories may have been in part due to his knowledge of Yiddish, for they were no doubt told to him with a Jewish accent. He notes "Judensprache hat etwas Pathetisches," and he was amused at the temperamental, enthusiastic manner of expression of an old Jewish beggar who was cured of cataract by Jung-Stilling, and who replied to the query whether the operation had been painful, that if he had a thousand eyes he would be willing to have them all operated on, one after the other, if he were paid for it, and who went along the street thanking God and Jung-Stilling, the magician, in a loud voice.

At the beginning of the new century the intellectual life of Berlin centred round the salons of a galaxy of brilliant Jewish women, such as Rahel, Henriette Herz and Dorothea Schlegel, the daughter of Moses Mendelssohn, who were connected with the Romantic Movement.

Goethe was on terms of intimate friendship with some of them, and it was they who contributed essentially to the spreading of an understanding of his works in the Prussian capital, which till then was a stronghold of the *Aufklärung*. He made the acquaintance of Rahel, who later became the wife of Varnhagen von Ense, in Karlsbad in 1795, and they were friends until his death. He had a very high opinion of her, which he expressed to a number of people, among them Riemer, to whom he said that she had been one of the first in Germany to understand him. Rahel's devotion may be judged by her description of an accidental meeting near Frankfort in 1815, when she saw him passing by: "Der Schreck, die Freude machen mich zur Wilden; ich schrei mit der grössten Kraft und Eile: 'Da ist Goethe. . . .'. Als er vorbei war, zitterten mir Kniee und Glieder mehr als eine halbe Stunde. Und laut und wie rasend dankte ich Gott in seine Abendsonne hinein." In her salon in Berlin the members of the Romantic School were to some extent brought under his influence.

Two Jewish women with whom he corresponded frequently were Marianne and Sara Meyer, the daughters of a Berlin banker. Marianne gave her hand in morganatic marriage to a Prince of Reuss and was known as Baroness von Eybenberg. After the death of her husband she lived in Vienna and did propaganda work for Goethe, who had met her, likewise in Karlsbad, in 1795. He appears, in fact, to have been in love with her for a time. In 1808 they met nearly every day for a period of about three months in Karlsbad, where they walked and talked, according to Goethe's diary, on matters of intellectual and political interest. Later in the same year he wrote to her: "Gedenken Sie mein im Stillen, denn es ist mir schon zu Ohren gekommen, dass man es nicht ganz gut aufnimmt, wenn Sie meiner in der Welt allzu vorteilhaft erwähnen. Wenn wir selbst nur wissen, was wir an einander haben, ist es völlig hinreichend." This seems to show that the interest was not wholly intellectual and political. On the 21st December of the following year he wrote that that was the shortest day of the year, but he had no intention or desire other than to spend the longest day in her company at Karlsbad. In 1810 he again met her in Karlsbad, but he wrote to his wife that they were not getting on as well as they used to: Marianne had grown very politically minded, and as her views on the subject were not the same as his, conversation was rather difficult, and they never met without her saying something that annoyed him. Nevertheless they seem to have seen each other every day. She died two years later. Goethe's correspondence with her sister Sara, who married a Baron Grotthuss, also lasted for many years, and she used to send him fish and caviar from Berlin.

In 1811 he made the acquaintance in Karlsbad of Simon von Laemel, a Jewish banker from Prague, and they discussed Jewish questions. Laemel complained to him that Schiller had pained and wronged the Jews through his

essay *Die Sendung Mosis*, showing that he completely mis-
understood his subject. Goethe in reply made the statement
from which I have already quoted at the beginning of this
paper: "The impression I received in my native town in
early youth was more a terrifying one. The people in the
narrow, gloomy Ghetto were to me very strange and incomprehensible figures, which occupied my imagination, and
I was unable to understand how this race had produced out
of itself the most remarkable book in the world. To be sure,
what stirred in me in my early youth in the form of abhor-
rence of Jews was mainly awe of the mysterious and the
ugly. The contempt I was accustomed to feel was more the
reflex of the Christians around me. Only later, when I got
to know many talented, cultured members of the race, was
my admiration for the people who had produced the Bible
and for the poet of the Song of Songs combined with respect."

This is the longest conversation with any of his Jewish
friends of which we have any record, but, as I have pointed
out, there is doubt as to its accuracy.

The last of Goethe's Jewish friends to be discussed is
the musician Felix Mendelssohn-Bartholdy. Though he was
baptised at birth, he was a Jew, the grandson of Moses
Mendelssohn. He was first introduced to Goethe by his
teacher Zelter in 1821, when he was only 12 years of age,
and the old man grew very fond of him and called him a
Wunderkind. Goethe made him pay frequent visits, and in
one letter the boy wrote to his parents: "Every morning I
receive a kiss from the author of *Faust* and *Werther*, and every
afternoon two kisses from Goethe my father and friend."
When Felix left Weimar, Goethe wrote to his father that
if the boy could see how he now and then turned his head
towards the piano, he would feel how sorely he was missed.
Felix visited Weimar many times in the following years, and
he dedicated a quartet to Goethe. His last visit was in
May, 1830, when he stayed a fortnight. He had only intended to stay for two days, but Goethe persuaded him to
remain, and he called every day and was made to play all

the great composers in historical sequence and explain them while the old poet sat in a dark corner "wie ein *Jupiter tonans*," as Felix put it, "und blitzt mit den alten Augen." There is something very charming about the relations between the young musician and the aged poet, and a delightful picture is conjured up of Goethe receiving a practical lesson in musical history. He once wrote to Felix: "You are my David; if I should grow ill and sad, banish my evil dreams by your playing. I shall never, like Saul, throw my javelin at you."

The single visit paid by Heinrich Heine is less cheerful. He came one day in 1824, having previously sent copies of his poems and tragedies when they were published. When Goethe asked him what he was engaged on now, he was either naïve, tactless, or impudent enough to say that he was writing a *Faust*, and Goethe took an early opportunity to bring the interview to an end.

When we come to consider the passages in Goethe's own works, in which he provides evidence of his attitude to the Jews and to Jewish thought, we meet with the difficulty that it is never possible to tell whether he is expressing his own view or merely putting into the mouth of one of his characters a statement that is consonant with the nature of that character. In the *Jahrmarktsfest zu Plundersweilern*, for example, the core of the piece consists of two scenes from the Biblical story of Esther, who with her uncle Mordecai saved the Jews from massacre at the hands of Haman. It has been suggested, though on no plausible grounds, that Goethe was acquainted with a Jewish Purim Play, dealing with the same theme, such as Jews were accustomed to perform at the festival of Purim. There is little in Goethe's Esther play that has much to do with the original story, but what concerns us is the conversation between Haman and King Ahasuerus, in which the former tries to persuade the King to agree to having Mordecai put to death by attributing to the Jews all sorts of iniquitous qualities. Is Goethe here really expressing his own views, as the anti-Semitic type of German literary historian would have us believe, or is he making fun of the anti-Semitic views of his own day that he does not share? There is, I think, no doubt that it is a burlesque, but I do not suggest that Goethe had any intention of taking the part of the Jews. He wrote it for fun, and it does not tell us anything about his own attitude to the Jewish question.

This we must look for in the short references which are scattered through his works, chiefly in the letters, diaries and conversations. In a review he wrote for the *Frankfurter Gelehrte Anzeigen* of a book called *Gedichte von einem Polnischen Juden* in 1772, he manifests a distinct sympathy with the author, who may, he says, have come from a foreign country to a strange world to practise his muse in a foreign tongue. But when he came to read the poems they disappointed him, for they achieved no more than a Christian "étudiant en belles lettres" might have done. In other words, he suggests that a Jew was capable of giving something fresh to German literature, something that a Christian poet could not.

One of the Venetian Epigrams, of the year 1790 or 1791, appears to be an exhortation to religious tolerance:

"Juden und Heiden hinaus! so duldet der christliche Schwärmer.
Christ und Heide verflucht! murmelt ein jüdischer Bart.
Mit den Christen an Spiess und mit dem Juden ins Feuer!
Singt ein türkisches Kind Juden und Christen zum Spott.
Welcher ist der Klügste? Entscheide! Aber sind diese
Narren in deinem Palast, Gottheit, so geh ich vorbei."

In the Notes to the *West-östlicher Divan* he says: "Die jüdische Religion wird immer einen gewissen starren Eigensinn, dabei aber auch freien Klugsinn und lebendige Tätigkeit verbreiten." In a short article he suggested that the tercentenary of the Reformation, to be celebrated in 1817, should be cancelled in favour of a celebration of the Battle of Leipzig, in which the whole nation could take part, not the Protestants alone but Jews, Mohammedans,

173

and Heathens, who had all fought on the same side, so that it would be more than a religious, more even than a national festival.

That is practically all he has to say that may be considered favourable to the Jews. When we look for quotations in which he expresses dislike or intolerance, the roll is much longer.

In one of his miscellaneous notes he suggests they are earthly minded; he says: "Keiner, auch nur der kleinste, geringste Jude, der nicht entschiedenes Bestreben verriete und zwar ein irdisches, zeitliches, augenblickliches."

In his essay *Zwo biblische Fragen* (1773) he makes a pastor say that he regards the Jews as a wild and unfruitful trunk, which stood amid a group of wild, unfruitful trees, and on which the Gardener grafted the noble branch of Jesus Christ that He might ennoble the nature of the trunk, which would then supply shoots to fructify all the other trees.

In *Wilhelm Meisters Wanderjahre* there are three different passages in which an opinion is expressed about the Jews, all of them unfavourable, but in two cases qualified either by an admission of their virtues or a caution not to treat them ill. When Wilhelm is being shown the picture-gallery which contains scenes from the Bible, he asks his guide why Jewish history in particular has been chosen for representation. He is told that at the judgment-seat of the Lord of Nations, the question that will be asked is not whether a nation has been the best, the most excellent, but only whether it has lasted, whether it has survived. The Israelitish race has always been good-for-nothing ("hat niemals viel getaugt"), as its leaders, judges and prophets have told it a thousand times; it possesses few virtues and most of the faults of other nations, but it is unequalled in independence, constancy, courage and tenacity. It is the most persevering people on earth; it is, it was, and it will be, to glorify the name of Jehovah throughout the ages. It has therefore been set up as an example, as the chief symbol for which the others only serve as a frame.

Later on in the book Lenardo is addressing the League of Wanderers, and mentions "the race which has appropriated to itself the blessing of wandering and understands, by its active mobility, how to outwit those who stay in the same place and to outstrip its fellow-wanderers. We should speak neither good nor evil of them : not good, because our League is on its guard against them; and not evil, because every wanderer is bound to treat everybody he meets in a friendly manner and bear in mind the possibility of mutual benefit."

And the summary of a conversation concerning a plan for the organisation of a new Christian community concludes with the statement that Jews are not tolerated, for how can they be granted a share in the highest form of civilisation, the origin and tradition of which they deny? That is to say, that as their religion is different, they cannot have the same outlook on life.

In a letter to Riemer in 1810 Goethe says that women, like Jews, have no *point d'honneur,* and in a letter to his wife in 1797 he writes that a Jewish dealer, who had brought him some inferior articles, had acted like "ein wahrer Jude."

There are other uncomplimentary references, but they add nothing to what we have already gleaned, and most of them are merely current generalisations. It is quite clear from what has already been said that, with the exception of a few personal friends, whom he no doubt did not think of as Jews at all, his attitude to the race was one of dislike. His hostility, however, is not always traceable to the same cause. In one reference, for example, he condemns Judaism because of its relationship to Christianity, which is antipathetic to his Greek ideal; elsewhere he decries it because it *denies* Christianity, which he says is the source of the highest modern civilisation. On the other hand, he once said to Riemer : "They are foolish descriptions—Paganism, Judaism, Christianity! There are Jews among the pagans—the usurers; Christians among the pagans—the stoics; pagans among the Christians—the worldlings!" And to

Boisserée he wrote towards the end of his life, in 1831, that he had never found any creed since the creation of the world to which he might have been able completely to attest; but he had just heard of a sect in the fourth century, called the Hypsistarians, who were hemmed in by Heathens, Jews and Christians, and declared that their system would be to admire and honour whatever they discovered to be most excellent and most perfect. It then suddenly dawned on Goethe that he had all his life been trying to qualify to become a Hypsistarian.

Goethe was not a Christian in the sense of subscribing to orthodox Christian dogma, but as a convenience for the smooth running of the social system he thought a state religion was necessary, and he would not brook any reform that he thought might give rise to a disturbance of law and order. During the years 1807 and 1808 he carried on a correspondence with Bettina Brentano (the daughter of the Maximiliane Brentano who had over thirty years before furnished him with some traits for the portrait of Werther's Lotte) about the efforts that were then being made in the direction of Jewish emancipation. He manifested considerable interest, but no particular sympathy or warmth. Bettina was very friendly to the Jews, and Goethe asked her to send him the Jewish pamphlets on the subject which were being published in Frankfort. The pamphlets arrived, and the interest with which he read them may be estimated from the numerous marginal notes which he made on them. His comment was that it was proper, no doubt, for an advocate of Jewish emancipation to consider what his people ought to be, but that the Governor of Frankfort could not be blamed if, in his treatment of them, he only took into account what they were and what they would continue to be for some time yet. Bettina also sent him pamphlets written by the Christian opposition, one of which met with his strong approval. It was a reply to a pamphlet written by a Jewish philanthropist named Israel Jacobson, and Goethe said he was very pleased to see

Jacobson so efficiently sent about his business. ("Es war mir sehr angenehm zu sehen, dass man den Finanzgeheimrätlichen, Jacobinischen Israels Sohn so tüchtig nach Hause geleuchtet hat.") He enquired the name of the author and declared that there were passages in the pamphlet which would not have disgraced a *plaidoyer* by Beaumarchais; but unfortunately it was not as lively, bold and amusing as it ought to have been in order to make what he calls "that humanitarian bore" (*Humanitätssalbader*) ridiculous, once for all, in the eyes of the whole world.

If further proof of Goethe's intolerance is necessary, there is the passage in his letter to Boisserée in 1816: "In Jena darf nach alten Gesetzen kein Jude übernachten. Diese löbliche Anordnung dürfte gewiss künftighin besser als bisher aufrecht erhalten werden." And there is the extraordinary outburst to which he gave vent in the presence of the Chancellor Müller in 1823, when he was 74 years old. In September of that year a decree had been issued by the Grand Duke of Weimar which gave the Jews greater freedom and permitted marriages between Jews and Christians. Goethe's diary on 23rd September of that year bears the entry: "Abends Kanzler v. Müller; über Christen- und Juden-Heiraten, unerfreuliche Unterhaltung." Müller himself relates the scene in greater detail: "I had hardly entered Goethe's room towards six o'clock," he says, ". . . when the old gentleman poured out his passionate wrath at our new law concerning the Jews, which permits marriage between members of the two faiths. He foreboded the worst and most jarring consequences, asserting that if the superintendent-general of the clergy had any strength of character he must prefer to resign his post rather than marry a Jewess in Church in the name of the Holy Trinity. All ethical family feelings, which, after all, were based on the religious ones, were undermined by such a scandalous law. Besides, he would like to see how it was proposed to prevent a Jewess from one day occupying the position of *Oberhofmeisterin*. Foreigners must really believe that bribery was at the bottom of it, otherwise they would find the adoption of such a law incomprehensible. Who knew whether the omnipotent Rothschild was not at the back of it!"

The sudden descent from his fears for the safety of the moral order to his realisation of the dreadful possibility that a Lord High Steward of the Grand Ducal Court might one day introduce a Jewess as his wife, is an example of bathos that must be rare in the recorded utterances of Goethe. It has been suggested that this outburst was only a method of giving vent to a general fit of spleen, and it is possible that it took place at a time when he was in a state of abnormal nervous irritation, but, however much we may discount, the residue is sufficient to illustrate his deep-seated general attitude. Yet, to conclude with two more quotations, one of which, however, is of doubtful authenticity, he could be very complimentary in statements about the Jewish mind. On one occasion, when he was managing the theatre, he is said to have forbidden one of the actors to portray a Jew as a figure of fun. "It is disgraceful," he said, "to pillory a race which has produced such excellent talents in the fields of art and science." And in his diary he noted (on the 15th March, 1808): "Augusts Besorgnis wegen des Band-wurms glücklich gehoben. . . . Deutsche gehen nicht zu Grunde, wie die Juden, weil es lauter Individuen sind." It is difficult to see the connection between August's tapeworm and the tenacious individuality of the Germans or the Jews, but he was sufficiently impressed with the latter idea to repeat it in almost the same words to Riemer.

I have so far tried to sift the mass of scattered data spread over the whole of Goethe's long life, and must now come to my conclusion. He noted in his diary time and again that he was reading books on the language or the history of the Jewish people; he was fond of visiting old synagogues and endeavouring to decipher the inscriptions he found there; he was interested in the literary, artistic and philosophical work of a number of his Jewish contemporaries; and he retained to the end his curiosity in regard to Jewish antiquities. But his whole interest in the Jews was no more than an intellectual curiosity. We look in vain for any touch of warmer feeling, for any hint of pity for their earlier sufferings or sympathy with their present lot. Even expressions of tolerance are rare, and Lessing might never have written the parable of the three rings for all the effect it seems to have had on Goethe, in spite of his openly expressed admiration for *Näthan der Weise* and the fact that he himself produced it on the stage. Goethe lived through two movements, each of which gave a new impetus to the spirit of religious tolerance—the *Aufklärung* in his youth, and the French Revolution with its sequels in his middle age. Great as was the influence of the *Aufklärung* on the development of his mind, he was not anxious to apply its ideas to the social order. Still less, those of the new age which dawned with the French Revolution. He was, at the most, lukewarm in his attitude to any suggestion of liberal or democratic institutions, such as the vote or the freedom of the press. German writers try to find excuses for him. They try to palliate his conservatism by such statements as that though he rejected the idea of reform when presented merely as a theory, yet he was an enthusiastic admirer of Napoleon because the latter was a great personality and therefore æsthetically attractive. This type of argument may throw some light on Goethe as an artist, but it does not make any more palatable the fact that in his later years he regarded unsympathetically the attempts of his countrymen to emancipate themselves from social and political bondage. If we are to regard Goethe as standing apart from the rest of mankind, that is to say, if we are to consider him solely as a poet to whom mundane things are of no concern, then we have no right to expect him to manifest what we nowadays regard as an enlightened attitude towards the less fortunate classes of humanity. But not only was he for a considerable period a statesman, the Prime Minister of Weimar. He is looked up to by his countrymen as a great leader, a guide to conduct

179

in both the private and the public affairs of life, and his views on the social order are therefore of the utmost importance. It only distorts the issue to speak, as one critic does, of the "limits of his social and political understanding which were conditioned by the peculiar greatness of the Goethean nature." Goethe's attitude to the Jews was typical of his attitude to his oppressed countrymen in general. As an artist and a thinker he, in some ways, transcended the limits of space and time. In other ways which we, in England, cannot help regarding as important aspects of a man's character, he failed to soar beyond the prejudices of a courtier in a small eighteenth-century German princedom. If German scholars will not recognise that fact it is, perhaps, desirable that it should not be ignored by students in other countries who have not been brought up to regard Goethe as beyond the reach of criticism.

THE ROMANTIC SYMBOL

NOVALIS AND THE BLUE FLOWER

THE purpose of this paper is to investigate the extent to which dream encroached upon reality in the life of one of the Romanticists. Novalis has been called the "key to the Romantic School," and as the most inspired of all the romantic writers he is likely to yield the most fruitful results in such an enquiry. As a poet is necessarily to some extent an idealist, the question must always arise as to how far he reconciles his ideals with his environment. Are those ideals fairly concrete, or are they vague and misty? Can the poet strike the balance between the two, and settle down to a more or less happy existence without losing his visions? If he is unable to reconcile the ideal and the real, will he withdraw from reality and find satisfaction in his imagination, or will he make demands on reality which are impossible of fulfilment, with serious results to his own mental health?

As Novalis was born two years before the publication of Goethe's *Werther*, he passed his childhood and boyhood during the most turbulent years of the *Sturm und Drang*. By the time he was old enough to go to the University, the Storm and Stress movement had gone underground, and German literature was dominated by the great twin stars, Goethe and Schiller. Novalis thus spent his teens and early manhood in the transition period between *Sturm und Drang* and Romanticism, and the whole of the twenty-nine years of his life were spent in the period above all in German literature when the inability of the poets to adapt themselves to reality found its most morbid expression. When the French Revolution broke out, Novalis was a youth of seventeen, the age when one would expect such an upheaval to have had a decisive influence on his mind and character. But it passed him by after a short period of enthusiasm and, like all the members of the Romantic School, he was hardly influenced by it. The psychic unrest of the previous generation, dimly foreboding coming changes, was expressive of the hope that a new world was about to rise out of the ashes of the old, and the burning resentment and bitterness which were induced by the failure of the Revolution to satisfy such hopes, found later expression, not in the Romantics, but in poets like Chateaubriand and Byron. The Romantics continued the tradition of the sentimental age which preceded and was contemporary with *Sturm und Drang*, and it was Novalis who gave them their symbol—the famous Blue Flower of Romanticism, the symbol of the unattainable, of the object of that vague longing which cannot be satisfied, or even defined, because its roots are in the unconscious. It was the Romantics who discovered the unconscious and insisted on its being appreciated. The eighteenth century had hitherto merely valued the conscious, and depreciated that which could not be rationalised.

Friedrich Leopold von Hardenberg, generally known by his pen-name of Novalis, was born on the 2nd May, 1772, at the Castle of Ober-Wiederstedt, as the second child of Baron Erasmus von Hardenberg. The father was a strange man. He appears to have sowed his wild oats, after the usual manner of a son of the nobility, but in middle life a sudden transformation took place. There is a document extant in which he has written down the following words: "After a wild and dissolute life, I was first aroused in the year 1769 by the violent shock of the death of my wife, and I conceived a violent uneasiness about the condition of my soul." He became a disciple of Count Zinzendorf, the leader of the Moravian Brotherhood, a community who laid stress on the necessity of concentrating on the inner life, and yielding passively to "the will of God." He endeavoured to bring up his children in these quietistic principles, and for their sakes he avoided all disturbing intercourse with friends and neighbours, so that they were thrown back upon themselves and the resources of the rambling old castle for amusement. On one occasion, when the poet Tieck was visiting his friend, he heard a terrific noise and the sound of swearing coming from the next room. He enquired of a servant what was the matter, and the man replied: "It is the master holding his religious lesson."

About a year after his wife's death he married a poor cousin, who appears to have been a frail and timid person, subservient to her husband, with whom she shared the same religious faith, and temperamentally colourless. Her naturally delicate health was no doubt transmitted to her eleven children, only one of whom survived its parents. Novalis was the second. If we knew more about the first six years of Novalis' life, we should be in a better position to understand his future psychic condition, but there is little doubt that both the spiritual and physical abnormality of his parents and the none too healthy environment of his childhood contributed materially, if not essentially, to give his mind the tendency it afterwards assumed. At the age of nine he is said to have fallen dangerously ill of dysentery, and whereas he had before been rather a dull child, after this physical crisis his mental gifts began speedily to develop. It will be noticed later that illnesses or death always formed turning points in his life. He was sent for a year to his uncle, a busy man of the world, who enjoyed the social pleasures of life to the full. In his house Novalis saw a very different world from the one he had known at home. In 1790, at the age of seventeen, he went to the *Gymnasium* at Eisleben, and in the autumn of the same year he entered the University of Jena, in order to study jurisprudence. The law, however, was little to his taste, and in Jena he appears to have led the wild life of a well-to-do student of the time. He is said to have fought many duels and to have cared but little for his professional studies, but his father grew uneasy at his behaviour, and sent him in the following autumn to Leipzig. It was in Leipzig that Novalis met Friedrich Schlegel, the thinker of the Romantic School, whose influence on him was great, but he continued the life he had begun in Jena. Wearying of this somewhat dissolute existence, he resolved to go away and become a soldier. He changed his mind, however, as quickly as he had made it up, and in the spring of 1793 he went to his third University, Wittenberg, concluding his studies in the summer of the following year. He then returned home, and in October of the same year he went to Tennstedt in Thuringia, to be instructed in the art of practical administration. One day in November he rode over to the neighbouring village of Grüningen, and met, in the house of a Herr von Rockenthien, the latter's stepdaughter, Sophie von Kühn, a girl not yet thirteen years of age, and it was his love for Sophie that coloured the whole of his subsequent mental experiences. It was the decisive factor of his life, and his mental attitude towards her was one of the strangest in the whole of literature.

We know little of Sophie herself. Her mental development was apparently meagre. Her Diary is childish, consisting of phrases such as "Hardenberg rode away again this morning, otherwise nothing happened to-day." On the following day she writes: "We were alone again to-day, and again nothing else occurred." On the next day she repeats the very same phrase. The writing and orthography are equally immature. One of her letters to Novalis runs as follows, without a single comma: "Husten und Schnuden habe ich aber offenes Leibes bin ich doch noch auch denke ich wenn es mir einfällt an Sie—Sophia."

Novalis has written down some of her characteristics. For example: "She does not care much for poetry. She does not yet appear to have come to the stage of reflection. Her fear of marriage. She does not want to let herself be incommoded by my love. My love often vexes her. She is thoroughly cold. She does not believe in a future life, but in the transmigration of souls. She does not let herself be called 'thou.' Her favourite foods—vegetable soup—beef and beans—eels. She is fond of wine."

In March 1795 Novalis and Sophie became secretly

engaged, but after a time his passion seems to have cooled. On one occasion Sophie reproached him for flirting, and his reply was, "Sie dreizehnjähriges Ding solle doch nur ganz ruhig sein," and German critics have pondered this phrase earnestly, and have written learned chapters to try to prove whether Novalis' love for Sophie was really likely to have endured. The truth is, I think, that he did not love the actual Sophie, but rather the illusion he had formed of her. They really appear to have been near to a break, when the decisive event happened. Sophie fell ill. The fear of losing her, and perhaps also the romantic halo cast around her by her illness, stimulated his love, and as he said himself, "I almost love her more on account of her illness." Her illness transformed her in Novalis' eyes into something ethereal. He likened himself to a despairing gamester, whose whole future depended on whether a petal fell in this world or in the other. When Sophie died, two days after her fifteenth birthday, he wrote, "The petal has now fluttered over into the other world." He commenced a Diary, which he dated from the day Sophie died, every entry being noted as so many days since her death, and this Diary he kept for about three months. With penetrating self-observation, which reminds us of *Anton Reiser*, the strangest psychological autobiography in German literature, he noted the most intimate impulses and emotions. He determined to die, but not by suicide. He determined to *will* himself to death, to concentrate on the thought until death came to him, and he was firmly convinced that as he belonged spiritually and absolutely to this dead girl, that as he was one with her, so he must eventually die from the very strength of this conviction. The soul was to consume the body. Novalis was at this time deeply influenced by Fichte's doctrine of the infinite power of the Will, the omnipotence of the ego and the unreality of the external world, all reality only being produced by the absolute ego. The will to die was what he called his *Zielgedanke*, his ultimate purpose, and again and again he recorded in his Diary the entry, "My final purpose kept pretty firm," or, "My resolve was firm." Then we read, "I still appear to be unable quite to accustom myself to my resolve. Fixed as it appears to be, yet at times I become distrustful, since it appears to be so unattainably far off, so strange." And later, "My resolve has often been the subject of discussion lately: I have often thought of Sophie, but I still have frivolous thoughts." The following day he records: "My resolve received new life, became more fixed." We begin to see the struggle between his emotions and his reason. The first impulse of despair gives way to a systematisation of his grief. He now nurses it consciously, and the registration of his emotions becomes almost scientific. On the sixty-fifth day after Sophie's death he writes in the Diary: "I must not start to reason closely about my resolve. Every argument based on reason, every illusive promise of my heart would be doubt, irresolution, and infidelity." Then he begins to find reasons *why* he should die: "My death shall be a proof of my feeling for the sublime; genuine sacrifice—not a refuge, not an expedient." Later he says, "I have once more affirmed my resolve," or, "My resolve has been quite firm. Only I still reason about it now and then."

The strange thing is that in the midst of these continual affirmations of his will to die, he gets worried about the state of his health, and even records in the same entry that he took a purgative in the morning and his resolve gained in strength in the evening. And just as he continually asserts his intention to die, so there is hardly an entry which does not record his obsession with the image of Sophie. He goes out to her grave, visualises her sitting in a characteristic attitude on the couch, or speaks about her with much emotion to her former French governess. He keeps close watch on himself to make sure that he remembers her every day. Novalis *wanted* to grieve for Sophie, and the question is, did he love the dead girl or did he love his grief? Like everyone else, he had a vision, somewhat vague and undetermined, of an ideal love-object. This dream is generally incapable of realisation, because the longing is not sufficiently concrete to receive concrete satisfaction: what *is* found, however, is a focussing-point, more or less temporary, consisting of a central figure in a veil of illusion, and towards this the longing is directed. It is only in the surrounding illusion that the spiritual part of desire finds gratification, though the physical element finds satisfaction in the actual love-object. When, however, the spiritual longing penetrates and disperses the illusory veil, it does not find satisfaction in the love-object, the longing is deflected, and the outward and visible sign is that the lover's ardour cools. If the love-object is unattainable, as in the case of *Werther*, then the illusion is never dispersed, and there are occasions when the lover sees no other way out than to commit suicide, since his spiritual condition is such that he cannot live without the object of his longing. In the case of Novalis, the matter is very different. Sophie was a child, and he was able to weave illusions round her which were not disturbed, since she never grew up, and it is easy to idealise a young girl.

In her lack of personality there was full scope for the imagination and sentimental dreaming. She was, it is true, sufficiently winsome to captivate Novalis' father and brother. She also interested Goethe, but as Goethe's taste in women was somewhat catholic, we may not deduce too much from this fact. It is obvious, however, that she was not able to enter into Novalis' spiritual world, as she did not care for poetry, and it is significant that his love reawakened when she fell ill. Novalis had a powerful impulse to idealise, and by her early death she was in his eyes transfigured. Henceforth his love for her became his religion. It will be remembered that it was by the death of his first wife that the mind of Novalis' father had been turned towards religion. Illness and death had a fascination for Novalis. He says that he saw in illness new possibilities of introspection and an opportunity to observe the soul. In his *Fragments* he declares that "Illness belongs to the human pleasures, like death." Grief should really be the natural state: it is joy that should be looked upon as the undesirable condition, and he carries the joy of grief a step farther even than the sentimental poets of the Göttinger Hain, for example, in consciously employing it to intensify his erotic emotion. He says in his Diary: "Whoever flees from grief no longer desires to love. The lover must always feel the deficiency, must always keep the wound open. May God ever preserve for me this indescribably dear grief, the melancholy memory, this spirited longing." He looks upon illness as perhaps the necessary beginning for an ardent union of two beings, as the indispensable basis of love. Whereas, when Sophie was alive, his power of imagination and his day-dreams constituted a danger to their love, when she was dead these served to strengthen the bond between them by intensifying his longing for her into a religion. He says himself, "What I feel for Sophie is religion—not love." The basis of religion and love is the same—a yearning which must eventually be centred on something or somebody. The early pietistic upbringing of Novalis left an imprint on his whole subsequent life, and he developed the power of picturing to himself an invisible world, of living in his imagination and evoking spiritual images under the influence of an exalted emotion. From early childhood he possessed the faculty of superimposing a busy imaginative activity on his ordinary practical life. In the case of complete introversion, the imagination is entirely divorced from reality, and if the introvert is indifferent to his environment, he is able to find happiness by yielding himself to his world of dreams. This type of introversion is hardly met with in German literature, though it is known in Russia as "Oblomovism," after the novel *Oblomov*, by Ivan Goncharov. One usually finds in German literature that the dreamer expects the world to conform to his dreams, and Goethe's *Werther* and *Tasso*, the poet Lenz, K. P. Moritz, and many other characters, both actual and fictitious, of the last third of the eighteenth century, are sufficiently frightful examples of what may happen when there is sudden and violent contact with reality. There were two great writers of the time who were able to keep their two worlds separate, to revel in their fantastic and often morbid visions without impairing the faculty for enjoying the material pleasures of physical existence. They were Jean Paul and Novalis. Though Jean Paul's psychic adaptation to reality remained incomplete, a spiritual condition to which he gave expression in his novels, he nevertheless did not demand from life what life could not give him, but contented himself with the limited satisfaction that reality had to offer.

Novalis really led a dual existence. After his death there grew up around him the tradition, which was fostered by the Romanticists, of the ethereal being, more seraph than man, who was too innocent to live and so was taken by the Gods. As a matter of fact, Novalis was a very efficient and conscientious official, with a healthy capacity for work, not a man of letters only, and this was an important factor in an age when poets were inclined to mental instability. He possessed a vividly sensual imagination, which was, no doubt, heightened by the dreams of longing whose possibility of realisation was prevented when Sophie died, and his erotic impulses are described quite candidly in the Diary he commenced after her death. For example: "My fantasy was a little lascivious, but nevertheless I felt fairly well"; "Felt lascivious from early in the morning till the afternoon"; "Very lascivious"; "Carried lasciviousness a bit too far"; "Yielded entirely to lasciviousness," and so on. There is hardly a page where he does not employ the word *Lüsternheit*. To judge also from the frequency with which he recorded the fact that he had had too much to eat, he was no doubt fond of the pleasures of the table. On the thirty-fourth day after Sophie's death he notes: "Early this morning sensual phantasies. Then fairly philosophical. . . . I have thought often of Sophie—but not with fervour. . . . I again had too much to eat to-day."

In this love for a young girl there was more of imagination

than physical desire, and thus during her illness, and still more after her death, the partition between love and religion became more and more shadowy, until eventually, as we shall see, he came to identify her with the Virgin Mary and to worship her with an erotico-mystical exaltation. Even in the Diary he puts down the phrase "Christ and Sophie." The connection between eroticism and religion, which is rooted in the most primitive instincts, comes to the surface in this love for a dead girl. The death of Sophie brought these unconscious instincts, so to speak, into Novalis' consciousness, though, of course, he himself did not recognise the significance of the identification.

The immediate literary result of the mood which was engendered by Sophie's death was the *Hymnen an die Nacht*, which may have been slightly influenced by Edward Young's *Night Thoughts*, a book that had a great influence on German literature in the eighteenth century, and which Novalis had been reading about this time. It is in these *Hymns to the Night* that Novalis depicts the successful consummation of his *Zielgedanke*, of his resolve to die. He found in his imagination a substitute for the failure to carry out his resolve in reality, and the *Hymns to the Night* are the literary expression of this substitute-fantasy.

There are six Hymns altogether, of which we need only deal with the first four, and the first one commences with the praise of Light, whose mild omnipresence reveals to men the wondrous splendour of the world. The poet then turns aside to the sacred, inexpressible, mysterious Night. The world lies far away, and in his breast is a deep melancholy. Distant memories, youthful desires, childhood's dreams, vain hopes and the short joys of all our long life hover around him like the grey evening mist when the sun has set. He laments the absence of Light. Then suddenly a presentiment stirs within him and disperses his sadness. Night also has favours to distribute—delicious balsam and the poppy seed. The poet is moved by a vague and inexpressible emotion, and the face of Sophie looks down upon him. He now despises the Light and blesses the departure of the Day. With the eyes which Night opens in us we are enabled to see into infinity. They can see farther than the stars, and they can look without the aid of Light into the depths of a loving heart. The poet then praises the Queen of the World, Night, the herald of sacred worlds within us, the guardian of blissful love, who has sent him his beloved. And he calls to his beloved: "Thou hast shown me that the night of death leads to eternal life. Consume my body with ghostly passion, that my union with thee may become more ardent and the bridal-night endure for ever."

The second Hymn opens with a lament that the morning must always return, that the secret sacrifice of love may not burn for ever. Light has a definite portion of time allotted to it, but the sway of Night knows neither time nor space. Sleep is eternal, and is to be found not merely in the darkness of *actual* night, but also in the golden juice of the grape, the miraculous oil of the almond-tree, and the brown juice of the poppy. It is Sleep which gives us the exaltation of the vine, the soothing balm of the oil, and the oblivion of the drug. It is Sleep which bears the keys to the Elysian Fields.

The third Hymn depicts the poet standing alone at the grave of Sophie, dissolved in grief and weeping bitter tears, hopeless and oppressed by unutterable fear. He looks around for help, unable to go either forward or backward, only clinging with infinite longing to his dead love, when suddenly the chain of Light, which binds him to the earth, snaps. The splendour of the earth disappears, and with it his grief; his sadness dissolves into a new, unfathomable world. The exaltation of Night, the slumber of Heaven comes over him, and his unchained, new-born Spirit floats up over the earth. The grave becomes a cloud of dust, through which he sees the transfigured features of his beloved. Eternity rests in her eyes, he seizes her hands, and their tears become a gleaming, indestructible tie between them. It was the first, unique dream, and it was only from then that he conceived an eternal immutable faith in the heaven of Night, and in his beloved, who was the moon of Night.

The poet now knows (fourth Hymn) when the last morning will be, when Light will cease to disperse Night and Love, when slumber will be everlasting and one inexhaustible dream. Whoever has stood at this grave, the boundary of this world, and gazed across into the domain of Night, will not desire to return to mundane turmoil. He will long and love until the most welcome of all hours, the hour of death, comes to draw him down again into the source of life. Light can still rouse the weary poet to the toils of the day, and inspire him with cheerful life, but it cannot tempt him from the mossy grave of memory. He will willingly carry out the duties ordained in this life, but his secret heart will remain faithful to the Night and to his beloved. The Light cannot give him the faithful heart, the pressure of the hand, the caressing word, and Life offers no pleasure which is not outweighed by the raptures of Death. Everything that exalts us bears the colour of Night. Night is the mother of Light, and it is to Night that the latter owes all its splendour. The day will come when Light will be extinguished for ever, and the poet feels that Light is ceasing to have any influence over him. Christ has shown that death is only the entry to real life, and has thus annihilated the resistance of Light to the ancient heaven of Night. The poet feels the rejuvenating flood of Death. By day he lives filled with courage and faith, by Night it is in the sacred ardour of Death that he is plunged.

We thus see how from the resolve to die there develops in Novalis an imaginative world, centring round the spirit of Sophie. Just as he declares he will do in the fourth Hymn, he carries out conscientiously the duties of his practical career. He is at home in two worlds, but the world which means most to him is the world of his dreams. He consciously and intentionally fosters this shadowy world of make-believe which is a compensation for reality. He expresses anew the ancient symbol of the conflict between Light and Darkness, but this time the victory is with Darkness, which is the home of the spirit. That is not to say that Novalis' conception is pessimistic. On the contrary, it is intensely optimistic. Though this life is vain and full of suffering, there is somewhere beyond a realm of Night, timeless and spaceless, of which the Night and Sleep of this ephemeral world are but dim shadows. It is for that immeasurable and eternal Night that Novalis feels his immense nostalgia; it is the great Mother, the *Urwelt*, the symbol of complete union; and in the centre of this Night is Sophie, his beloved, with whom he will celebrate an eternal bridal-night, with whom he will consummate the marriage that was denied him in this world. There is a strange connection between Love and Death. His longing for Sophie was at the same time a longing for Death. The different elements of eroticism and the death-cult which we saw in the Diary as definitely separate emotions have in the *Hymns to the Night* become fused into one emotion, or at least, if one may not psychologically refer to them as one emotion, they are so bound up with each other that they cannot be separated. The thought of death inspires in him an erotic emotion, and his love is at the same time a *Liebestod*, a love-death.

The third element in the mystic trinity of Novalis' fantasy is Religion. Religion, Death, and Love. The love for his dead bride becomes fused with the love for Christ, and the final *Hymn* concludes with the words "Let us descend to the sweet bride, to Jesus, the Beloved!" and as has already been mentioned, one of the notes in his Diary consists of the three words "Christ and Sophie." In the *Fragments* he says, "Love is thoroughly pathological: hence the wonderful significance of Christianity"; while a number of his *Spiritual Songs* afford further proof of the bond between the erotic and the religious emotions, and show how the one decisive event of his life fused in him love and religion.

The most considerable work of Novalis is the novel he wrote during the last two years of his life, and which he never lived to complete. Even if he had lived, it would probably have remained a fragment. *Heinrich von Ofterdingen* was to be the romantic counterpart of Goethe's *Wilhelm Meister*. As the hero of Goethe's novel gradually emerges from his world of dreams into the active stream of life, and comes through disillusionment more and more into touch with reality, so Novalis' hero is to start from an ordinary mundane existence to arrive eventually in a world of dreams. Goethe strikes the balance between the poet and the man of the world, but Novalis as a poet has no use for the world. He was at first an ardent admirer of *Wilhelm Meister*, which he read again and again with the utmost enthusiasm, since he regarded it as a portrayal of the æsthetic education of the idealist, but the more he studied the book, the more was he impressed by a tendency which inspired him with aversion. Goethe demonstrated the danger of that vague idealism which is lacking in thought and harmony, and in his novel Romanticism comes to grief. The Romanticists affected to despise the rational side of man's nature, while Goethe stands with feet firmly planted on the earth. Novalis therefore proposed to write an "apology for poetry," a novel where the hero should turn from the world of action to the world of poetry, instead of the opposite, as Wilhelm Meister had done. This attitude of Novalis towards *Wilhelm Meister* epitomises the attitude of the Romantic School towards Goethe. They were attracted by Meister, since he also was possessed by longing, but they looked upon his rejection of their vague idealism as a betrayal of poetry. Both Goethe and Novalis wrote *Bildungsromane*, but the education of Ofterdingen was towards a goal that Meister definitely rejected.

Novalis' novel is divided into two parts, of which the first is entitled *The Anticipation*. The youth Heinrich lies restlessly on his couch, thinking of a strange visitor who has related a story about a Blue Flower. He falls asleep and dreams of this flower, but is awakened suddenly by his mother. His father tells him that "Träume sind Schäume" (dreams are bubbles), but it appears that he also had once had a dream about a mysterious flower, without, however, pursuing the matter any farther. Heinrich is to prove that dreams have a significance after all.

The greater part of the first book is taken up by a journey which Heinrich makes with his mother in company with a band of merchants to the city of Augsburg. On the way he has various adventures, including a meeting with a captive Eastern girl, and with a hermit named the Count of Hohenzollern, who shows him a book where he sees pictured himself and incidents of his past life. He sees his parents and his friends, and even the Eastern girl, but they wear different clothes and they seem to belong to another epoch. A large number of figures seem familiar to him, but yet he cannot say who they are. Then he sees his own future, among other pictures one of himself with a guitar on his arm being presented with a laurel-wreath. The end of this mysterious book is missing. At last the company arrives in Augsburg, at the house of old Schwaning, Heinrich's grandfather, and here, during a feast, Heinrich meets and falls immediately in love with Mathilde, the daughter of the poet Klingsohr, for whom Novalis evidently took Goethe as his model. The praise of poetry runs like a thread throughout the story. It is the *Leitmotiv*, and the first book concludes with the relation by Klingsohr of a fairy-tale, which prophesies the return of a Golden Age through the instrumentality of Poetry.

The second part of *Heinrich von Ofterdingen* is called *The Fulfilment*, and the world of reality disappears more and more, to give place to the supernatural. Mathilde has been drowned in some unexplained way, and Heinrich is in despair. He meets a young girl, Cyane, who says she is the daughter of the Count of Hohenzollern, and that she is sent to him by the Virgin Mary. She leads him to an old man, the physician Sylvester, and the story breaks off abruptly in the midst of a conversation between the two men. The poet

Tieck has endeavoured to give an idea of the continuation of the story from conversations with Novalis, and from the latter's papers. It appears that Sylvester is the same old man who had entertained Novalis' father when the latter dreamed of the Blue Flower. Cyane is the daughter of the Count of Hohenzollern, had lost her brother at an early age, and had herself been saved in some strange way from death. She tells Heinrich his own story, as though she had once heard it from her mother. She sends him to a monastery inhabited by dead monks, and after living with these for a time, he suddenly finds himself in Italy, which is now split by internal wars. He takes part in these wars, but is later thrown by a tempest on the shores of Greece, where his mind is filled with the treasures of antiquity. He then visits the Orient, and finally returns, sated with experience, to Germany, where he makes the personal acquaintance of the Emperor Frederick II, and becomes a great Minnesänger. Thus, in a new and larger way than in the first book, he experiences life and death, war, the Orient, history and poetry, and then turns back into the world of the spirit. After discussing with Klingsohr strange tokens and presentiments, he arrives in an allegorical world, a world out of time and space. He hears somebody singing an old song, describing a deep pool in some secret place. There awake in him long-forgotten memories, he goes to the pool and finds a golden key, which a raven had once stolen from him, and which he had never been able to find again. It had been given him shortly after Mathilde's death by an old man, who had told him to take it to the Emperor, and that the latter would tell him what to do with it. This Heinrich does, and the Emperor shows him an old document, which says that the man who brought the key would find in a hidden spot an old talismanic jewel, a carbuncle belonging to the crown, in which the empty space was still unfilled. On the way to find this jewel, Heinrich meets the old man who had first told him and his parents about the Blue Flower. He goes into the mountains, and is followed by Cyane. Soon he comes to a wonderful country, in which air, water, birds, and animals are of a quite different nature from those in this world. The fairy world becomes visible, the real world is looked upon as a fairy-tale. He finds the Blue Flower, and it is Mathilde, who is asleep and holds the carbuncle. A little girl, the child of Mathilde and Heinrich, is sitting by a coffin, and through her he becomes rejuvenated. This child is the *Urwelt*, the Golden Age which is to come at the end. Heinrich plucks the Blue Flower and releases Mathilde from her enchantment, but he loses her again and becomes literally petrified with grief. After further adventures he again meets Mathilde, and becomes monarch in a kingdom where the seasons are united and the sun never sets.

The strangest thing about the story is the way in which various characters are identified with each other. Mathilde is also Cyane and the Eastern girl, and also the Blue Flower. Klingsohr appears again as the King of Atlantis. Sylvester is, among other incorporations, the Count of Hohenzollern, and probably also Heinrich's father. And in a similar way, all the experiences which existed in the first book merely in the boy's imagination as presentiments occur again, and are realised as actualities, in the second part, in *The Fulfilment*. The past, the present and the future are bound up together. At the beginning of the second book Heinrich had gone out into the world as a pilgrim after the death of Mathilde, and in a new love he found again the old one, for Cyane was also Mathilde. Novalis had early occupied himself with the question of the transmigration of souls, and it is possible that he regarded these different incarnations of the same spirit in that light. The development of Heinrich von Ofterdingen is a symbolical representation of Novalis' own development, and demonstrates the importance of love and poetry for the re-creation of the Golden Age. As in the *Hymns to the Night*, the fulfilment is to be an eternal celebration of love. The characterisation of Mathilde is perfectly colourless, and she does not give us any clue to the character of Sophie von Kühn, but, just as in Novalis' own life, it is the death of this girl that starts Heinrich on his poetic career, and, as in the case of Sophie, the idea of the dead Mathilde becomes fused with the idea of the Madonna.

After the death of Mathilde, Heinrich hears her voice bidding him take the girl (Cyane) who will come to him, as she will be a consolation while he still remains on earth. Novalis appears here to express the conviction that there was no contradiction between his eternal love for Sophie and his attachment to another woman, Julie von Charpentier, for, strange to say, Novalis had again become engaged only eighteen months or so after the death of Sophie. It is hardly possible that he regarded the spirit of Sophie as having migrated into Julie, since the latter was the older of the two, and the question would have arisen as to whose soul was occupying Julie before Sophie died, though the category of time may not hold good for the spirit-world. To judge by this passage in *Heinrich von Ofterdingen*, Novalis might have looked upon her as a substitute during his mundane existence, but it is quite likely, since it was rather a symbol that he was in love with and not Sophie herself, that he to some extent identified her with Julie, finding in both the common element of *das Ewig-Weibliche*. Not that there is any permanent, absolute quality which can be designated as the "eternal feminine," any more than there is an "eternal masculine," but these qualities which each sex seeks in the other are symbols of the same thing— they are both aspects of the "Blue Flower." When Heinrich dreamed of the Blue Flower, he saw in it a woman's face, and when he at last found it, it was Mathilde. It is significant that when Novalis describes landscapes, he describes distant landscapes, and his motives are mostly distant themes, such as the Orient, Antiquity, the Golden Age, etc. The reason why distance lends enchantment to the view is that illusion is essential for dreams, and the Blue Flower can never be found; it is only to be sought.

There is no doubt that in *Heinrich von Ofterdingen* Novalis attempted to solve the problem of reconciliation between

his fidelity to Sophie and his attachment to Julie. His solution was that in this world of reality, which was for Novalis
only the dream-world, they appeared as two separate individuals; in the next world, which was for Novalis the real
world, the world of fulfilment, they would be one and the
same. It is an open question whether Novalis was more or
less intentionally and successfully deceiving himself, or
whether he really had arrived at the mystic conclusion that
Sophie and Julie were but corporeal aspects of the same
being. It is significant, in connection with what has already
been said on the subject, that it was only when Julie fell
ill that the idea occurred to him, as he says, to dedicate
his life to her. He must have identified her to some extent
with Sophie.

There is little more to relate. In August 1800 Novalis was
promoted to a post which enabled him to look forward to
an early marriage with Julie, but his hopes of domestic
happiness were no more to be fulfilled this time than they
were before. As Maeterlinck says in his introduction to one
of Novalis' works: "Quand nous sentons trop vivement notre
bonheur, c'est qu'il nous frappe en passant sur l'épaule pour
nous faire ses adieux." He had betrayed symptoms of consumption five years before, and Sophie's death had helped to
accelerate the progress of the disease. His condition now
became steadily worse, and on the 25th March, 1801, in
the twenty-ninth year of his age, he died. His life, like his
work, remained a fragment, and another was added to the
long list of German poets who were cut off before they could
fulfil the promise of their youth. He was the prophet and
genius of the Romantic movement, and he did not live to
see its decay. Practically the whole of his literary work falls
within the last three years of his life, and when one considers the contrasts that appear so vividly even within that
small compass, it is impossible to say with what riches he
might not have endowed German literature. A man who
could frame for himself such a vivid inner psychic world

and yet not lose his grip on reality, who could "dream and not make dreams his master," might have been a creative influence in an age when the old world was falling to pieces and the new epoch had not yet arrived. Many dreams were being shattered, and the way was being prepared for the age of philosophic Pessimism, but as yet there was no systematisation of Weltschmerz into a philosophy. It was because they were unable to express concretely what they only felt vaguely, to give plastic representation to the super-sensuous, that so much of the work of the Romanticists remained fragmentary. It is fruitless to enquire how far the germs of consumption, which was no doubt inherited, affected Novalis' mental attitude towards life and its problems. As Heine says, the rosy hue in the writings of Novalis is not the hue of health, but perhaps it is true that illness provides new opportunities to observe the soul. There are mental and spiritual characteristics which appear with greater prominence in the sick than in the healthy, and it is in Novalis, its most problematical figure, that the psychology of the Romantic movement can best be studied.

EXPRESSIONISM IN GERMAN LITERATURE

WHEN in the 'eighties of the nineteenth century it became evident that the older writers had shirked the realities of life and drawn over them a veil which gave to ugliness the illusion of beauty, there was a revolt of the younger generation, and modern German literature may be said to have begun. A new theory of Naturalism sprang from sources which have since done more than anything else to change the trend of European thought—the then recent discoveries in the field of science, more especially the theory of Evolution, and the ideas of the early political, socialist writers such as Marx and Lassalle. In addition, there was the cumulative effect of the new tendencies in French, Scandinavian and Russian literature. The new generation was imbued with the conviction that literature may not dispense with the depiction of life as it is, but, as so frequently in Germany, theory preponderated over practice. In the bustle of activity necessary for the discussion and settlement of weighty questions of style and the relations between science, life and art, with the consequent important business of setting up programmes and laying down rules, they had little inspiration left for creating works of art in consonance with their theories.

The relations between literature and social revolution have always been close. The Storm and Stress of the eighteenth century was really a social struggle fought on the bloodless field of literature, and throughout the nineteenth century there were reflections in literature of discontent with the structure of society. To mention but one of these, Hauptmann's early drama *Die Weber* was particularly appreciated after the Revolution of 1918, and since the Naturalist generation the connection in Germany has come more and more in evidence, until in recent years there has been a tendency to mistake the political manifesto for a form of drama.

In attempting to survey the general tendencies in contemporary German literature, it becomes more and more obvious that the aspect which must be emphasised is literature in its attitude to the accepted forms of society.

Naturalism never had undisputed possession of the field, and the most important counter-influence was that of Stefan George and his circle, which, grouped in the early 'nineties round the periodical *Blätter für die Kunst*, cultivated formal artistry, art for art's sake, than which nothing could be more opposed to the view of the Naturalist writers that poetry must approximate as closely as possible to life. The precursors of George were the Pre-Raphaelites in England, and Baudelaire, Verlaine and Mallarmé in France. The pre-War currents in German literature between the two poles of Naturalism and the George circle are too numerous to be explained shortly without recourse to artificial groupings, and it is only possible to mention by name those older writers whose influence has survived the War and the younger ones who before 1914 were beginning to show promise.

In the half-dozen years which preceded the War there was a perceptible calmness in literature. Among those whose reputations were already made, and have since endured, were Hauptmann and Wedekind in the field of drama, Dehmel, George and Rilke in poetry, Thomas Mann and Jakob Wassermann in fiction. Schnitzler and von Hofmannsthal, different yet alike as they are, were the most celebrated of the Viennese writers who had achieved an international reputation. The bubbling of ideas had considerably abated, and literature pursued an even course, troubled only by occasional stirrings of uneasiness at the materialistic tendencies of civilisation and the subordination of spiritual to economic values. The turbulent blood of the writers who had been the hotheads at the turn of the century had now cooled, and the younger generation had not yet found its feet. Hauptmann and Sudermann were still spoken of in one breath, but Hauptmann's post-War writings have done nothing to increase his reputation, while Sudermann, as a dramatist, is now regarded as little more than a master of stage technique.

There were poets at that time who seemed to have an inkling of the coming cataclysm, which is foreshadowed, for example, in the fine poem "Umbra Vitæ" of Georg Heym, who was drowned at the age of twenty-four in 1912 :—

> "Die Menschen stehen vorwärts in den Strassen
> Und sehen auf die grossen Himmelszeichen,
> Wo die Kometen mit den Feuernasen
> Um die gezackten Türme drohend schleichen."

The humanity and fellow-sympathy for the rest of creation, which was later to be so strikingly demonstrated in German literature, is already seen in the poetry of Franz Werfel, the most considerable of the younger poets of to-day. This humanity, coupled with a devout searching for God, is expressed in a poem which he published in 1913 at the age of twenty-three :—

> "O Herr, zerreisse mich!
> Was soll das dumpfe, klägliche Geniessen?
> Ich bin nicht wert, dass Deine Wunden fliessen.
> Begnade mich mit Martern, Stich um Stich!
> Ich will den Tod der ganzen Welt einschliessen.
> O Herr, zerreisse mich!"

There is something of the humility, the mystic pantheism and yet the consciousness of his own individuality that we find in an older Austrian poet who came from the same town of Prague, Rainer Maria Rilke.

In 1913, the year of the centenary celebration of the War of Liberation from the yoke of Napoleon, and the twenty-fifth year of the Kaiser's reign, Gerhart Hauptmann received a commission to produce a *Festspiel*, to be staged by Reinhardt, and he wrote a play which lauded the spirit of Peace instead of hymning the patriotic fervour of 1813. There was much objection to the play, and a protest from the Crown Prince led to its withdrawal. A year later came the War, and, in common with the writers of all the other belligerent countries, those of Germany felt the thrill of patriotism which inspired them to outpourings of the most ephemeral and flatulent type. The poetic resources of the country were, so to speak, adapted to war-work. It has been estimated that the number of patriotic poems published in Germany in the first year of the War amounted to a million and a half. There is no reason to suspect that many of them possessed higher worth or dignity than the majority of those which were produced simultaneously in this country. They could not have possessed less. It is a question whether the verse of this period even reached the level of mediocrity attained by the war poetry of 1870. As in England, where older poets descended to the writing of such pathetic stuff as showed them to be entirely out of touch with the soul and attitude of the men in the trenches, so in Germany the older writers tried their hand at verses which would have suited admirably the bellicose spirit of the wars of a hundred years ago. They were completely foreign to the mentality of the citizen soldier, who realised that the men in the trenches opposite were also human beings, and had little use for the bombastic claptrap produced amid the artificially created atmosphere at home. It is significant that the real soldiers' song was a quaint sentimental medley based on Uhland's famous Volkslied, "Ich hatt' einen Kameraden," which is supposed to have originated before the War and been spread by the Wandervögel; it concludes with the lines:—

> "Die Vöglein im Walde,
> Sie sangen all so wunder-wunderschön,
> In der Heimat, in der Heimat,
> Da gibt's ein Wiedersehn."

In this song there is no more of the jingoism of the truculent old gentlemen at the *Stammtisch* than there was in "Tipperary," and the best of the War poetry is in the same Volkslied tradition.

The literature of the War can be divided into two phases,

of which the second began in 1917, or slightly earlier. Even in 1914 there were voices raised against war. The group of writers whose mouthpiece was the periodical *Die Aktion*, founded in 1911 and edited by Franz Pfemfert, took their stand against the War from the beginning. A second important Expressionist periodical, of a more abstract tendency, was *Der Sturm*, founded in 1910 and edited by Herwarth Walden.

When we come to deal with the second phase, which began with weariness and culminated in despair, it must be borne in mind that whereas in England we speak of "the War" and its effect on the mentality of the younger generation, the Germans speak about "the War and the Revolution," and the difference is vital. The effect of a lost war *and* a revolution was catastrophic. There was in England no upheaval of the national soul as there was in Germany, an upheaval which explains the ecstatic, mystic, even apocalyptic nature of much of the literature produced between 1917 and 1921, the period of chaos.

There was, of course, a very strict censorship, which was afterwards abolished by the Revolution, but the first literary signs of the change of mentality came from the poets at the front, mainly from those of *Die Aktion*, which had been the chief exponent of political poetry, but had been compelled by the outbreak of war to eliminate the political element. After the War it became for a time the literary mouthpiece of the Spartakist movement. One of the most violent of those who raged against the War and its horrors, and at the same time heralded a fraternity which should embrace the world, was the poet Johannes R. Becher.

The new literature appeared under the banner of Expressionism, which, though by no means a new art form, only became popular with the change of spirit about 1917, and reached its climax during the Revolution period. By 1921 it was practically dead. The name "Expressionism" came from the sister art of painting, and was used in the first place to denote the opposite of Impressionism. As

Kasimir Edschmid, one of the leaders of the movement, explains:—

"The world is there. It would be absurd to reproduce it. The greatest task of Art is to search out its intrinsic essence and create it anew."

Each object has its profounder aspect, which our eyes are too blinded by experience of its external qualities to see. Everything should be related to eternity. For example, a sick man is not only seen as an individual sufferer, but becomes the symbol of illness itself; his suffering is but a reflection of the suffering of the whole of creation, and when an artist wants to depict a sick man he must depict the very quality of sickness. A house is not seen as a mere construction of brick and mortar, an angular object with qualities of beauty or ugliness, as the case may be, but its actual nature is studied until its profounder aspect is revealed, until it is freed from the restraint of reality and appears as an *expression* of its ultimate character, even if it thereby lose all resemblance to that which generally comes into our mind when we think of a house. Similarly, in Expressionistic art, a man ceases to be an individual, he becomes a concrete representation of the abstract conception *Man*. The work of art is the medium by means of which the spectator or reader is enabled to enter into the emotional mood in which the artist created it. Therefore, if the spectator looks only with his physical eye, he may see things which appear to him absurd or grotesque. The Impressionists tried to reproduce the variety of life, and give an optical impression which was momentary. The Expressionists sought to visualise the eternal, and abstained from painting pictures of the external world of appearances.

This art is really an attempt to escape from the ugliness and suffering of life by diving beneath the surface, which appears shifting and worthless, in order to find the true basis of the cosmos and something fixed and essential to grasp. The War fostered this tendency, but there is something very similar in Greek philosophy in the theory of Platonic ideas.

In poetry and drama writers tried to obtain their effects primarily by concentration, and to this end they laid violent hands on the language. Articles, prepositions, grammatical inflections and prefixes were regarded as unnecessary and could be omitted. Substantives could be used to form new and unusual verbs, or verbs to form new substantives. The natural consequence was that each poet tried to create his own language, and since Expressionist drama or poetry is not in any case easy to understand, confusion became worse confounded. The tendency to reduce verbal expression to its most primitive form reached its *reductio ad absurdum* in the revolt against intellectualism known as the Dada movement. As one Dadaist poet has said: "We write without taking into account the meaning of words!"

An example of abbreviation and concentration is given by one of the theoreticians of the Expressionist movement. The phrase "Die Bäume und die Blumen blühen" can be abbreviated to "Bäume und Blumen blühen." This can further be concentrated to "Baum und Blume blüht," and still more to "Baum blüht Blume," till eventually the utmost concentration is attained in the single word "Blüte," which represents the complex idea of both tree and flower in blossom.

The most celebrated of the anthologies of Expressionist poetry is called *Menschheitsdämmerung*, a title which expresses both the realisation of the twilight of the world which is at the turn and the hope of a new dawn for humanity. The anthology is divided into four sections, headed respectively "Sturz und Schrei," "Erweckung des Herzens," "Aufruf und Empörung," "Liebe den Menschen," titles which explain themselves. It contains not only the work of many of the most celebrated poets of the new school, but also some extraordinarily convulsive efforts.

The following is an example, by no means extreme, of the

abstract poetry fostered by the periodical *Der Sturm*. It is by August Stramm, who fell on the Russian front in 1915, and is called "Schwermut" :—

> " Schreiten Streben
> Leben sehnt
> Schauen Stehen
> Blicke suchen
> Sterben wächst
> Das Kommen
> Schreit!
> Tief
> Stummen
> Wir."

The poet is obviously striving for ultimate concentration and simplicity, using hardly any punctuation except exclamation marks, and we can understand why this particular poem appears in the section "Sturz und Schrei." Stramm is the classic example for this obscure, staccato, stammering kind of verse, to which we cannot attribute much importance, for it is difficult to believe that the emotions or thoughts of these poets were too profound or complicated for expression by the various ordinary media of poetry.

There were poets innumerable, but in addition to those who have already been mentioned, or who will be mentioned later, it will suffice to note the group of labourer poets, some of whom achieved considerable celebrity, such as Karl Bröger, Gerrit Engelke, Max Barthel and Heinrich Lersch, the tinsmith, who wrote one of the most popular of the War poems with the refrain "Deutschland muss leben, und wenn wir sterben müssen."

The endeavour to be original at all costs was perhaps due to a self-consciousness which is characteristic of the majority of minor German poets. They possess too keen a realisation of their poetic nature to be able to produce effortless poetry, or even the appearance of effortlessness. The reader has a continual, uneasy feeling that he is being present during the pangs of creation. In a recent anthology of living poets called *Saat und Ernte*, each poet was asked to choose those of his own poems which he desired to have included, and has prefixed in each case a short autobiographical sketch. To show what I mean by the self-consciousness of these poets, I will quote extracts from two of the autobiographies :—

". . . an old priestly race bequeathed to me an inclination for the next world. The fighting energy of my ancestors rests in the dreamy veins of their descendant. If these are the elements of my being, they are also the elements of my poetry."

And in another case, after a few words about his lyrical disposition, the poet continues in the following strain :—

"I early felt the superior force of my environment and the incompatibility of my personal, spiritual disposition with the mysterious and dangerous forces of existence."

These quotations are typical of the autobiographies. We may expect such an objective attitude to his own ego in a Goethe summing up at the end of a long life, but the effect is very different in a young poet at the outset of his career.

Thomas Mann is reported to have said in conversation that the young generation during the War was not revolutionary but loud. That is unjust; but the intense earnestness with which they took themselves would, in a less serious nation than the German, lead one to suspect the profundity of their feelings. It is to be explained by the fact that whereas the older generation looked upon the War as an incident in history, the younger generation regarded it as a definite turning-point in civilisation. Their humanitarianism was large; they no longer took for their themes their merely personal emotions and sufferings. Their sympathy was cosmic, and their compassion covered the whole of humanity. That is why their dramatic characters were types, but they were inclined to mistake reformatory enthusiasm, religious fervour, and even political rhetoric for poetry; to consider tempestuous emotion and obsession by ideas a surrogate for a sense of form or beauty.

The fact that characters appear mostly as types, coupled with a strong tendency to allegory, is perhaps the most striking feature of Expressionist plays. Walter Hasenclever, in his drama, *Der Sohn*, one of the pre-War Expressionist dramas, treats the father-son conflict, which appears again and again in the dramatic literature of this period, and is, of course, of fundamental importance in psycho-analysis, as typical of the father-son conflict which appears anew in every generation. The father represents the principle of authority, against which the son, the symbol of the repressed section of humanity with its urge for liberty, rebels. Parental love is regarded as selfishness. These young men wanted themselves to be a beginning, and not heirs to the past, with which they wanted to break more completely than any previous generation had wished to do. It is extraordinary how frequently we find the death-wish against the father in the works of this period. As a contrast we sometimes see the attempt to weave a new myth round the mother, as in Fritz von Unruh's drama, *Ein Geschlecht*. The same attitude towards the father appears in Franz Werfel's *Spiegelmensch*, Arnolt Bronnen's *Vatermord*, Ernst Toller's *Die Wandlung*, Georg Kaiser's *Die Koralle*, Anton Wildgans's *Dies Iræ*.

Characters are often given mere type-distinctions, as in *Ein Geschlecht*, where the characters are The Mother, The Eldest Son, The Cowardly Son, The Youngest Son, The Daughter and a Leader of the Soldiers. Reinhard Sorge's *Bettler*, which is the earliest of the Expressionist dramas, having been written in 1910, introduces typical groups such as Newspaper Readers, Prostitutes and Aviators, who speak in chorus. Allegorical characters appear in various forms— as a Stranger representing Death in Wildgans's *Armut*, as a Friend representing Rebellion against parental authority in Hasenclever's *Sohn*—but this is not particularly novel. In von Unruh's non-Expressionist play, *Offiziere*, there appears a strange officer among the other officers on board ship who are on their way to fight in South-West Africa, and he represents Death, while as long ago as 1891 Wedekind had introduced a "Vermummter Herr," as a representation of the life impulse, into the last scene of *Frühlings Erwachen*.

The endeavour to create types instead of individuals results often in the creation of a false psychology. Actions do not follow logically from character and environment, and the characters are not drawn in their natural *milieu*, since they are abstract and not dependent, as real people would be, on fortuitous conditions of place and time. Actual scenes alternate with dream scenes, and instead of a dramatic representation we get a lyrical one. The new art, in fact, found its best expression in the lyric, and between 1910 and 1920 it was the lyrical mood which predominated in literature, even the drama being pervaded with lyricism. The dramatists, in their convulsive search for a new style, often employ an extreme conciseness of phraseology, and their characters speak in jerky sentences which at times remind one forcibly of Mr. Alfred Jingle in *The Pickwick Papers*. The tendency to exaggerated concentration gave rise to a whole group of what are known as *Schreidramen*, where the characters speak either in monosyllables or in incoherent screams. Sometimes the stage directions occupy more space than the text, and here there can, perhaps, be traced the influence of Mr. Bernard Shaw, who in Germany is classed with Shakespeare and Oscar Wilde as one of our three great dramatists.

The logical outcome of Expressionist drama, if it had not died an early death, would have been its approximation to the film, for which the frequent change of scene, the gradual elimination of language in favour of action, the complicated lighting and the alternation of reality with dream scenes seem peculiarly to qualify it. In Hasenclever's *Sohn*, everything that happens is supposed to be seen from the standpoint of the son himself, as in the film *Dr. Caligari* everything is seen through the eyes of a madman, and the whole action and scenery given the requisite twist.

The majority of Expressionist writers were socialists, and the object of their contempt and hostility was the bourgeois, the representative of the existing order, who was regarded as the upholder of an effete economic and ethical system. Frank Wedekind, who with Strindberg was one of the chief founts from which Expressionist drama drew its inspiration, had already done pioneer work in the pillorying of the bourgeois, and the two outstanding satirists of the day, who never tired of holding up the bourgeois, his views and foibles, to ridicule, were Heinrich Mann the novelist and Carl Sternheim the writer of comedies. Heinrich Mann is celebrated for the trilogy of novels in which he mercilessly lashes German society in the reign of William II, *Der Untertan*, *Die Armen* and *Der Kopf*. *Der Untertan* was first published in 1918, having been prohibited by the censor four years earlier. Mann traces the decadence of the ruling classes in Wilhelmine Germany to the instinct of servility, of deference to the man above. Sternheim has turned out comedy after comedy burlesquing the hypocrisy and other failings of the bourgeois, but his method is purely destructive, and his satire entirely intellectual. The extreme revolutionary attitude was represented by Johannes R. Becher, who appeared to confuse the mission of the poet with that of the political orator and leader of the proletariat. The capitalist, as a stockbroker or banker, appears in grotesque guise in Kaiser's *Von Morgens bis Mitternachts* and in Toller's *Masse Mensch*. In Kaiser's *Die Koralle* both the son and daughter of the milliardaire are socialists. Among the poets who actually took part in the Revolution it is only necessary to mention Kurt Eisner and Ernst Toller, the former of whom was assassinated, while the latter spent five years in prison for his part in the Communist outbreak in Munich.

A striking feature in this rejection of modern civilisation was hostility to the large town. The developing sense of realism in German literature during the nineteenth century, which culminated in the Naturalist movement, had hitherto paid admiring tribute to the mechanical forces invented by man to overcome his natural limitations. Now there came a change of attitude. Mechanical forces came to be regarded as the means by which the workers are kept in subjection in gloomy, smoky towns, where they are unable to obtain a glimpse of green fields or even of the sun. The poets who had sung hymns in praise of machines now switched over to the opposite extreme. The voracious appetite of the towns which destroy everything green and smiling and swallow up the creatures of the countryside, human and animal, is expressed most powerfully by Armin T. Wegner. He sees a vision of towns which reach to the sky and spread over the face of the earth in one vast, endless town :—

> "Euch Ebenen, die in das Endlose führen,
> Alle verschlingt unserer Mauern zermalmender Mund.
> Bis wir zum Saume der Meere uns strecken,
> Nie sind wir müde, wir werden nie satt,
> Bis wir zum Haupte der Berge uns recken
> Und die weite, keimende Erde bedecken :
> Eine ewige, eine unendliche Stadt !"

Bound up with this nostalgia for simple forms of existence were disappointment and disillusion at the result of the Revolution, I will not say of the War. The majority of the Expressionist poets were highly, if vaguely, idealistic and opposed to the materialism of the age. The abuses against which they had protested disappeared apparently with the Revolution, but too much of the old mentality still remained with those in authority, and the hopes of the young men, who saw the same old world rising like a phœnix from its own ashes, were scattered to dust. A reflection of this disillusionment is to be seen in many of the revolutionary dramas written about the year 1920, in which a character is acclaimed by the masses as a leader, only to be rejected by them since they are incapable of sympathising with his high ideals; he is martyred by the very people he sought to save. Johannes R. Becher had already warned the poets that the masses would swirl over their heads and that they would be the first to be crucified. It may not be out of place in connection with this atmosphere of pessimism to note that the first volume of Spengler's *Untergang des Abendlands* has now passed its hundredth edition and the second volume its ninetieth. Although the title of this book was originally intended as a protest against the optimism of the pre-War mentality, it was seized upon as a catchword after the collapse, when the view was eagerly welcomed that the cultural possibilities of the Western world were exhausted.

It is tempting to draw a parallel with the eighteenth-century Storm and Stress movement, and one thinks involuntarily of Karl Moor's outburst against his ink-spilling century. In the eighteenth century literature provided a substitute for political activity; in the twentieth century literature preceded revolution. The Storm and Stress movement lacked the all-embracing compassion of the twentieth-century writers. But the most striking difference between the Expressionist movement and all that had gone before was in the attitude to women. Love no longer played the dominant rôle. The relations between man and woman appeared intellectual rather than emotional. Perhaps nothing showed the gulf between Gerhart Hauptmann and the younger generation more than the former's satiric idyll, *Die Insel der Grossen Mutter*. Schnitzler continued to produce psychological and erotic studies of neurotic characters. Stefan George stood at the opposite extreme, and his school appeared to be more interested in the friendship of man for man. There was even an apparent lack of sympathy among the Expressionists for the important place given to women by Goethe; and they were, of course, even farther out of touch with the smouldering passion of Dehmel. An exception must be made in the case of Fritz von Unruh, in whose work the relation of man and woman was of primary importance. When the sexual element appeared in

Expressionistic work, it was generally in the form of abnormality.

The ideas germinating in the minds of writers at this time can best be seen in four or five typical works. Reinhard Goering's drama, *Seeschlacht*, reproduces the spirit in the Navy which culminated in the mutiny of 1917 and the later revolt at Kiel; Fritz von Unruh's War-book, *Opfergang*, is a mirror of the coming change of mind in the Army; Clara Viebig's novel, *Töchter der Hekuba*, and its sequel, *Das Rote Meer*, where nearly all the characters are women, describe the terrible conditions at home, and Ernst Toller's *Hinkemann* shows something of the post-War conditions.

Seeschlacht contains seven characters, all sailors, and the scene of action is the armoured turret of a battleship which is steaming towards the Battle of Jutland. The drama reproduces the morbid atmosphere of expectation and the conflicting thoughts in the men's minds. The fifth sailor expresses the awakening sense of revolt against the idea of military duty, and this is perhaps the very first sign, in the works which the Censor allowed to be made public, of the coming collapse. But when the battle begins, the incipient mutineer is the bravest fighter. The crew of the turret is wiped out, and the dying words of the fifth sailor are:—

> "Ich habe gut geschossen, wie?
> Ich hätte auch gut gemeutert! Wie?
> Aber schiessen lag uns wohl näher? Wie?
> Muss uns wohl näher gelegen haben?"

When it came to the crisis, it was easier to fight than to mutiny, so the drama really ends on a question-mark.

Fritz von Unruh's *Opfergang* was written in the trenches before Verdun in 1916. It describes the preparation for and the actual attack of his company on the fortress; the change from hope to the realisation of failure, and the careless lack of understanding of the people at home when the soldier goes on leave. It crystallises the change in the mentality of von Unruh himself, a regular officer in the Prussian cavalry, whose earlier plays idealised the orthodox sense of duty in the German Army, but whose later works are ranked among the finest expressions of that pacific idealism which sprang from the War. *Opfergang* demonstrates the ultimate realisation of the tremendous sacrifices which were made for infinitesimal gain, or even for none at all. It is best compared with Henri Barbusse's *Le Feu*. The French novel is sober and realistic, even cynical; the German book is full of fire and emotion; together they give a better idea of what the War on the Western Front was like, both materially and spiritually, than anything else that was written during the War years in the field of imaginative literature.

The scene of Clara Viebig's novel, *Töchter der Hekuba*, is a suburb of Berlin, whence all the men have gone, and the author pictures the tragic combination of monotony and fear of what the day may bring for the women whose husbands, fathers and sons are at the War, with the accumulating misery of lengthening casualty lists and food queues; the sense of primitive reality gradually breaking through the old prepossessions and artificial barriers.

Toller's tragedy, *Hinkemann*, is supposed to take place about 1921. Hinkemann has returned from the War as a sexual cripple. The man who could not bear to see an animal hurt is compelled to earn a living by biting rats and mice to death at a fair to amuse the spectators. This cripple is presented to the audience with profound irony as the "incarnation of German strength." He is seen by his wife, who feels the deepest sympathy for her husband reawakening, but a man whom he had looked upon as his friend lies to him that she had laughed. In the street he sinks to the ground and people collect round him, but when military music is heard in the next street people rush to see the soldiers. On the way home he purchases a bronze statue of Priapus, who appears to him to be the god of the present age. His wife tries to bring about a reconciliation, but he no longer has either hope or the will to live. His wife throws herself out of the window. And when her body is brought in Hinkemann prepares a noose with which to commit suicide. "Warum . . . trifft es mich, gerade mich?" he asks. "Wahllos trifft es. . . . Was wissen wir? Woher? . . . Wohin?" It is the tragedy, intensified to the extreme limit, of the man returned from the War to find himself estranged from the rest of humanity.

When these works are considered as typical manifestations of the state of mind produced by the events of 1914 to 1923, they are as terrible an accumulation of documents as it would be possible to collect.

The most important dramatic work of this period is to be found in three trilogies by Fritz von Unruh, Franz Werfel, and Georg Kaiser respectively.

The literary career of von Unruh has been rather out of the ordinary. He sprang from an aristocratic family with a long tradition of service to the throne as high officials or army officers, and was, as has already been mentioned, an officer of Uhlans. When he was a cadet, eight years of age, he is said to have been put under arrest for referring to a sunset as "wunderschön," it being argued that expressions in use in girls' boarding-schools were not suitable in the mouth of a future officer. His two pre-War plays, *Offiziere* and *Louis Ferdinand*, were in the old tradition. The production of the latter was prohibited in 1913, but in the same year von Unruh was awarded the Kleist Prize. During the War the three works, *Vor der Entscheidung*, *Opfergang*, and *Ein Geschlecht*, were prohibited by Army General Headquarters. In 1920 von Unruh was nominated by Gerhart Hauptmann, as President of the Schiller Prize Committee, for the Schiller Prize, but the nomination was rejected by the Prussian Minister of Culture. In 1927 the Schiller Prize was divided between Hermann Burte, Fritz von Unruh, and Franz Werfel.

Von Unruh's conception of duty to the monarch, or to military superiors, which was the inspiration of the earlier plays, where it was shown in conflict with the personality of his characters, underwent a fundamental change. It became transformed into the conception of duty to one's fellow-men. The germ of the change is seen in the "dramatic poem" *Vor der Entscheidung*, written as early as the autumn of 1914, and in the trilogy von Unruh attempted to give dramatic form to his inward experience, with his hatred of war and his idea of the new era that was to come. Only the first two parts of the trilogy have so far appeared. The first part, written in the field in 1915 and 1916, is called *Ein Geschlecht*; the second part, finished in 1920, is called *Platz*. In the former the characters are all types; the mother who defends the existing order though she protests against war, the unbalanced daughter, the eldest son, imbued with the life-force and fretting against traditional restrictions, the cowardly son, and the youngest son, who is still immature. This family—the mother, the daughter, and the sons—is a microcosm of the human race.

The scene is at the entrance to a graveyard on the top of a mountain during a war. The whole scene takes place between night and morning. In the valley a battle is raging, while in the cemetery the mother is burying one of her four sons who has been killed in the fight. With her are her daughter and her youngest son. Her two other sons appear under the escort of soldiers. The eldest son has attempted to violate a woman, the cowardly son has refused to fight. They are tied to the cemetery gate, and the youngest son is taken away by the soldiers to be steeled in battle. Between the eldest son and the two women there is a violent scene. The son's nerves have been unstrung by the war, and he manifests a forbidden love towards his own sister, who reciprocates his desire and loosens his bonds. He reproaches their mother, their dead father, religion, law, everything which has hitherto been held sacred. He protests against the setting up of his father as an idol for him to worship, until he hurled the idol down and strode on over its ruins. He despises the mothers who say they wish they had more sons to sacrifice for the Fatherland. "I must go," he says, "where truth prevails, and falsehood no longer like a slug draws its slime over the purest of my impulses." The mother defends the existing order, but also apostrophises all mothers to mobilise against the madness of war. When the morning dawns, the eldest brother tears the cross from his brother's grave and then hurls himself from the wall to his death. Soldiers approach with news of victory; they pay homage to the dead soldiers in the cemetery, but prepare to drag away the corpse of the eldest son. The mother tries to prevent this, and tears his baton, the symbol of authority, from the hands of one of the officers. She announces the coming of a new generation that will make a more worthy use of the staff, and then is killed in a struggle. The soldiers revolt and, led by the youngest son, rush down into the valley. The cowardly son is freed by one of the officers, because he is not worthy to die, but the other officer, uncertain whether the revolting soldiers can be restrained, begins to doubt the blessings of war. He throws away his red cloak, the symbol of war and its horrors, to be bleached by the sun of a new day.

The youngest son and this second officer foreshadow the new era. The conflict in the poet's soul between his earlier conception of duty and his newly won realisation of man's duty to mankind is solved in favour of the latter. The new humanity of the future is to be held above the narrower conception of nationality. But though von Unruh had a clear consciousness of what he hated and wished to destroy in the old system, he had no clear view of what he wanted to take its place. Yet he did sincerely believe in a better future. The sufferings of the War were only to be justified if a new humanity was to be the result, and in the second part of the trilogy von Unruh tried to come to closer grips with his Utopian ideal. Unfortunately, his creative power was not equal to the passion and enthusiasm which filled him. His characters are too abstract; they are incorporated ideas, lacking in the flesh and blood necessary for the stage. There is too much declamation, and it is a fault common to most of the Expressionist dramatists that they talk glibly of humanity but have not succeeded in creating a plausible human being. The characters of Expressionist drama have been compared to the rather wooden medieval drawings which have balloons issuing from their mouths to denote what they say. The dramatists overestimated the intellect, but at the same time they put forth their ideas in an emotional, ecstatic manner which was unsuitable for the presentation of abstract conceptions.

The scene of *Platz* is in a square surrounded by Government buildings. Most of the characters are given names, which are, for the most part, symbolic. The youngest son is Dietrich; the commandant is called Graf Gutundblut; a profiteer, whose opportunism permits him to adapt himself to all changes, is called Christlieb Schleich; and the daughters of the ruler of the State are Irene and Hyazinte. The action is involved and fantastic. The hero of the piece is Dietrich, now no longer the tempestuous revolutionary who seeks his ends by political means. He has undergone an inner transformation, his ideal has moved on to a higher and more abstract plane. He sees in Irene ("peace") a symbol of the future. Humanity is to be regenerated by a new relationship between man and woman. But the action is still insufficiently plastic, the characters still abstract types. In *Ein Geschlecht* the poet's inward experience has obviously been poured hot and glowing into dramatic form, but *Platz* is too much a product of the intellect, and fails to achieve the immediate appeal of the earlier play. Neither is the thought particularly clear, and it is not obvious whether Dietrich rejects the revolution and democracy for Irene's sake or not. When von Unruh was unable to fall back on immediate experience, his inventive talent was too weak to hide the creaking of the mechanism. The work is pervaded with the idea of the regenerating power of love, but this has not prevented von Unruh from inserting incidents where eroticism assumes the form of macabre perversion.

There was to be a third part of the triology, called *Dietrich*, that was to solve the problem of the new humanity which had not been solved in the first two parts. It is still unpublished, and perhaps unwritten, and it is doubtful, at this stage, whether von Unruh possesses the staying-power to round the trilogy off with the third part. He was a visionary, and, as was shown by the tactless book of travel-sketches, *Flügel der Nike*, based on a very short stay in France and a few days in England, which he published in 1924, he was rather out of touch with reality. The more radical minds in Germany considered that von Unruh's pacifism did not accept the logical consequences; that it was too abstract and lacking in a clear understanding of the facts, a view with which the English reader of *Flügel der Nike* is inclined to agree.

Franz Werfel's trilogy, which was first performed in the autumn of 1921, is called *Spiegelmensch*. It illustrates Werfel's view of the double nature of man, the two conflicting aspects of the Ego upon which much of his poetry is based. In the young Goethe it was the emotion and the reason, in Werfel it is the higher and the lower Self. Thamal, the chief character, retires, wearied with life, to a monastery, where the abbot explains to him that he is not yet ripe to shun the world. He must first experience it. When Thamal is left alone, his glance falls on his reflection in a mirror; he is overcome by a feeling of repulsion and shoots at the reflection, thereby releasing from the smashed mirror Spiegelmensch, his other Ego, the incorporation of his lower instincts. Spiegelmensch becomes his constant companion, his Mephistopheles, and together they set forth into the world. With every new act of guilt committed by Thamal, Spiegelmensch gains more strength. They go to the house of Thamal's father, whom Thamal kills by the mere wish. Eventually Thamal and Spiegelmensch reach the country ruled by Ananthas, the serpent demon, the embodiment of all evil. Ananthas is conquered by Thamal, who, at the urging of Spiegelmensch, allows himself to be deified by the people. This is a triumph for Spiegelmensch, that a noble deed should be followed by vanity and the lust for power. Spiegelmensch now thinks that he has turned the tables and can treat Thamal as his servant. In the third part of the trilogy, Thamal separates from his companion and, after various adventures, delivers himself voluntarily for trial. He takes upon himself full responsibility for his misdeeds, and utters his own fatal sentence, in spite of the efforts of Spiegelmensch to entice him again by visions of power, pleasure, and the fear of death. He drinks a cup of poison, which delivers him from his double, who steps back into the mirror. Thamal finds himself back in the monastery, and the mirror he now sees as a window, through which he looks out into a higher life.

There is an obvious resemblance to Goethe's *Faust* and to Ibsen's *Peer Gynt*, to say nothing of Grillparzer's *Der Traum ein Leben*. Thamal has, by his various adventures and experiences, to arrive at a realisation of his higher Self. The piece has many faults; the metaphysical ideas are too much in evidence, the construction is sketchy, but the effect on the stage is nevertheless impressive. Werfel's work is that of a profounder mind and a richer imagination than that of von Unruh, who poses questions but does not succeed in solving them. Werfel's work is more tangible, and he achieves a synthesis of emotion and intellect which in von Unruh appear to work separately.

Werfel calls his play a "magic trilogy." Kaiser's trilogy is of a very different kind. It is a tragedy of capitalism, of the curse of money, a subject which had already been treated in *Von Morgens bis Mitternachts*. The first part is called *Die Koralle* and the other two *Gas*, parts one and two, and Kaiser shows, in the fate of a gigantic gas factory and its workers during successive generations, how the masses prefer to keep their necks to the yoke, and are prepared to crucify their would-be saviour. They prefer to remain slaves to the machines.

The idea which runs through all Kaiser's dramas is the

awakening of man from money slavery and drudgery to the realisation of a worthier life. His characters are products of the intellect, incorporated ideas, and, perhaps even more than other Expressionist dramatists, he needs a thoroughly expert producer.

Ernst Toller has also tried to express the tragedy of capitalist civilisation in *Masse Mensch* and *Die Maschinenstürmer*. In the former play, it is a woman who leads the people and ultimately sacrifices herself for them. In *Die Maschinenstürmer*, which has as its theme the rising of the Nottingham weavers against the introduction of machinery about a hundred years ago, Toller again presents the idea of humanity and fraternity; but both these plays suffer from overweighting with matter more suited to the political tract than to the stage. He treats men in the mass, but in *Hinkemann* he shows a distinct advance in plastic power, in the ability to create an individual.

The general impression of Expressionist literature is that it was feverish and morbid, intensely impatient, chaotic, but fundamentally idealistic. It was too near the War and the Revolution to be anything but subjective. The War and the subsequent period were treated ecstatically, and the time had not yet come when sufficient distance had been gained for objective, or even satiric, treatment. Expressionist literature revealed the anguish of the German soul, but the pessimism which appeared to darken nearly all the imaginative writing of this time had reference only to the past and the present. With regard to the future it was fundamentally optimistic, even though this optimism was not based on very sound premises. The purpose was vague, and as Germans always need an intellectual purpose and a spiritual leader, the blind groping in an atmosphere of chaos was bound to give place before long to a more tangible aim and a definite direction. The post-Expressionist painters and writers grew tired of types, abstractions, and symbols, and by 1924 there appeared signs of what was termed a "New Objectivity."

But this was hardly a movement; it was mainly a convenient label for the return to a less emotional way of writing.

Expressionism has contributed much to literature which does not appear on the surface. It signified a new way of looking at and expressing things, and sprang from an intenser feeling and a profounder insight. Short-lived as the Expressionist movement was, it ensured that a superficial realism can never again be taken for literature. The reaction to a more objective way of writing did not sweep away the benefits rendered by Expressionism, any more than the classical Goethe and Schiller or the Romantics could deny their debt to the preceding *Sturm und Drang*. The philosophers, the psychologists and the scientists are all showing us a very different world from the one which the nineteenth century knew. Modern research in psychology and physics, in particular, has shown that the outward and visible phenomena represent only the surface of life and creation, and it is but natural that the present and the coming literary generations should seek to interpret these in different terms from those employed by their predecessors. This is not to belittle the significance of tradition, but merely to emphasise the fact that German literature is passing through a transitional stage of peculiar interest, and that criticism and research, for their own well-being, must recognise that the centre of gravity has shifted.

THE GERMAN DRAMA, 1914-1927

THE writers who belonged to the Naturalist movement towards the end of the nineteenth century had disclosed an interest in social matters which, in so far as it concerned the poorer or working classes, was of short duration. From the 'nineties onwards literature again shrank from close contact with the "lower orders"; and though the cult of art for art's sake, which is connected with Stefan George and his circle, was not widespread, the divorce of literature from the life of the people was sufficiently marked to restrict its appeal to a comparatively small percentage of the nation. Social and political problems ceased to have the importance they had for a short time enjoyed, and the uglier sides of life receded into the background. The movement for the emancipation of the theatre, which began in 1889, the year in which Gerhart Hauptmann's Naturalist drama, *Vor Sonnenaufgang*, was produced, continued however to bear fruit; and it eventually gave the German theatre the position in Europe which it now holds.

The feeling of despair which was engendered during the second half of the War, together with the bitterness and hope inspired by the final catastrophe, sought an outlet in a literary movement of unparalleled violence and intensity. Expressionism had already made some headway in Germany before the War; but it did not reach full tide until the couple of years which followed the revolution and the collapse of the old regime. German literature from 1916 reflected for about eight years a surging desire for the establishment of society on a new basis; and this is still evident, though in considerably diminished force, in the literary production of to-day. The Expressionist movement was moulded by a new interest in social and political matters, and in the relations between the thinking individual and the accepted forms of society.

Bitterness and hope were the two poles—bitterness at the old world which had culminated in the War, and hope in the new world which was to result from four years of suffering. But hope was far outweighed by embitterment, which was nourished and intensified by the realisation that the new world was at bottom little different from the old, and that the poets were to have no share in shaping the new order they had helped to establish.

It was a period when the younger generation—those who had passed through the War at an age when they were young enough for their whole mind to be moulded by it for good or ill—wanted with all its soul to finish the smashing of the old order and to rebuild on a new basis. What that basis was to be was not at all clear. German ideals are in general lofty, but vague. In estimating the extent to which the younger generation lost touch with hard facts, it must be borne in mind that the lost War was followed by a revolution, which was by no means so bloodless as is generally thought. The Germans had been taught to expect a short and victorious campaign; but it lasted four years, and the result was catastrophic. The years of peace were initiated by a continuance of the blockade and civil war, followed by the nightmare episode of inflation, when the people starved as they had not starved during the War. Unless this social background is taken into consideration, it is not possible to survey in the proper perspective the German drama during the period under review. Æsthetic appreciation of literary forms is of little significance without reference to the essential fact that Expressionist drama was rooted in the generation's absorbing longing for a new world order, for the revaluation of traditional ethics.

Expressionist literature was in its main features a literature of ecstasy, even of mysticism. It was both destructive and creative; and what it wanted to do with the world was epitomised in what it did to the language. The latter was to be broken up and recreated. The effect aimed at was concentration. Grammatical inflections and prefixes were

regarded as unnecessary. Articles, conjunctions and prepositions could be omitted. Each writer tried to fashion the
language he needed for the expression of what he wanted to
communicate, and did not hesitate to invent new words
when he found those already available inadequate. This did
not, of course, make an already obscure art-form any the
more easy to understand; and the attempt to reduce the
expression of the essential to the most primitive and simple
form resulted, in most cases, in a but vaguely intelligible
indication of thoughts and emotions which we are bound to
infer were themselves far from lucid.

While the Naturalists tried to reproduce the visible world
in a way which bordered on the photographic, and the
Impressionists only reproduced fleeting or incomplete
aspects of life, the Expressionists wanted to bring forth the
ultimate reality which lies behind that which can be grasped
with the physical senses. They were not content to reproduce
the outward phenomena. In the words of Kasimir Edschmid,
"Art must be able to penetrate the world before our eyes in
order to seek out and recreate the intrinsic essence." The
Naturalists revealed the facts behind the veil with which an
unfeeling or prudish society had covered them up, but said
nothing about the *Wesen eines Dings*, nothing about the
ultimate truth of which the visible facts were only an
outward aspect. They did not show the relation to eternity
of the things they revealed. The Expressionists, on the other
hand, endeavoured to solve the problem of man's relation
to the absolute.

Their way of arriving at an understanding of the absolute
was not by psychology, but by direct personal feeling,
which, in their view, went deeper than psychology. The
attempt to express the intrinsic essence resulted in the
appearance on the stage of figures which, to the eye of the
average spectator, were far removed from his ordinary
conception of reality; but they were genuine men and
women, stripped of everything merely incidental to the
individual and not a part of his true nature. They were

Urmenschen, as God created them, and it was the spectator himself whose true nature was covered up and hidden.

"Whoever does not recognise his own brother in each of these figures is lost," says Paul Kornfeld, one of the Expressionist dramatists, "for he knows nothing of his own actual nature, and is, in the real sense of the word, unconscious; he has fallen like rotten fruit from the tree of humanity, for he no longer has any association with the world and its focus, and his existence will never be anything but merely terrestrial."

The artist, Kornfeld goes on to say, must be humanity's conscience, and the actor who presents his figures on the stage has to strip off the attributes of outward reality and represent an idea, an emotion or a destiny. The last thing an actor should do is to imitate. If he has to die on the stage, he should not go to a hospital to learn how to do it; if he has to be drunk, he should not go to a tavern to look for a model. He must not be ashamed to *act*, for to be able to show *how* a man dies is only a matter of observation and a certain virtuosity, while to show *what it means* to die is a matter of personal feeling and demands creative power.

Expressionist art is then, to a great extent, intuitive, for the artist must deduce the universe from his own ego. Though he expresses his own soul, the result is not to be regarded as personal experience but as the essential experience of humanity. Expressionist writers are interested in man in general, not in individuals; and therefore their plays tend to be allegorical and their characters mainly types, which are given not names, but type-distinctions, such as The Father, The Son, The Mother, The Prostitute, The Gentleman with a Top Hat, The Nameless One; or there are groups, such as Aviators, Soldiers, or Those Condemned to Death. The hatred of war and longing for the betterment of the world infused Expressionist literature with a spirit of profound compassion, with a sympathy for humanity that transcended the bounds of nationality. The motive of love between man and woman was practically eliminated from the drama, and the relations between the sexes were no longer emotional but intellectual. Woman was seen as the equal of man, with the same rights and claims.

There was a demand for a complete break with the past, and this was typified in the conflict between father and son which is to be found in nearly every important Expressionist drama. The son does not hesitate to utter a death-wish or even to kill the father. The motive appears in the first of all the Expressionist dramas, Reinhard Sorge's *Der Bettler*, which was written in 1910, published in 1912, when it was awarded the newly established Kleist Prize, and produced by Max Reinhardt in 1917, and is also found in Walter Hasenclever's *Der Sohn*, which likewise dates from before the War; Rolf Lauckner's *Predigt in Litauen*; Franz Werfel's *Spiegelmensch*; Fritz von Unruh's *Ein Geschlecht*; Arnolt Bronnen's *Vatermord*; Joachim von der Goltz's *Vater und Sohn*, which treats of the relations between Frederick the Great and his father; Georg Kaiser's *Die Koralle*; and Ernst Toller's *Die Wandlung*.

Expressionist dramas are generally built up not so much in acts as in a series of scenes. Toller, for example, divides both *Die Wandlung* and *Masse Mensch* into a number of "pictures," interspersed with "dream pictures," and in the former the pictures are grouped into a number of "stations." The phraseology is often so concise that single words are rapped out one after the other with breathless intensity. The chief exponents of this so-called "telegram style" are Carl Sternheim and Georg Kaiser. Emphasis is laid on gesture and action rather than on language; and it is not difficult to see in all this an approximation to the film, which at a later stage played a great part in the productions of Erwin Piscator. The effect is not one of carefully planned development, but of spasmodic movement. The most exaggerated and incoherent of the Expressionist dramatists was August Stramm, whose *Kräfte*, written in 1915, was produced by Reinhardt in 1921. His dialogue, for pages at a time, consists only of monosyllabic exclamations.

The chief dramatists of the Expressionist period were Kaiser, Werfel, von Unruh and Toller; and as a typical example of Expressionist dramatic production we may take Kaiser's *Die Koralle* and the two parts of *Gas*, which are to be regarded as a trilogy, though the connection of *Die Koralle* with the other two plays is loose. As in the earlier *Von Morgens bis Mitternachts* the theme is the tragedy of capitalism. The trilogy contains all the features of Expressionist drama—the characters are types, the son is in violent conflict with the father, has a preference for the proletariat and cherishes plans for the betterment of humanity, while the language is reduced to the utmost conciseness.

The chief character in *Die Koralle* is a milliardaire who owns the gigantic factory in which his father was once a labourer. He cannot forget the dreadful experiences of his childhood, when his father, prematurely worn out, went away after being dismissed from the factory and his mother committed suicide. He was urged to work his way up to his position of stupendous power by the thought that, if he did not conquer the machines which had used up his father's energy and then cast him away, they would crush him. His journey to the summit was thus a constant flight from the vision of his childhood, and he still avoids contact with the world from which he sprang. He only comes in contact with his workmen through his secretary, who is his double, and from whom he can only be distinguished, even by intimates, by a coral which the secretary wears on his watch-chain. He tries to bring up his son in the same way to avoid contact with the plebs, but when he thinks the son is a passenger in a luxury steamer he is actually acting as stoker in a cargo-boat, for his sympathies are with the proletariat. There ensues a dispute between the father and son; and the son confesses that he once called his father a murderer on the occasion of an accident in the factory and

had cherished the thought of shooting him. The milliardaire
sees his hopes crashing to the ground. Shortly after the break
with his son and his daughter, who has taken her brother's
part, he murders his secretary and takes from him the coral,
which he puts on his own watch-chain, so that he might be
taken for the secretary, whose happy childhood he has
envied. This actually happens, and he is accused of murder-
ing himself. In prison his outlook on life becomes clarified,
and he walks calmly to the scaffold.

The next two parts of the trilogy are called *Gas*, Parts I
and II. The gigantic gas factory now belongs to the milliardaire's son, who manages it on a co-operative system,
all the workers sharing in the profits. The factory provides
the industry of the whole world with gas, and the work does
not cease for a moment. But one day there is a terrific
explosion and the whole works are destroyed. The defect
cannot be discovered; but although the gas formula is
correct, the workmen demand the dismissal of the chief
engineer before they will return to work and resume the
supply of gas for which the world is clamouring. The
milliardaire's son points out to them that the formula was
correct and another explosion would inevitably occur; but
the workmen will not listen to him and he agrees to dismiss
the engineer. He has a new plan to save the workers, in
spite of themselves, by turning the site of the destroyed
factory town into a rural settlement, where the green spaces
will be a contrast to that which formerly covered the site.
He preaches the return to nature; but when he explains his
scheme to a mass-meeting of the workers, the engineer also
addresses them and urges the reconstruction of the factory.
The workers, under the influence of mass-suggestion, cry
out that the engineer shall be their new leader, the engineer
whom they have just wanted to make the scapegoat. The
milliardaire's son still tries to prevent the men from recon-
structing the factory; but the Government threatens to
deprive him of his property if he persists in trying to stop the
supply of gas, thus holding up the manufacture of arma-

ments which are particularly necessary as a war is imminent. The milliardaire's son realises that it is more than ever his duty to prevent the workers from forging weapons against themselves; but he is compelled to give way; and the workers, who are once more to work for the inevitable explosion, indulge in shouts of joy.

We see in this piece how the milliardaire's son, who appeared in *Die Koralle* as the apostle of humanity, endeavours to transform ideal into deed. But the masses prefer to keep their necks to the yoke, and are prepared to sacrifice their would-be saviour. They prefer still to be slaves to the machines. At the end of the play the daughter of the milliardaire's son declares that she will bear the new man, the new leader who is to come.

In *Gas*, Part II, we are at the centre whence gas is distributed for the waging of a great war. The supply is giving out and the army on the verge of defeat. All want peace; the workers strike, and the cry is "No more gas." The opposing army, however, does not respond to the demonstrations of peace, and demands the handing over of the gas factory, requiring at the same time that the workers resume work in its interests. The workers assemble to make their decision. The son whose birth was heralded at the end of the first part is now working in the factory, and urges the men to resume work; but the chief engineer wants to continue the fight against the enemy. He shows them a new weapon, a little red ball in which is a new poison gas he has invented. The people decide to resume the fight with the new gas, but the milliardaire worker seizes the ball and hurls it among his own people. At the same time the enemy bombardment begins. Even the milliardaire worker, who came to fulfil the ideals of his grandfather, the milliardaire's son of the first two parts of the trilogy, was powerless to save the people against themselves, and the only way out he saw was annihilation.

Compassion with the masses ground under the capitalist heel is seen also in Toller's *Masse Mensch* and *Die Maschinen-*

stürmer; and in both plays the leaders of the people, in the former a woman, are sacrificed by or for those whom they set out to save. Their fate is similar to that of the idealists in Kaiser's *Gas*. Toller declaims with passionate intensity of purpose the ideal of human brotherhood, but he labours under the inability to subordinate the politician to the dramatist. The fact that much of his work was written as a political prisoner has exaggerated his fervour, but has kept his outlook narrow.

Von Unruh used to be put in a class by himself as a Prussian Regular officer, whose early plays were concerned with the conflict between military duty and personal inclination, but who was converted by his War experience to pacifism. His chief dramas are *Ein Geschlecht*, written during the War, and *Platz*, which was completed in 1920. They are part of a trilogy, of which the remaining play is still to come. The characters in *Ein Geschlecht* are types, consisting mainly of a mother with her daughter and three sons; and the action takes place in a graveyard while a battle is being fought in the valley below. The characters in *Platz* are not anonymous, but their names are partly symbolic. Von Unruh has expressed in the two plays his intense conviction of the curse of war and the essential rottenness of the old order, with its hypocrisy and hide-bound worship of authority. The ideal of duty to superiors has given place to the ideal of duty to one's fellow-men. The hero, Dietrich, the youngest son of the first piece, sees a hope for the regeneration of mankind in a new relation between man and woman. The important place given to woman in the future development of the human race strikes a new note in German literature; but the thought is vague; and though there is no doubt of von Unruh's sincere and fervent desire for a new world order which will justify the sufferings of the War, it is equally certain that he does not yet possess the clarity of thought or the plastic power to represent his ideas in dramatic form. His characters are mere abstractions. Though *Ein Geschlecht* was written while the author's

233

emotions were hot and tense, they had obviously cooled by the time he wrote *Platz*, and his failings as a creative writer leap to the eye. If he should ever produce the third part of the trilogy, it will be interesting to see whether it will regain for him the reputation which his subsequent works have not helped to maintain. As with Toller, the ascendancy of the emotions over the intellect prevents the control of the creative capacity within the bounds of artistic form.

The most important work of Franz Werfel, apart from his poems, is also a trilogy; and though its debt to Goethe's *Faust* and Ibsen's *Peer Gynt* is evident, it is the work of a more profound mind than either Kaiser, Toller or von Unruh. *Spiegelmensch* is the clearest expression of the ideal of renunciation which we find at this period side by side with, though not to the same extent as, the impulse to revolutionary action. The hero is Thamal, who attains to a realization of his higher self after a series of experiences in the company of a Mephistophelian character who comes out of a mirror and is Thamal's own double, or the incorporation of his lower self. This trilogy also is too abstract and too loosely constructed for a dramatic work of art; but it has proved effective on the stage. Werfel's gifts, like those of von Unruh, are lyrical rather than dramatic. They both have the quality of pity; but Werfel has the greater creative imagination, and while von Unruh lets his emotion run away with him, in Werfel it is held in check by his intellect.

Though the Expressionists wanted to make a break with the past, their art owed not a little to predecessors. The two older dramatists from whom they learned most were Wedekind and Strindberg, both of whom had been fighters against the existing *Gesellschaftsmoral*, though the German dramatist had acclaimed the rights of the flesh while the Swede regarded man's fleshly instincts as the source of his unhappiness. From the point of view of style, the influence of the unreal, dreamlike, macabre nature of some of Wedekind's plays is clearly evident in the dramas of Expressionism. Wedekind expressed ideas about man and society by incorporating them in stage figures; but the Expressionists are more abstract; for with Wedekind, as with Strindberg, there is still characterisation and psychology, which the younger men have abandoned. Wedekind's powerful and influential play *Frühlings Erwachen*, though divided into three acts, is really constructed as a long series of consecutive scenes; and this method was inherited by the Expressionists, as was also the way in which he makes his characters talk mechanically, in compressed sentences, with no apparent relation between the several remarks. The "Vermummter Herr" in the same play is the progenitor of similar allegorical characters in plays by Hasenclever, Wildgans, Kaiser and von Unruh.

Another dramatist who came into his own during the Expressionist period was Georg Büchner, who lived from 1813 to 1837, and forms a kind of link, through Wedekind, between the eighteenth-century *Sturm und Drang* dramatists and the Expressionists, who rediscovered him after many years of neglect. In addition to his comedy *Leonce und Lena*, his chief work consists of the two tragedies *Dantons Tod* and *Wozzeck*. The swift succession of short scenes, the forceful, turbulent nature of his language, his revolt against bourgeois society and compassion for the under-dog are all reflected in the dramatic literature of Expressionism.

Among those who first learned from Wedekind how to pour scorn on the bourgeois and the Philistine was Carl Sternheim, who, like Georg Kaiser, was about forty years of age at the end of the War, and therefore no longer to be counted among the younger generation. Kaiser developed Sternheim's telegraphic style and shows further evidence of Sternheim's influence in his satires on the bourgeois; but his scope is wider, while his fertility is amazing, for he has written nearly thirty plays of various categories in about twelve years. There seems to be no idealism behind the purely intellectual satire of either Sternheim or Kaiser, and they have nothing of the passionate feeling of von

Unruh and Toller; but they both possess a far better sense of the theatre.

Unlike many of the Expressionist dramatists who achieved celebrity at the height of the iconoclastic enthusiasm, Kaiser's talent shows no sign of flagging. He is the most inventive craftsman of all contemporary German dramatists. In addition to plays which revive the themes of *Gas* and *Von Morgens bis Mitternachts*, he has produced a drama on the relations between de Musset and George Sand and one on the relations between Gilles de Rais and Joan of Arc. The three acts of his *Nebeneinander* have nothing to do with one another except that they have the same starting-point. A pawnbroker, while cleaning a coat that has been pledged with him, finds in a pocket a letter to a girl from which he gathers that the owner of the coat has thrown her over and that she is going to kill herself. He decides to try to save her; and the three acts show the separate fates of the pawnbroker, the girl and the man. The pawnbroker becomes involved, through his compassionate impulse, in misfortunes which lead him to commit suicide, while the other two achieve happiness along their separate paths. It is an interesting experiment which, from a dramatist whose sympathy for those who are crushed by the chance of fate or the inequity of social justice was dictated more by the heart, might have made a much deeper impression. One of his latest plays, *Gats*, produced in 1925, resumes the theme of the regeneration of the world, which is this time to be brought about by the voluntary consumption on a large scale of a drug, discovered among an unknown race in the heart of a primeval forest, the effect of which is to produce sterility. Human society is to organise its future along Malthusian lines; but when the discoverer, finding his idea unwelcome, causes the only woman who has remained loyal to him to take the drug unwittingly, she betrays him to the authorities who have forbidden its use. He is one of the latest in the long series of leaders of the people who have been sacrificed by those whom they have sought to save.

Kaiser's subsequent plays are little more .than light entertainments.

The fever of Expressionism had already begun to abate
by 1921; and about three years later it became evident that
there was to be a fairly wholesale return to what was called
a new realism or a new objectivity—*Neue Wirklichkeit* or
Neue Sachlichkeit. If this was to be only a reaction from the
ecstatic nerve tension of the post-War years and if there was
to be no constructive purpose underlying the new movement, it would be merely, as Professor Walzel puts it, a
case of *Katzenjammer* after a period of intoxication. It began,
as always in Germany, with the setting up of a programme.
Types, allegories and symbols were to give place to something less removed from everyday experience. The urge to
emancipate the proletariat by an upheaval of the social
order ceased to be the principal motive in the drama,
though plays continued to be written and produced which
showed no advance on the ideals or methods of 1919. The
diminished absorption in cosmic ideas, and the return to
simplicity and restraint, have made possible a welcome
revival of straightforward comedy. Characters of flesh and
blood are appearing on the stage again in place of incorporated ideas, and motives have become more concrete. A
large number of dramatists have turned to history for their
subjects, and are attempting to revaluate decisive events of
the past. Von Unruh has written a play called *Bonaparte*;
Werfel deals with the ill-fated Emperor of Mexico in *Juarez
und Maximilian*; a few dramatists have found a congenial
theme in Frederick the Great, among them Bruno Frank,
the author of *Zwölftausend*; Hanns Johst brings the American
War of Independence and the French Revolution into his
Thomas Paine; and Alfred Neumann, the author of the
novel *Der Teufel*, has written, in *Der Patriot*, a drama about
Paul the First of Russia and Count Pahlen, which has been
seen in this country both as a stage play and as a film. An
outstanding historical drama, one of the best produced in

237

Germany since the War, is Wolfgang Goetz's *Neidhardt von Gneisenau*.

The subject of love between man and woman has been rediscovered as a fruitful source of plots, though some dramatists, like Brust in *Die Wölfe*, are obsessed by the attempt to represent the instinct of sex in its most primal and brutal form. Bertolt Brecht's *Trommeln in der Nacht* concerns a soldier, thought to be dead, who returns on the eve of the revolution when the girl he loves, who has waited for him for four years, has just become engaged to a war profiteer. The first two acts show a power of characterisation and a theatrical sense which, when the play appeared in 1922, led to Brecht being acclaimed the rising hope of the German stage; but he has done little since then to justify the title. The remaining acts of *Trommeln in der Nacht* fall off into Expressionist incoherence, and only come back to something like reality at the end, when the returned soldier leaves the mob which is attacking the newspaper quarter of Berlin and goes away to find happiness with the girl. The inability of the Expressionist dramatists to mould bitterness into tragedy, and the insufficiency of ecstatic feeling as a surrogate for plastic power, are again seen in the way this play runs to seed after the first two acts. Nevertheless, it was the first real sign of the return to a more realistic treatment of problems which the War has brought close to the soul of humanity. Brecht has poetic genius and creative power, and his development will be watched with interest.

Two dramatists who are generally mentioned together with Brecht, though they have little more in common than the first two letters of their names, are Arnolt Bronnen and Alfred Brust. Bronnen's first play was *Vatermord*, which dealt with the Oedipus theme. His later plays are less Expressionistic, but he retains a liking for violent theatrical effects, and his partiality for topical subjects is seen in *Rheinische Rebellen*, which deals with the Separatist movement in the Rhineland a few years ago. The sexual element is strong in his works, and there appears to be a search for the presentation of primitive brutality. The attempt to reduce everything to the primitive is a sign that Expressionism is still exerting its influence. The most interesting of his plays, from the point of view of both subject and technique, is *Ostpolzug*. Brust has a similar liking for brutal action, as in *Tolkening*, a series of three one-act dramas of which the above-mentioned *Die Wölfe* is the first. He combines the depiction of extreme sensuality with mystic asceticism, without being able to fuse the two; and the effect is therefore generally artificial and unplausible. One of his most successful plays is *Der singende Fisch*, the scene of which is on the Lithuanian coast. There is a legend that the soul of the Saviour entered into a fish after the Crucifixion, and that the Madonna asked that hers might live in a succession of women until the end of the world. Only the one in whom her soul has taken up its temporary abode is able to hear the fish when it sings, and she then knows that the soul of the Holy Virgin is living in her, for she does not know it before. Brust has utilised this legend in his drama of a girl who looks forward with horror to her approaching wedding. The sensual and the ascetic in the lives of his Lithuanian fishermen are presented with the same power of characterisation as in *Tolkening*, but with greater restraint and a more credible combination of the realistic with mystic elements.

Hasenclever, von Unruh, Werfel and Toller are continuing to produce plays which enable us to judge the extent to which they have developed either in imaginative or dramatic power; but the only one of these who has maintained his former reputation is Werfel. His two latest plays, *Juarez und Maximilian* and *Paulus unter den Juden*, both have historical subjects, the former being a "dramatic history" in three "phases" and thirteen "pictures," and the latter a "dramatic legend" in six "pictures." In *Juarez und Maximilian* Werfel has chosen his theme from the comparatively recent past, opposing the well-meaning Royal idealist, a tool in the hands of politicians and business men, and the cool and purposeful Mexican leader, Juarez, who never appears on the stage. In *Paulus* he has tried to depict the decisive moment when Christianity detached itself from the mother religion. He explains in an afterword that history and religion are irreconcilable opponents, since history rationalises the moment of the divine miracle by which every newly instituted religion is initiated; but *Paulus* is an historical tragedy in the sense that it attempts to reconstruct an historical happening, the great tragic hour of Judaism, with the object of showing its profound significance, the protagonist being Israel itself. Hasenclever, the author of the first Expressionist drama to be produced (*Der Sohn*, published 1914, produced 1916), was also one of the first to abandon Titanic defiance and moral indignation for lighter weapons. He turned to irony and comedy, as others turned to history, in search of *Neue Sachlichkeit*; but his later plays are of little literary value.

Von Unruh has abated the tumbling excitement of words which he poured out with such abundance of emotion, but he does not give any sign of increased dramatic power. His Festspiel, *Heinrich von Andernach*, written during Passion Week in 1925 for the Rhineland millenary celebrations, shows a certain power of dramatic purpose and testifies again to von Unruh's humanity. But *Bonaparte*, produced in 1927, in which he has made a definite attempt to abandon abstractions, to create individuals and to dramatise a decisive episode in the career of Napoleon, lays bare the mediocrity of his dramatic talent, while the endeavour to keep the dialogue within the bounds of the new objectivity makes it read in places like a stilted translation. Von Unruh has not yet found the right form for what he wants to say.

Ernst Toller, less cosmic in his scope than von Unruh, has at three periods of his career written plays to express his disappointment at the course of contemporary history. *Die Wandlung*, written in 1917 and 1918, was due to the blighting of the enthusiasm with which he had joined in the War three years before. In *Hinkemann*, written in 1921 and 1922, during imprisonment in a fortress for participation in the

Munich revolt—which is the only play in which he has succeeded in getting away from types and creating individuals—and in *Hoppla! wir leben*, written after his release and produced in 1927, he gives vent to his bitter disappointment at the turn events have taken since the Revolution. Neither Hinkemann, the sexual cripple, nor Karl Thomas, the hero of *Hoppla!*, who goes out of his mind while in prison and is only released after eight years, is able to adapt himself to the changed conditions. Even *Masse Mensch* was an expression of the disappointment of an idealist at the way the Revolution had proceeded. *Hoppla!* has made evident what has for some time been suspected. It affords no proof that its author has made progress either in depth of thought, constructive purpose or dramatic power. Toller's new hero is still nothing but the incorporation of an idea. The period which has elapsed since the War has not diminished his passionate hatred of the social order and social morality; and until he is able to take a more objective view of the world around him it is to be feared that Toller will continue to be unable to distinguish between the stage and the political platform. He needs a constructive purpose and an inspiration less artistically sterile than disappointment at the slowness with which the social order is changing. Having seen Toller's plays produced with the inadequate means at the disposal of the English stage, we are perhaps in a better position than the Germans to appreciate how much he owes to his producer. The poetic quality of his dramas is small, and they depend for their effect in the theatre on the modern methods of stage production in which Germany leads the world.

The mention of other dramatists who have come to the fore during the last three years could only be in the nature of a catalogue; for it is impossible, in the case of such recent work, to obtain even the inadequate perspective that gives us the courage to review the dramatic production of the period immediately following the War, when there was a certain outward unity in the Expressionist method and the prevalent hostility to the three great bulwarks of the bourgeois—militarism, capitalism and "middle-class morality."

Nothing has been said about the older writers like Hauptmann, Schnitzler and Hofmannsthal because, though their older works continue to appear on the stage, they have done little since the War that has any relation to the new orientation. Karl Zuckmayer became famous in 1925 on account of his comedy *Der fröhliche Weinberg*; but it did not owe its sensational success to any literary quality, in spite of the award of the Kleist Prize. It presented a slice of life, entirely free from any suggestion of ideology and realistic to the point of coarseness, with characters indulging their senses instead of exercising their intellects, to a public which was tired of abstractions. An artist who took to the drama late in life is Ernst Barlach, who had already made a name as a sculptor long before he received the Kleist Prize in 1924 at the age of fifty-four. He combines a sense of reality with spiritual vision, and possesses the creative power to become a classic of the German stage.

There are two organisations which have done work of importance in disseminating popular interest in the theatre. The *Bühnenvolksbund* encourages the Catholic drama, and publishes the plays of a large number of Catholic authors, of whom the most gifted is Leo Weismantel. The *Verband der deutschen Volksbühnen* comprises between two and three hundred *Volksbühnen* in various German towns, with more than half a million members. The movement has developed out of the *Freie Volksbühne*, which was founded in 1890 with the purpose of bringing the drama to the workers.

The founding of the *Freie Bühne* in 1889, which disturbed the complacency of the fossilising German theatre, initiated a development which has in the course of time led to a state of affairs where it may be said without hesitation that the importance of the drama as literature during the last twelve years is small compared with the importance of stage production. The dramatists have supplied material for the real genius, the producer. Max Reinhardt had already brought into the theatre a staff of architects, sculptors, scene-painters and other technicians, but he did not pre-dominate over the author. Expressionist drama required a new kind of production; and original producers like Leopold Jessner, Jürgen Fehling and Erwin Piscator have by their methods achieved striking effects with plays which were weak in inspiration and poor in construction. They have supplemented and given concrete form to the sometimes obscure vision of the dramatist. To take an example of the difference production could make even to a fine play like Hauptmann's *Die Weber*, the Expressionist production soon after the War turned the despairing weavers, whose revolt was not guided by any dominating purpose, into purposeful protagonists of a class war such as were certainly not con-templated by the author when he wrote the play. The producer is able, if he so desires, to give a play such a twist that the effect is contrary to that which the author intended. Piscator's production of Schiller's *Die Räuber* in modern dress made Karl Moor into an undecided democrat of the type of Kerensky, while the real hero was Spiegelberg, who was intended as a portrait of a Bolshevist and was made up to look like Trotsky. Piscator, of course, used his theatre in the interests of Communist propaganda, but whether or not we regard his treatment of Schiller's play as trespassing on the prerogative of the author, the methods of this brilliant young producer are of considerable import for the art of the theatre. It was Piscator's production which made a success of Toller's *Hoppla!*—a typical example of the way in which a producer can seize the opportunity to fill out an uninspired play with all the means at his disposal. Piscator uses the film to portray events in various countries and to get the effect of a mass of people appearing on the scene, thus providing in *Hoppla!* a world-background for the stage action. Whether this intensifies the dramatic effect or has the opposite result of dispersing it, and whether the dis-proportionate participation of the producer will in the long run be advantageous to the drama, or will reduce the dramatist to the comparative unimportance of a scenario writer—these are matters the implications of which require separate discussion. The tendency in Expressionist drama has been for the actors to be reduced to puppets; but artists like Werner Krauss and Fritz Kortner have known how to fit themselves into the scheme and yet make the audience realise that here were great actors.

Expressionism has not passed by without leaving permanent traces. It not only treated old themes in a new way, but it brought the German stage into closer touch with the ultimate problems of life than it had ever been before. The lack of interest in the relations between individuals, including the love relationship between man and woman, rendered it certain that the Expressionist movement would have only a short life; but while it lasted it was like an intense flame that burned away much of the dross that had accumulated during the years of self-satisfied prosperity. It did not, however, denote the complete break with the past that its advocates proclaimed; for it contained elements such as mysticism, belief in the ultimate goodness of human nature, pity for the proletariat and scorn for the bourgeois which go back to the eighteenth century.

THE SPIRIT OF REVOLT IN GERMAN LITERATURE FROM 1914 TO 1930

THE purpose of this paper is to trace in German literature the change of attitude towards the War which began even before the first wave of enthusiasm had subsided. A recent German writer has said that the younger writers of England immediately after the War were not interested in social and political problems, or else considered them with a superior irony; that they experienced a certain emotion when they thought of the War and the aftermath, but, like the aristocratic company in *The Decameron*, they turned their backs on the painful subject and spent their time telling stories. This is, of course, not the whole truth, but it would not be possible to make the same reflection about the writers of the same age in Germany. The combatant generation there was ruthless and outspoken practically from the start, and German literature mirrors the emotional effects of the War to an incomparably greater extent than does that of England.

The year 1913 was celebrated in Germany as the centenary of the War of Liberation, when the people rose in an outburst of patriotic enthusiasm which culminated in the defeat of Napoleon Buonaparte at Waterloo. The occasion called forth two literary productions of very different types. Gerhart Hauptmann's *Festspiel in deutschen Reimen*, which was written to order, was not quite what those who controlled the nation's destinies had expected, and it had to be withdrawn. They had looked forward to the patriotic effusion of a laureate, but Hauptmann's play breathed the spirit of humanity and concluded with a procession symbolic of the activities and blessings of peace. Ernst Lissauer, in his cycle of poems entitled *1813*, celebrated in song the heroism of that epoch and set it up as a model for his contemporaries.

Younger poets than Lissauer also had a foreboding of the coming War, but their reactions were not the same. Georg

Heym wrote powerful poems in which he brooded over the vision of an imminent world catastrophe. He had a presentiment of the War in all its horror three years before it broke out, and expressed what he felt in the uncanny verses of "Umbra Vitæ" and "Der Krieg."

When the War came, in 1914, it was greeted with enthusiasm and patriotic fervour in Germany as it was, of course, in the countries of her enemies, and nearly every poet of reputation, to say nothing of the others, applied himself to the duty of turning out verse which should remind his countrymen of the sacredness of their cause, and spur them on to rise in their might and crush the disturbers of the peace. Just as we were urged to regard the War as a crusade, to stamp out the evil teachings of the unholy trio Nietzsche, Treitschke and Bernhardi, so the Germans were told by Church and Government that they were fighting for Christianity against a horde of heathens of various colours. The fact that they later had an ally in Turkey was a little awkward, but it inspired a professor of theology to prove that the Turks were imbued with the same Christian spirit of humility as the Germans themselves. The clergy never tired of quoting in their sermons the lines of the poet Geibel to the effect that the world may once more be healed by that essence which is to be found only in the Germans: "Und es mag am deutschen Wesen / Einmal noch die Welt genesen." One pastor sent forth a fiery poem, in which he addressed the God who dwelt in Heaven high above the Cherubim, the Seraphim and the Zeppelins. But some of these efforts were too much even for the 1914 stomach of Germany.

Gerhart Hauptmann composed a "Reiterlied" which he dedicated to the Uhlan officer and poet Fritz von Unruh. Richard Dehmel, though he was over age for military service, insisted on joining the Army and going to the Front, and he saw service in the trenches. He was rather hurt, however, when the Emperor awarded him, one of the most famous living German poets, the Order of the Red Eagle of the fourth class, and the progress of his disillusionment after his preliminary enthusiasm can be traced in his War-diary *Zwischen Volk und Menschheit*, which was published in 1919. Even Ernst Toller, who was abroad at the time, rushed home to throw himself with ardour into the struggle and volunteer for service in the belief that his country had been wilfully attacked. Fritz von Unruh wrote patriotic poetry, in the traditional manner, which might have come from a Körner, a Schenkendorf or an Arndt.

A typical volume of verse was Rudolf Herzog's *Ritter, Tod und Teufel*, from which I may, perhaps, quote an example of that sickening combination of sentimentality and un-thinking brutality which has parallels in this country, though the Latin races appear mercifully to be immune from it. He describes, in a poem written in 1914, how the sergeant-major comes to him waving a telegram and shouting his congratulations on the birth of a daughter:—

"Telegramm aus der Heimat! Schafft Platz, ihr Tröpfe.
Bei unsrem Dichter—grad hab' ich's vernommen—
Ist ein Kriegsmädel angekommen!"

The poet is naturally delighted; and the German Army, far and near, ceases work, while officers and men gaze up to Heaven and listen for the distant lisping of childish lips. Everybody stands in smiling bliss as though the enemy did not exist, and yet all that has happened is that on the German Rhine, in an old castle lost amid the trees, a dear little German girl has been born:—

"Und war doch nur am deutschen Rhein,
In alter Burg unter Bäumen verloren,
Ein klein lieb deutsches Mädel geboren."

This same Rudolf Herzog, in a poem printed a few pages farther on, urges his comrades to keep their blood cool and thrust their lances in the enemy's bowels—the enemy who is taking the bread out of the mouths of women, children and old men:—

"Nun schlingt es zur Mästung der räubrische Gauch—
Drauf! Stosst ihm den Speer in den prallen Bauch."

The most celebrated poem expressive of this mentality was, of course, Ernst Lissauer's "Hassgesang," which was reproduced in millions of copies and even distributed by an army order of the Crown Prince of Bavaria. The author protested later that the notoriety he obtained by this poem both in his own country and abroad gave a false view of his poetic achievements, and he regretted that he had not expressed his anxiety for his country in a song of love for Germany instead of in the negative form of a song of hate against England. But the "Hassgesang" is exceedingly well constructed, it possesses concentration and force and, whatever we may think of hate as a theme for poetry, it at least lacks the banality of idea and execution which is to be found in most of the patriotic poetry of the time.

The German passion for thoroughness, for *Gründlichkeit*, is seen in a poem which may be quoted because of the extraordinary refrain:—

> "Wir spiessen den Bären und rupfen den Hahn,
> Sie wolltens nicht anders, nun wird es getan,
> Aber gründlich!
>
> Wir treiben das brüllende Untier zu Platz,
> Den britischen Löwen, die falsche Katz,
> Aber gründlich!
>
> Wir üben das edle Weidwerk noch so
> Wie die alten Germanen, Halli und Hallo!
> Aber gründlich!
>
> Und früher, bei Gott! wird Rast nicht gemacht,
> Bis das letzte Wild wird zur Strecke gebracht!
> Aber gründlich!"
>
> ["Jagdlied," by Gustav Falke.]

It is, of course, easy to laugh at this kind of verse, but it would not be difficult to find equal cause for ridicule in our own literature. There was in Germany a finer kind of patriotic poetry which avoided both the vapourings of the armchair warriors and the romantic illusions of the young soldiers who did not yet know what a modern European war was going to be like. The poetry which struck the deepest chord in the heart of the people was that of the small group of poets known as the *Arbeiterdichter*. These workmen poets were not inspired by hate. They seemed to see more clearly than their fellows that the War was not calculated to bring nearer the fulfilment of spiritual ideals, and they regarded the enemy as a human being who might be imbued with an equal idealism to their own and who was, in any case, a brother. Gerrit Engelke, who came home from Denmark to fight and was killed only just before the Armistice, wrote at the outbreak of war: "For the time being I am still unclear and vague in my mind. . . . My feeling still resists the War instinctively. Murder is murder. If it were not for the one fact that we were acting in self-defence, I would have flatly rejected it all and stayed in the land where the pepper grows. . . . Such a war is not made by any man—it is always the gigantic, invisible hand of Fate, of God, of the power that controls Heaven or earth, or whatever other name we like to call it." At Whitsun, 1915, he wrote that the all-compelling necessity which inspired people and poets in 1813 to rise up and hurl off the yoke of a powerful tyrant was lacking a hundred years later, and that was why the national soul was not so completely inflamed and the poets had not been adequate to the occasion. In the last year of the War he said that the sudden development of Germany into a *Weltvolk* would only have implied a new and gigantic triumph for materialism. She was being thrown back by Destiny upon her own centre, which was the realm of the mind, by means of which she would always dominate the world. This may, perhaps, be regarded as the general conviction of those who succeeded in coming to grips with their own souls before the country and the Army collapsed.

The finest of these workmen poets, one who will have a permanent place in German literature, is Heinrich Lersch. His famous poem "Soldatenabschied" was published a fortnight after the outbreak of war in the *Frankfurter Zeitung* and achieved immediately enormous popularity. Like all the best of Lersch's verse, it is in the simple manner of the Volkslied. It begins:—

> "Lass mich gehn, Mutter, lass mich gehn!
> All das Weinen kann uns nichts mehr nützen,
> denn wir gehn das Vaterland zu schützen!
> Lass mich gehn, Mutter, lass mich gehn.
> Deinen letzten Gruss will ich vom Mund dir küssen:
> Deutschland muss leben, und wenn wir sterben müssen!"

And the same line forms the conclusion of each of the five stanzas—"Deutschland muss leben, und wenn wir sterben müssen!" An equally famous poem is the "Bekenntnis" of Karl Bröger, with its fine expression of a simple man's love for, and faith in, his country. The last stanza was often quoted:—

> "Immer schon haben wir eine Liebe zu dir gekannt,
> bloss wir haben sie nie bei ihrem Namen genannt.
> Herrlich zeigte es aber deine grösste Gefahr,
> dass dein ärmster Sohn auch dein getreuester war.
> Denk es, o Deutschland."

It is a striking fact that the poems and songs which appealed most to the people were those that were most akin to the folk-song. The "Österreichisches Reiterlied" of an Austrian, Hugo Zuckermann, with its parallelism, the soldier's foreboding of death and his resignation, is wholly in the Volkslied manner:—

> "Drüben am Wiesenrand
> Hocken zwei Dohlen—
> Fall ich am Donaustrand?
> Sterb ich in Polen?
> Was liegt daran?
> Eh sie meine Seele holen,
> Kämpf ich als Reitersmann.

Drüben am Ackerrain
Schreien zwei Raben—
Werd' ich der erste sein,
Den sie begraben?
Was ist dabei?
Viel hunderttausend traben
In Öst'reichs Reiterei.

Drüben im Abendrot
Fliegen zwei Krähen—
Wann kommt der Schnitter Tod,
Um uns zu mähen?
Es ist nicht schad'!
Seh' ich nur unsere Fahnen wehen
Auf Belgerad!''

The most popular of the songs sung by the soldiers was a medley of a number of songs : "Ich hatt' einen Kameraden," "Gloria, Viktoria," "Die Vöglein im Walde" and "In der Heimat, da gibt's ein Wiedersehn." This combination made a sentimental ditty about the spirit of comradeship, the little birds that sang in the woods, and the prospect of seeing their friends and relations when they got home again. Another exceedingly popular song was "Annemarie," in which the soldier sang that he might possibly see his sweetheart soon, but on the other hand the whole company might be in their graves on the following day. If a bullet should shoot him dead, Annemarie was not to redden her eyes with weeping, but to seek another lover, though, he suggested, it need not necessarily be one from his own company. This combination of sentimentality, stoicism and humour was not, of course, a monopoly of the German soldier, but was equally characteristic of the British Army.

The reader who tries to find his way among the overwhelming mass of writings during the first two years of the War is soon struck by the astonishingly early period at which the signs of revolt began to appear, and by the volume of poems, dramas and stories in which the protest against war and militarism became articulate. The Expressionist periodical *Die Aktion*, edited by Franz Pfemfert, which was founded in the year 1911, was opposed to the War from the beginning, and even before 1914 it was the organ of those who declined to see in any war anything exalting or sacred. It fought against what the editor called the *Völkerkrankheit* of patriotism, and when, during the War, it was compelled to cease its political activities, it devoted itself to promoting the international spirit. It published an anthology of lyrics, written on the battlefields between 1914 and 1916, some of them by youths who had been killed, which is as different as possible from what we ordinarily find in a war anthology. It is, in fact, an anti-war anthology, and Pfemfert added an afterword to the effect that he sent the book forth in opposition to the spirit of the time, as the asylum of a homeless ideal. He attacked what was known as *Hurrapatriotismus*, and in the pages of *Die Aktion* appeared some of the first signs of the change of mind, all the more significant since they came from the Front. Take, for example, the poem by Erwin Piscator, in which he tells the mother to weep for her son when she receives the news that he has fallen, since she herself shares the blame for his death in having let him play as a child with his lead soldiers:—

> "Musst nun weinen, Mutter, weine—
> Wenn du's liesest: 'Starb als Held.'
> Denk an seine Bleisoldaten . . .
> Hatten alle scharf geladen . . .
> Starben alle: plumps und stumm. . . ."

Or the heartfelt cry of the soldier for but one day when he might sink his head among the cooling flowers; when he might give himself up to dreams; for but one day when he might be free from killing:—

> "Einen Tag lang in Stille untergehen!
> Einen Tag lang den Kopf in Blumen kühlen
> und die Hände fallen lassen
> und träumen: diesen schwarzsamtnen, singenden Traum:
> Einen Tag lang nicht töten."
> ["Loretto," by Edlef Köppen.]

Or the poem addressed to a wounded Frenchman in which
the poet sees only the man in agony and not the enemy:—

" . . . mein Herzblut wallte
Um dich, den Blutenden, gleich IHM ans Kreuz geschlagen."
["Einem verwundeten Franzosen," by Jomar Förste.]

Austrian poets found a mouthpiece in the periodical *Die
Fackel*, edited by Karl Kraus, which, like *Die Aktion*, was
hostile to the War; and René Schickele, an Alsatian,
devoted his paper *Die Weissen Blätter*, which he edited and
published in Switzerland, to a like purpose. Schickele's
drama *Hans im Schnakenloch* shows the psychological struggle
in an Alsatian who is torn between both countries, and it
was prohibited by the Censor, though not before it had
been successfully performed.

The *Arbeiterdichter*, who had stood out as the least assailable,
the most humane, of those who wrote patriotic verse, were
also in the front rank of those who proclaimed the gospel
of humanity when the time had gone by for the hymning of
the military spirit. The two most gifted of these poets were
Heinrich Lersch, who has already been mentioned, and
Max Barthel. The former's volume *Herz! Aufglühe dein Blut!*,
published in 1916, contains some of his finest poems. The
lyric entitled simply "Im Schützengraben" gives expression
to the feeling that Frenchmen and Germans were in the
same way bound to the wheel of Fate, that both the soldier
and his enemy were the instruments of a destiny which
marched on over their dead bodies. In another poem,
"Brüder," he says that every dead man has the face of a
brother. Bitter hatred of the profiteer at home breaks out
in "Die toten Soldaten"—the dead soldiers go about in the
night as spirits, consoling the kin of the fallen and encourag-
ing the faint of heart; but they would like to show terrible
visions to those who coin gold out of heart's blood and
wealth out of tears. A poem which Lersch dedicates to a
friend, in memory of the spring of 1915, describes the effect
of the awakening of spring on a soldier who had spent the

autumn and winter in the trenches. Until then he had hardly realised what the War had done to the earth, but the voice of the first lark shook him out of his torpor, only to make him oblivious of his surroundings and able to realise nothing except that a lark was singing. In "Der Kriegs-invalide" the ex-soldier, who has lost an arm, thinks of the dead lying on the battlefields and exults in the mere fact that he is alive, that he can revel in the supreme happiness of no longer being in the line:—

> "Ich aber lebe, und die Welt ist mein.
> Es gibt auf Erde ja kein grösseres Glück,
> als nicht Soldat, als nicht im Krieg zu sein!"

And elsewhere Lersch says that whoever returned home from the War was a gleaming island of happiness in the ocean of mourning humanity—"Jeder, der heimkehrt vom Kriege, der ist im Meere der trauernden Menschheit eine leuchtende Insel von Glück." The tone is very different from that which was prevalent in 1914.

Lersch wrote what is, in a way, the loveliest poem of the War—"Die Mutter Gottes im Schützengraben." The naïve sincerity of its inspiration is in the pure tradition of the folk-song. It was composed at Christmas-time, when the poet asked the Mother of God to visit him in his dug-out in the front-line trenches, where he and his comrades would stand guard before her door and protect her with their lives. She would bring them the King of Peace, to put an end to all suffering. On the Holy Night the rifles in their hands would turn to green branches, and the cartridges to blossoms; the whining shells would become singing birds, the guns sink into the earth; hate would disappear from the hearts of the leaders of the enemy, and they would come like the three wise kings, black, yellow and white, to offer her their homage.

Heinrich Lersch was, and still is, a tinsmith. Max Barthel has tried a dozen trades and tramped through many of the countries of Europe. He spent four years fighting in the Army, and took part in the Revolution. Like Lersch, he was able to regard the man in the opposite trenches as a brother:—

"Der du den sausenden Tod aus deinem Graben herüberspeist:
Dennoch nenne ich dich 'Bruder' im Geist!"

His poem "Vor der Schlacht" is addressed to the enemy, this time the Russians. He says the Germans were also under the subjection of Tsarism and the knout, but they reacted like tame dogs and wagged their tails. Fate was more powerful than their yearning, more powerful than their will; their dying was tragic, for they knew the stake they had to pay, but were ignorant of the goal; and the poet asked for the kiss of brotherhood before they were driven to attack and mutilate each other like cattle.

It is interesting to note that, except during the first patriotic outburst, or in such verses as are not worthy of a second glance, there is no lauding of military leaders or heroic deeds. Walter Hasenclever, on the contrary, launches a most bitter accusation of callousness against those in authority. Although his poem is open to the accusation of being exaggerated, for the purpose of propaganda (it is called "Die Mörder sitzen in der Oper"), it is a striking example of the feeling against the military hierarchy, which culminated in officers having their epaulettes torn off in the street when the Revolution broke out:—

"Der Zug entgleist. Zwanzig Kinder krepieren.
Die Fliegerbomben töten Mensch und Tier.
Darüber ist kein Wort zu verlieren.
Die Mörder sitzen im Rosenkavalier.

. . . . .

Der Mensch ist billig und das Brot wird teuer.
Die Offiziere schreiten auf und ab.
Zwei grosse Städte sind verkohlt im Feuer.
Ich werde langsam wach im Massengrab.

. . . . .

Verlauste Krüppel sehen aus den Fenstern.
Der Mob schreit: 'Sieg!' Die Betten sind verwaist.
Stabsärzte halten Musterung bei Gespenstern;
der dicke König ist zur Front gereist.

'Hier, Majestät, fand statt das grosse Ringen!'
Es naht der Feldmarschall mit Eichenlaub.
Die Tafel klirrt, Champagnergläser klingen.
Ein silbernes Tablett ist Kirchenraub.

.   .   .   .   .

Der Unteroffizier mit Herrscherfratze
steigt aus geschundenem Fleisch ins Morgenrot.
Noch immer ruft Karl Liebknecht auf dem Platze:
'Nieder der Krieg!' Sie hungern ihn zu Tod.

Wir alle hungern hinter Zuchthaussteinen,
Indes die Oper tönt im Kriegsgewinn.
Misshandelte Gefangene stehn und weinen
am Gittertor der ewigen Knechtschaft hin.

Die Länder sind verteilt. Die Knochen bleichen.
Der Geist spinnt Hanf und leistet Zwangsarbeit.
Ein Denkmal steht im Meilenfeld der Leichen
und macht Reklame für die Ewigkeit.

Man rührt die Trommel. Sie zerspringt im Klange.
Bier wird Ersatz und Blut wird Bier.
Mein Vaterland, mir ist nicht bange!
Die Mörder sitzen im Rosenkavalier.''

A German writer in one of the volumes issued by the Carnegie Endowment for International Peace states that the letters of soldiers from the Front since 1916 showed a patient weariness and apathetic resignation. This is borne out by a recently published volume of letters by German students who fell in the War. This book, *Kriegsbriefe gefallener Studenten*, is the most poignant War-book that has appeared in any country and, as a document, its value is equal, if not superior, to any literary production since 1914. We can trace in these letters, from the beginning of the struggle until the final catastrophe, the change of mood, from enthusiasm to despair, which we may take as being characteristic of the German front-line soldier—at any rate, of the intellectual. The very first of the letters in the volume is dated the 3rd of August, 1914. It is to the writer's parents, and begins as follows:—

256

"Hurrah! At last I have my orders. . . . When we think of ourselves and our families we become small and weak. When we think of our nation, of the Fatherland, of God . . . we grow courageous and strong."

Four days later, in the railway train on the way to the Front, he writes of the impressiveness of their departure. The experiences of months and years seemed to be crowded into a single hour. The soldiers decorated their uniforms and helmets with flowers, and handkerchiefs were waved from every window. "This hour," he says, "which strikes so rarely in the lifetime of the nations, is so powerful and affecting that it alone makes up for many exertions and deprivations." A month later he is in the line, and the tone has changed. "This terrible battle is still raging. It is the fourth day. The shells were dropping so frequently to-day, in front of us and behind, that one must regard it as a dispensation of God if one came out uninjured." Eleven days later he writes from hospital. "Oh! how happy I am to see once more a brighter world than that world of terror. At last I am freed from the haunting thought, which all the time enveloped me, that I should never see you and your world again." Four days later he was dead from lockjaw, caused by the septic state of his wound.

A letter from another soldier, dated the 28th of October, 1914, begins: "With what joy, what pleasure I went out to the battle, which seemed to me to be the finest opportunity to allow my love of life and the life impulse to achieve impetuous fulfilment. With what disillusionment am I now sitting, cold horror in my heart."

I have quoted these letters, which are typical of many, to show that experience of the reality soon quenched the feelings of high romance with which many youths set out for the War. The one thing that strikes the English reader is the intense idealism by which a number of the writers were animated. If many English soldiers felt the same emotions, I think they would, in the majority of cases, not have consciously admitted it to themselves—and they would certainly not have expounded those emotions in their letters home. It is difficult to think of the average English soldier, even one who had gone to the Front straight from the University, writing in this strain :—

"But we are Germans; we are fighting for our people and are shedding our blood, and hope that those who survive will be worthy of our sacrifice. It is for me the struggle for an idea, the *fata morgana* of a pure, loyal, honourable Germany, without baseness or falseness. . . . I will fight, and perhaps die, for a beautiful, great and exalted Germany, from which baseness and selfishness are banned, and where loyalty and honour are restored to their ancient rights."

The Englishman, with his natural reserve so far as his idealistic emotions are concerned, would be inclined to call this priggishness. But we must not judge it from our conventional point of view. It was in accordance with the deepest instincts of the German mind, when they threw themselves into a war on such a gigantic scale, that they should endeavour to seek a philosophical basis for their military enthusiasm. The Germans also tend to think on paper, and in the work of a number of their poets we find such an intense and conscious realisation of their poetic mission that the reader feels he is being admitted to watch the poet's soul in the throes of composition, instead of being presented with the finished product, and that·is why the impression induced in the mind of the non-German reader is sometimes far from comfortable.

Of the War stories written before the Armistice I need mention (with the exception of one by Fritz von Unruh, which will be dealt with later) only two as representative of many—Leonhard Frank's *Der Mensch ist gut* and Andreas Latzko's *Menschen im Krieg*.

Frank's book, which was written in 1916 and 1917, is a collection of five short stories in which he shows the effect of the War on a number of people, each of whom eventually initiates, or joins in, a procession which demands the cessation of hostilities. They are brought by their own suffering to a realisation that the War is futile. The first of them, an old waiter who has lost his son, breaks into the speech of the chairman at a meeting of workmen who are being informed that there are no more funds available for the unemployed or the sick. He tells them that the enemy is in themselves, that the cause of all wars is the non-existence of love, that the whole of Europe has gone mad and is weeping because the whole of Europe has lost the power of love. "We cry out with grief, or our eyes remain dry with grief, when a son has fallen. So long as we do not likewise cry out with grief when a Frenchman falls, there is no love in us. So long as we do not feel that a human being, who has done us no harm, has fallen and is dead, so long are we madmen. For this man had a mother, a father, a wife who are crying out with grief. He so wanted to live. And he had to die. Why? For what reason? We, his murderers, let him die because we do not love. . . . We only need to love, and the last shot will have been fired. Then peace will come." The result of the waiter's speech is that they all follow him out into the street to demand that the War shall cease.

In the second story a woman, who has just received news that her husband has fallen, thinks of the number of women who are in the same situation as herself. "Ja wieviel Frauen sind's denn? Zwei Millionen vielleicht, die in ihrem Zimmer sitzen und, wie ich, an ihren toten Mann denken? Zum Fenster hinaussehen und an ihren toten Mann denken, Staub wischen, Kinder warten, Strümpfe stricken, kochen, auf die Arbeit gehen und an ihren toten Mann denken, an ihren toten Mann denken, toten Mann denken. Sich abends ins Bett legen und an ihren toten Mann denken."

In the third story a mother reads, after her son's death, a letter he has written to an imaginary person in which he ventilates the thoughts that are torturing him. He compares his state of mind with that of a man who is descending in the

dark a flight of steps which are perfectly familiar to him,
yet who, before he reaches the last one, thinks he is already
at the bottom and receives a shock when his outstretched
foot sinks into empty air. This physical and mental shock
of stepping into a sudden abyss had been lasting for three
years, and the only antidotes to it were either that the
soldiers got used to it or, if the dulling of the senses by
custom was not possible, went mad. He gives a further
example—that of a man who has rented a room on the
fourth storey of a house, opens the door leading on to the
balcony, and is precipitated into the depths because the
balcony does not exist. An onlooker, who sees the man fall,
will experience the same mental shock as the man himself
when he realised the absence of the balcony and the fact
that nothing could stop him from crashing down to the
pavement below. When one spends days watching people
falling from the fourth storey, one at last begins to laugh,
that is to say, one goes mad; or one closes one's eyes, that is
to say, one gradually gets used to seeing people falling from
the fourth storey. If one imagines these shocks occurring
uninterruptedly and in an incalculable crescendo for three
years, it is obvious what the eventual effect must be.

The final story describes how an army surgeon, unable
to endure any longer the unending operations and amputa-
tions, leads a vast, ghastly procession of mutilated soldiers,
which swells into a procession of the whole nation demand-
ing and compelling peace.

The book suffers from its abstractness, the figures being
incorporated ideas rather than living characters, but it is
inspired by a great vision—of a peace to come about by the
realisation of the brotherhood of humanity and a world in
which man's inhumanity to man shall be eliminated. It
shows the hollowness of such phrases as "the altar of
the Fatherland," "the field of honour," "sacred cause," and
the rest.

Andreas Latzko, in the powerful short stories which
constitute his book *Menschen im Krieg*, describes the horrors

of modern warfare as outspokenly as any: of the novels which appeared ten years later. It was dedicated "to friend and enemy," but it contains nothing of the hope which is implicit in Frank's book, if we except the motto which he set at the beginning: "Ich weiss gewiss, die Zeit wird einmal kommen, wo alles denkt wie ich." Latzko is bitter at the militarists, where Frank refuses to lay the blame at anyone's door, except that of unrepentant humanity itself, and by his very title links his faith with that of Rousseau in the ultimate good that lies in the depths of man's nature. Latzko, on the other hand, seems to have written his book with a twisted and sardonic grin.

In the drama, the first signs of a change of spirit came even before the superficial, literary outpourings at the outbreak of war had subsided. In the autumn of 1914 von Unruh wrote the "dramatic poem" *Vor der Entscheidung* after it became evident that there was no hope of peace by Christmas. An officer of Uhlans is ordered to set fire to a village and execute the inhabitants, who are said to have shot some German soldiers. He enters a house where the young wife of the mayor of the place is lying in travail, and takes away her husband, her father and her brother to be shot. The woman dies before his eyes, and he is unable to free himself from the impression which these events have made upon him. In an open field behind the battle line he has a vision of the spirit of Shakespeare, who appears as an apostle of peace and serenity of imagination. Refugees go past, freezing and hardly alive, full of hate for their conquerors, and later he sees, in a church which has been shot to pieces, a number of mourning women, also obsessed by hatred, praying at the altar. A veiled figure, symbolic of mourning, appears to him, and he follows it into a vault which leads to the realm of the dead, where he is surrounded by shades that are longing to get back to the upper world. The veiled figure leads him to an inner chamber, in which he sees the sarcophagi of the Hohenzollerns, and he pays homage to those of the Great Elector and Frederick the

Great. He also speaks with the spirit of the poet Heinrich von Kleist, who opposes the ideal of the power of the sword to the Uhlan's world-embracing love. The veiled figure adjures him, however, to follow the path that will lead to full ethical development, in order that he may, in consciousness of the "letztheilige Dinge," be able to fulfil his mission as a human being. He then finds himself in the open once more, and, after a battle scene, he greets the rising sun as the dispenser of mortal happiness, which is to spring from humility and love of humanity. He calls upon the soldiers to become the shining liberators of our suffering race, and while the sun fills the whole firmament, they all unite in proclaiming that the gods of lies have come crashing to the ground :—

> "Lügengötter stürzen nieder!
> Sonne! Sonne leuchtet wieder."

It will be seen that this allegory is inspired by a somewhat nebulous idealism, and it is only remarkable from the fact of its having been composed when the War was hardly three months old, and by a poet whose family traditions and previous literary work offered no clue to the lines along which his mind was to develop. This regular officer in the Prussian cavalry, whose pre-War dramas gave evidence of his preoccupation with the conception of duty, suddenly evinced an antipathy to war, and proclaimed that the military ideal of duty should be transformed into the ideal of duty towards our fellow-men.

A work which may be mentioned in the same breath as *Vor der Entscheidung* is Ernst Toller's play *Die Wandlung*, the first draft of which he wrote down in 1917. It is preceded by a prologue called "The Barracks of the Dead," in which we see a row of soldiers' graves, arranged according to companies, with the graves of the officers placed separately at the side. There enters Peace-time Death, wearing a top-hat on his skull, with War-time Death, who wears a steel helmet, is covered with orders and carries a leg-bone as his

field-marshal's baton. War-time Death takes command of
the officers and soldiers, who rise from their graves, wearing
helmets, and commence to do the goose-step and other
military exercises. Peace-time Death is surprised to see that
even when they are dead the distinction is still preserved
between officers and other ranks. The actual play begins in
a small room at Christmas-time, where a young sculptor,
who feels himself spiritually uprooted, comes to the decision
to go to fight in the colonies. This he feels as a relief, and
he cherishes the hope that the fighting will provide a bond
between him and his fellow-countrymen. We see him again
on a troopship and later in a desert after sunset. After we
have seen a weird dance performed by some skeletons
that have been caught in the barbed wire, the sculptor
appears in a number of scenes where he gives expression to
his disillusionment. He has been engaged on a statue
representing the victorious Fatherland, but he smashes it,
for he has conceived a greater ideal of a world in which
there shall be no war and no hate. He becomes disillusioned
of this ideal also and, in the final scene, where he addresses
a crowded throng, he utters an accusation against humanity.
"You have buried the spirit," he says. "Thousands of spades
are continually in movement to pour more and more
debris on the spirit. You implant hate in your children, for
you have lost all knowledge of love. You have carved Christ
in wood and nailed Him on a wooden cross, because you
yourselves did not want to tread the path to the cross which
led Him to redemption. . . . You are no longer human
beings but caricatures of yourselves. Yet you could be, if
only you had faith in yourselves and in man." The people
respond to his flaming oratory, and he calls on them to
march towards their rulers and tell them that their power is
an illusion; to bid the soldiers forge their swords into
ploughshares; to tell the rich that their hearts are but heaps
of rubbish, but to treat them kindly, for they also are poor
creatures who have lost their way. The piece concludes
with the masses calling for revolution. The action is sup-

posed to take place "vor Anbruch der Wiedergeburt" and there is no doubting the intensity of feeling with which Toller composed this indictment of civilisation.

During the heavy fighting in the attempt to capture Verdun, von Unruh wrote his War-book *Opfergang*, which describes his company's experiences during the preparation and the attack, in the course of which hope gave way to the realisation of failure and the consciousness of the immense and futile sacrifice in human life. The book is written in an ecstatic manner which is in striking contrast to the War novels that have been appearing in Germany during the last two or three years. It was composed with a burning emotion which allowed little or no room for reflection, and like *Vor der Entscheidung* it mirrors the change in its author's outlook as the professional soldier gave way to the pacific idealist. *Opfergang* was written in the early part of 1916 and printed in the summer of the same year, but it was not allowed to be published until the War was over. Von Unruh's soldiers are not realistic characters, but idealists like himself, and his descriptions are imaginative. Like Remarque in *Im Westen nichts Neues*, he draws attention to the inability of the people at home to understand the sufferings of the troops. During 1915 and 1916 he composed his drama *Ein Geschlecht*, which was the first part of an intended trilogy. In this concentrated and powerful play he shows the consolidation of his conversion to pacifism and sees a vision of a new world, though the vision is necessarily vague as to what is to replace that which is to be destroyed.

It was not only in the Army that underground rumblings were becoming audible. The Navy was rusting at its bases; and the mutiny which eventually unbalanced the toppling edifice of the State is foreshadowed in a drama by Reinhard Goering called *Seeschlacht*. Seven sailors are penned up in the armoured turret of a battleship just before the Battle of Jutland. The atmosphere is overcharged with expectation of the coming trial of strength, and the men's minds are a welter of conflicting thoughts. One of them is hovering on the verge of revolt, but when the battle begins he is the keenest of them all. The turret and its crew are destroyed, and the sailor who might, had there been no battle, have been the leader of a mutiny, dies with the words on his lips that he had been a good shot, but he might also have been a good mutineer. Only it was easier to shoot. And so the conflict between personal liberty and the military organisation is solved in favour of the latter, though it is really no solution at all, since the potentiality of revolt is merely stifled, on account of the immediate urgency of warding off the enemy. It is remarkable that the Censor allowed the play to be published during the War. A more recent account of the state of things in the German Navy up to the Revolution is to be found in the novel *Des Kaisers Kulis*, by Theodor Plivier, which was published in 1930.

By the time the German nation collapsed, the revolt against militarism was developing into a revolt against society. The years 1919 and 1920 were characterised by a flood of ideological dramas written in the Expressionist style. I have discussed in the previous two papers the methods and aims of Expressionism, and it must suffice to say here that the movement would have become a force in German literature anyway. The first two years of the War interrupted the natural development, but it set in again with intensified zeal once the young generation had been brought into forcible contact with elementals. I am here concerned chiefly with the revolutionary and social aspects of Expressionism, and these may be summed up briefly. We must bear in mind the nature of the social background, conditioned, as it was, by the circumstances of the continuation of the Blockade, which kept Germany short of food and other necessities; the instability of the new regime; and the creeping paralysis of the period of financial inflation.

It is not easy to draw a line between the literature of revolt that was produced during the War and that which was produced afterwards, but there seem to be roughly three stages in the process of rejection of the mentality which developed in Germany with the prosperous years after the three successful wars and the founding of the Empire. Wedekind and Sternheim in their plays, Heinrich Mann in his novel *Der Untertan* and Hermann Burte in his novel *Wiltfeber* had before 1914 attacked without mercy the aspects of German civilisation which they detested. The experiences of the War implanted in the minds and hearts of the younger men an intense desire to replace the old order by something of which they had a vague vision and which could only be achieved by a revolution. When the revolution came, preceding the Armistice by a couple of days, it was disappointing in its results; and it is disillusionment with the *revolution* which constitutes the third stage and distinguishes the Expressionist dramas after 1918 from the Wartime literature which mostly had to await the abolition of the censorship before it could be made public. While the War lasted there was hope of a radical change to come. The failure of the Revolution to fulfil those hopes tinged the minds of the dramatists with pessimism. The Expressionists had helped to call the revolution into being, and one would have expected an outburst of satire when the Republic fell so far short of what they wanted. But though there was considerable bitterness, no great satirist has yet arisen from their ranks.

In an essay on the War generation, Heinrich Mann summarises the feelings by which they were animated. During their sensitive years they had learned not to love but to hate. Their all-embracing love was an idea with which they armed themselves against the hate which was consuming them. Their elders had hated, but they themselves fought passionately against the blood of their elders which flowed in their own veins, and they wanted to recognise no foe, unless it were their elders themselves. The hatred of the sons for the fathers has nowhere appeared with more annihilating force than in the generation of young Germans that was sacrificed by its fathers and led to destruction, and it was the only vital element in a hundred works by young writers. All else was merely an effusion of the will, each of their characters merely a lyrical idea, and only the hatred was tangible. This view, coming from one who influenced his juniors to no inconsiderable extent, throws valuable light on a generation which was more familiar with death than any that had preceded it since the Thirty Years War; and it is not a matter for surprise that the moral rejection of the achievements of industrial civilisation was symbolised, in a large number of dramas, in a conflict between father and son which did not hesitate at parricide. The Expressionists hated the bourgeois and the civilisation for which he stood, they hated the great city which, like an octopus of brick and mortar, was spreading its tentacles over the countryside and overlaying the face of Nature; and, could they have done so, they would have initiated a frenzied smashing of the machines which, like the large overgrown towns, were symbols of the mechanical, soul-destroying forces that had gained the upper hand during the nineteenth and twentieth centuries. Those who saw the German film *Metropolis* may have recognised something of the same idea. The fact that the War was predominantly a matter of machinery helped to consolidate their hatred. Georg Kaiser, in his trilogy of the gas factory, and Ernst Toller, in his play about the Luddites who tried to wreck the weaving machines at the beginning of the Industrial Revolution, have depicted, in powerful scenes, attempts to rebel against the manifestations of Capitalism; and it is significant that in each case the rebellion was futile.

With the exception of the bourgeois, however, and the materialism with which he had surrounded himself, these writers appeared prepared to love everything that breathed. The literature of the generation which began to write just before or during the War is suffused with a quality of pity that raises it to a higher plane than it would otherwise have attained. The poets take upon themselves the sufferings of the world, and sometimes make their heroes a sacrifice for those who are to come after them. Von Unruh saw in a lamb which was being carried to slaughter, past two soldiers lying dead in a corner of a churchyard, a symbol of the Lamb of God which was to bring the kingdom of Heaven back to earth :—

> "Lamm Gottes, ich sah deinen wehen Blick,
> Bring 'Frieden uns und Ruh,'
> Führ' uns bald in die Himmel der Liebe zurück
> Und deck' die Toten zu."

The chief apostle of humanity was Franz Werfel, who, in a succession of poems, dramas and stories, has, since before the War, advocated the faith that man can only find salvation in love for his fellow-men. His poems, in particular, are inspired by a limitless compassion for all suffering things, and it finds utterance in continual variation. He feels his oneness with all who are condemned to pain, toil or humiliation, until he seems at times to revel in the thought, or emotion, of silent martyrdom on behalf of the rest of creation :—

> "Hier Gesicht und Brust!! Mit jedem Stosse
> Bin ich ja dem Tempo Gottes näher!"

In another of his poems he enumerates the agonies which man is called upon to endure, and appeals to God to give him the grace of martyrdom, so that he may comprise, in himself, the torment and death of all living things. If it is not putting it too crudely, he appears at times to want to identify himself with the figure of Christ. One of his best-known poems is "Jesus und der Äser-Weg," in which Jesus wreathes His hair with a horrible putrefying mass in order to overcome His own disgust, and show that love can conquer everything—"Ist das denn Liebe, wo noch Ekel ist?" These poems were written before the War, but the same theme inspires his later poems and dramas.

This ideal of humanity was carried, by some, to the point of exaggeration where the sublime descends to the level of the ridiculous—when a poet, for example, likened a dog to a saviour digging a grave for a corpse with his teeth, because the dog swallowed a mouse that had been run over by an omnibus.

It was not long before there was evidence of bitterness at the thought that the mentality of the people had not changed. I have already referred to the dramas which represent the idealist going under, because the people are not prepared to follow him to the rather indeterminate goal to which he wishes to lead them. Toller showed in *Hinkemann*, and later in *Hoppla!*, the tragedy of the soldier who returned under abnormal personal conditions and found that he was unable to adapt himself to the new situation. Bert Brecht, in his drama *Trommeln in der Nacht*, treated a similar theme and took the opportunity of giving a picture of a couple of War profiteers. He added, as a sort of afterword, "Die Ballade vom toten Soldaten," a bitter satire which pretends that in the last year of the War, when men were running short, a military medical commission was sent to disinter a dead soldier from his grave. The result of their examination was that he was found fit for military service, and the ballad then describes an uncanny, grotesque march through the night which seems to have been inspired by Bürger's "Lenore."

The new movement which took the place of Expressionism about the year 1924 was known as the "New Objectivity." Authors manifested a desire to descend from the bleak plateau of ideas, and deal with things that they could grasp with their five senses. The new plays and novels were peopled with real characters and real situations, which were presented to the public in language of comparative simplicity. There was a renewal of interest in celebrated figures of the past, though there was still, in the new historical novels and dramas, an attempt to elucidate present-day problems in the guise of history.

Dr. Kurt Pinthus, the editor of the anthology of Expressionist poetry, *Menschheitsdämmerung*, has published recently

269

a suggestive essay[1] in which he contrasts the literary production after 1925 with the literature of Expressionism. He says that in post-Expressionist literature interest is centred on *men*, while the central figures of Expressionist works were *youths*. The unsentimental, unadorned style of the most recent dramas and novels is very different from those in which the protagonist was the youth, with his vehement protest against the past and his insistent urge to model the future. Writers have abandoned the attempt to represent the infinite and the unattainable, concerning themselves with what is tangible and near to hand; with facts rather than ideas. Ernst Glaeser in *Jahrgang 1902* and Remarque in *Im Westen nichts Neues* both declare that their intention is only to "report" what they have themselves experienced. Dr. Pinthus suggests that youths like Remarque, who were still adolescent when the War broke out, saw things more clearly than those who had outgrown that stage and, young though they were, had to switch over to a new mentality. The generation which was still in its teens in 1914 was never really young, but sprang into manhood at a bound. When it reveals the destroying of its illusions, it does so not in the tense, high-pitched manner of the Expressionists, who wanted to smash the conditions which caused the catastrophe, but with the objectivity of the historian, whose purpose is to record what happened.

This does not mean that the new generation does not, in places, give imagination its due and make the actual facts serve the purpose of artistic truth. We need only compare *Opfergang* with *Im Westen nichts Neues* to see immediately the difference between the two types of War-book. We must, of course, take into account the distance from the War at which the latter novel was written and the difference in perspective. If we look below the surface, there are even points of resemblance. Von Unruh was struggling to find some meaning in what was happening, and could only do

---

[1] "Männliche Literatur," in *Das Tagebuch* [Jahrg. 10: Heft 22. June, 1929].

so by the introspective method, by looking within himself to see whether man still retained his human attributes. To Remarque the War had become a meaningless massacre, and his questioning was consequently more hopeless and passive. In the case of the later writers the necessity was no longer urgent to find the answer which, to those who were in the thick of the struggle, involved sanity itself. The Expressionists saw visions of a world cataclysm and rebirth. Remarque and his successors described what they saw of the War from the "frog's eye" point of view.

The farther we are removed from those years by the natural progress of time, the easier does it become to regard the War as an historical incident, and, though it does not become more acceptable morally, it does become more acceptable aesthetically. It is therefore not improbable that the literary treatment of War is about to enter a third stage, which will have a certain kinship with the attitude of the Expressionists in that the relation of the War to the general destiny of humanity will again be emphasised, though in a different way.

Though Remarque says that his book is not intended as an accusation, it *is* an accusation, while Glaeser takes as his motto the phrase: "La guerre, ce sont nos parents." From this point of view, many of the most recent War-books, written from memory or on the basis of diaries, or even predominantly imaginative, link up with those which were produced in the full heat of immediate experience. There is nothing to be said, from the point of view of the subject of this paper, about the whole class of novels already in existence which link up with the pre-War mentality in the glorification of armed force as an instrument for the realisation of cultural ideals. The majority of them are worthless as literature, and their inspiration is to a great extent propagandist.

Those who were young enough when the War broke out to take an active part in it, and whose lives have had imparted to them by the experiences of those years a permanent colouring, are now middle-aged or approaching middle age. Those who were writing from 1914 to, say, 1923 are no longer the younger generation, while the children who were in the nursery or at school during those years are becoming articulate, and to them the War is almost a legend. From 1914 until about 1923 the main stream of literary production in Germany was wholly coloured by the War and the calamitous events which were the consequences of defeat. The poems, the dramas, the novels that are being written to-day are cast in a calmer mould. They lack the vigour, the fierceness, the insanity perhaps, of the short eruptive period that we may conveniently label the years of Expressionism, when writers were grimly trying to come to grips with life and seeking in the embitterment of disillusion to make as complete a break as possible with the past. But short as was the period during which the reaction of the War generation took such an unprecedentedly explosive form, Expressionism has left an indelible mark on German literature. In spite of its apparent newness, its themes and fundamental inspiration were linked with those of the past; but its deepened consciousness of the ultimate significance of problems which previous generations had treated with less searching insight, will render necessary a revaluation of the literature of, at any rate, the nineteenth century and the first decade of the twentieth.

A SELECT BIBLIOGRAPHY OF BOOKS

which deal with German literature since 1914. The ordinary literary histories are omitted.

K. EDSCHMID: *Ueber Expressionismus in der Literatur* (E. Reiss. Berlin, 1919).

M. MURET: *La littérature allemande pendant la guerre* (Payot. Paris, 1920).

G. MARZYNSKI: *Die Methode des Expressionismus* (Klinkhardt und Biermann. Leipzig, 1920).

F. LANDSBERGER: *Impressionismus und Expressionismus* (Klinkhardt und Biermann. Leipzig, 1920).

R. FRANK: *Das expressionistische Drama* (herausgegeben vom Bühnen-Volksbund in Frankfurt am Main. Verlag Dr. Filser & Co. Augsburg, 1921).

M. FREYHAN: *Das Drama der Gegenwart* (E. S. Mittler & Sohn. Berlin, 1922).

J. BAB: *Die Chronik des deutschen Dramas*, 1900–1926 (5 Vols. Oesterheld. Berlin, 1922–27).

FANNY JOHNSON: *The German Mind* (Chapman & Dodd. London, 1922).

CAMILLE POUPEYE: *Les dramaturges exotiques* (The article *Le théâtre expressioniste*. La Renaissance d'Occident. Brussels, 1924).

H. W. HEWETT-THAYER: *The Modern German Novel* (The last two chapters, *The Novel of the Great War* and *The War Unheeded*. Marshall Jones Co. Boston, 1924).

A. SOERGEL: *Dichtung und Dichter der Zeit—Im Banne des Expressionismus* (R. Voigtländer. Leipzig, 1925).

B. DIEBOLD: *Anarchie im Drama* (Frankfurter Verlags-Anstalt. Frankfort on Main. 3rd ed., 1925).

C. H. HERFORD: *The Post-War Mind of Germany* (Clarendon Press. Oxford, 1927. Also in *The Bulletin of the John Rylands Library*, Vol. X, No. 2. July, 1926).

W. WORRINGER: *Nach-Expressionismus* (Klinkhardt und Biermann. Leipzig, 1926).

S

K. Breysig: *Eindruckskunst und Ausdruckskunst* (G. Bondi. Berlin, 1927).

S. D. Gallwitz: *Der neue Dichter und die Frau* (F. A. Herbig. Berlin, 1927).

F. J. Schneider: *Der expressive Mensch und die deutsche Lyrik der Gegenwart* (J. B. Metzler. Stuttgart, 1927).

W. Knevels: *Expressionismus und Religion* (J. C. B. Mohr. Tübingen, 1927).

E. Utitz: *Die Ueberwindung des Expressionismus* (F. Enke. Stuttgart, 1927).

F. Bertaux: *Panorama de la littérature allemande contemporaine* (Kra. Paris, 1928).

H. Ihering: *Reinhardt, Jessner, Piscator oder Klassikertod?* (E. Rowohlt. Berlin, 1929).

H. Koch: *Das Generationsproblem in der deutschen Dichtung der Gegenwart* (H. Beyer & Söhne. Langensalza, 1930).

J. Bab: *Arbeiterdichtung* (Volksbühnen- Verlags- und Vertriebs-Gesellschaft. Berlin, 1930).

H. Kindermann: *Das literarische Antlitz der Gegenwart* (M. Niemeyer. Halle a.d. Saale, 1930).

P. Fechter: *Deutsche Dichtung der Gegenwart* (P. Reclam jun. Leipzig, 1930).

C. E. W. L. Dahlström: *Strindberg's Dramatic Expressionism* (University of Michigan. Ann Arbor; Michigan, 1930)

Kurt K. T. Wais: *Das Vater-Sohn Motiv in der Dichtung* (2 Vols. W. de Gruyter. Berlin, 1931).

J. Knight Bostock: *Some Well-known German War-Novels, 1914-1930* (Blackwell. Oxford, 1931).

H. Cysarz: *Zur Geistesgeschichte des Weltkriegs* (M. Niemeyer. Halle a.d. Saale, 1931).

R. Müller: *Die idealistischen Grundzüge der expressionistischen Weltanschauung* (F. Dietzler. Berlin, 1931).

A SELECT BIBLIOGRAPHY OF BOOKS

ANTHOLOGIES

F. PFEMFERT: *1914–1916: eine Anthologie* (Verlag der Wochenschrift *Die Aktion*. Berlin-Wilmersdorf, 1916).

F. PFEMFERT: *Das Aktionsbuch* (Verlag der Wochenschrift *Die Aktion*. Berlin-Wilmersdorf, 1917).

A. WOLFENSTEIN: *Die Erhebung* (2 Vols. S. Fischer. Berlin, 1919 and 1920).

K. PINTHUS: *Menschheitsdämmerung* (E. Rowohlt. Berlin, 1920).

B. DEUTSCH and A. YARMOLINSKY: *Modern German Poetry* (Lane. London, 1923).

A. SERGEL: *Saat und Ernte* (Bong. Berlin, 1924).

O. HEUSCHELE: *Junge deutsche Lyrik* (P. Reclam jun. Leipzig, 1928).

W. R. FEHSE and KLAUS MANN: *Anthologie jüngster Lyrik* (Gebrüder Enoch. Hamburg, 1927).

Reihe der deutschen Arbeiterdichter: A series of volumes containing the poetry of workmen poets (Arbeiter Jugend-Verlag. Berlin, various dates).

ACKNOWLEDGMENTS

I DESIRE to offer grateful acknowledgment to Messrs. George Routledge & Sons for permission to reprint the first four papers (which appeared as Introductions to volumes in the series of Broadway Translations), *Expressionism in German Literature* (from the volume entitled *Contemporary Movements in European Literature*, edited by J. Isaacs, M.A., and myself), and *The Romantic Symbol* (from the quarterly review *Psyche* for June, 1924, where it first appeared in condensed form); to The Scholartis Press for permission to reprint *The Historical Background of Goethe's "Werther"* (which appeared as the Introduction to my translation of the novel); and to the Editor of *The Times Literary Supplement* for permission to reprint *The German Drama, 1914–1927* (from the "Recent German Literature Number" of April, 1929). *The Romantic Symbol* was also printed in condensed form in the *Publications* of the English Goethe Society for 1924.

INDEX

A

Adriatic Rosemund, The, 90
Aegidius Albertinus, 91
Æsop, 12–14, 16
Agrippa von Nettesheim, 61
Albertus Magnus, 61
Aleman, Mateo, 91
Amadis of Gaul, 88, 89, 91
Anhalt, Prince of, 61
"Annemarie," 251
Anton Ulrich, Duke of Brunswick-Lüneburg, 90
Arbeiterdichter, 250–3
Arcadia, 89
Argenis, 89
Aristotle, 42
Arminius and Thusnelda, 90
Armut, 210
Arnout, 32
Asiatic Banise, The, 90
Assenat, 90
Aufklärung, 166, 179
"Auf Miedings Tod," 167
Avianus, 13

B

Bab, Julius, 157
Babrios, 13
Balduinus, 34
"Ballad of . . . Doctor Faustus, A," 70
Bamberg, Bishop of, 44, 52, 53
Barbusse, Henri, 216
Barclay, John, 89
Barlach, Ernst, 242
Barthel, Max., 208, 253, 254
Baudelaire, C., 202
Baumann, Nicolaus, 34
Beast Epic, Æsop and the, 16
— —, France and the, 11, 14, 18, 19, 25–27, 29, 31, 32, 33

Beast Epic, Germany and the, 11, 12, 14, 25, 29
— —, Greece and the, 12, 13
— —, Grimm and the, 11–13
— —, the Latin, 13, 16, 20, 27, 28, 31
— —, Monastic influence on the, 11–14, 18 ff.
— —, Origin of the, 11 ff.
Beast Stories, 16–18, 21–27, 30–31, 33
Beaumarchais, P.-A. C. de, 177
Bebel, H., 122
Becher, Johannes R., 205, 212, 214
Beer, Michael, 167
Begardi, Philipp, 44
Belsavage Playhouse, 73
Benedict of Aniane, 18
Bernhard, Prince of Weimar, 103
Bernhardi, 246
Berno, 19
Bethmann, 168
Beuther, Michael, 35
Bidermann, Jacob, 123
Bielschowsky, A., 155
Blätter für die Kunst, 202
Bobertag, F., 100
Boisserée, S., 164, 176, 177
Bonaparte, 237, 240
Book of Chronicles, 61
Böttiger, 164
Brecht, Bertolt, 238, 269
Brentano, Bettina, 176
Brentano, Maximiliane, 134, 136, 138, 176
Brentano, P. A., 134, 136, 138
British Museum, 109, 110
Bröger, Karl, 208
Bronnen, Arnolt, 210, 229, 238, 239
Bruce, James, 123
Brust, Alfred, 238
Brydone, P., 122